Prentice Hall *LITERATURE*

PENGUIN EDITION

Unit Four
Resources

Grade Nine

PEARSON

Upper Saddle River, New Jersey
Boston, Massachusetts
Chandler, Arizona
Glenview, Illinois
Shoreview, Minnesota

BQ Tunes Credits

Keith London, Defi ned Mind, Inc., Executive Producer
Mike Pandolfo, Wonderful, Producer
All songs mixed and mastered by Mike Pandolfo, Wonderful
Vlad Gutkovich, Wonderful, Assistant Engineer
Recorded November 2007 – February 2008 in SoHo, New York City, at
Wonderful, 594 Broadway

This work is protected by United States copyright laws and is
provided *solely for the use of teachers and administrators* in
teaching courses and assessing student learning in their classes
and schools. Dissemination or sale of any part of this work
(including on the World Wide Web) will destroy the integrity of
the work and is *not* permitted.

Copyright© by Pearson Education, Inc., or its affiliates. All rights reserved. Printed in the United States of
America. This publication is protected by copyright, and permission should be obtained from the publisher
prior to any prohibited reproduction, storage in a retrieval system, or transmission in any form or by any
means, electronic, mechanical, photocopying, recording, or likewise. The publisher hereby grants
permission to reproduce these pages, in part or in whole, for classroom use only, the number not to exceed
the number of students in each class. For information regarding permission(s), write to Pearson School
Rights and Permissions Department, One Lake Street, Upper Saddle River, New Jersey 07458.

Prentice Hall® is a trademark, in the U.S. and/or in other countries, of Pearson Education, Inc.,
or its affiliates.

13-digit ISBN: 978-0-13-366453-9
10-digit ISBN: 0-13-366453-8

1 2 3 4 5 6 7 8 9 10   12 11 10 09 08

CONTENTS
Unit 4

For information about the Unit Resources, assessing fluency, and teaching with BQ Tunes, see the opening pages of your Unit 1 Resources.

© Pearson Education, Inc. All rights reserved.

© Pearson Education, Inc. All rights reserved.

Poetry Collection: Walter Dean Myers; Alfred, Lord Tennyson; and May Swenson

Poetry Collection: Yusef Komunyakaa, Lewis Carroll, and Edgar Allan Poe

Poetry Collection: Yusef Komunyakaa, Lewis Carroll, and Edgar Allan Poe

Poetry by Mary Tall Mountain, Naomi Shihab Nye, and Student Writers

Poetry Collection: Ernest Lawrence Thayer, William Stafford, and Sandra Cisneros

Poetry Collection: Edgar Allan Poe, Edwin Muir, and Richard Wilbur

Poetry Collection: Ernest Lawrence Thayer, William Stafford, and Sandra Cisneros

Poetry Collection: Edgar Allan Poe, Edwin Muir, and Richard Wilbur

Poetry Collection: Edgar Allan Poe, Edwin Muir, and Richard Wilbur

Poetry Collection: Robert Frost, Emily Dickinson, and T. S. Eliot

Poetry Collection: Robert Frost, E. E. Cummings, and William Shakespeare

Poetry Collection: Robert Frost, Emily Dickinson, and T. S. Eliot

Poetry Collection: Robert Frost, E. E. Cummings, and William Shakespeare

Poetry Collection: Robert Frost, E. E. Cummings, and William Shakespeare

Poetry by Alice Walker, Bashō, Chiyojo, Walt Whitman, and William Shakespeare

Communication, performed by Blip Blip Bleep

We're kicking off the **communication**

by talking 'bout the things that we think about
And the words are open to **interpretation,**

Yeah we just try to listen as we're hanging out

And think about the **meanings** of all of these things
Discuss all our feelings of what is going on here
And we start to become **aware,** of what goes on around us
and the things we share

We can **exchange**

For a little bit of an **understanding,**

illuminate why sometimes we whisper, sometimes we shout,
Sometimes you'll disagree but find **resolution,**

And kid I know you'll work it out, work it out

React and put yourself in someone else's shoes
and feel some **empathy** for someone else's blues

And **respond** with your point of view
That shows some **comprehension** and shows some understanding
We're kickin off the **communication,**

so we can stay **informed** of what's happening
With all our friends and all of our family,

relationships that help us learn how to live

We think about the **meanings** of all of these things
discuss and we talk about what is going on here,

What is going on here . . .

Song Title: **Communication**
Artist / Performed by Blip Blip Bleep
Vocals: Sean Han
Backing vocals: Sarah Lee
Drums: Brett Thomson
Lyrics by Sean Han
Music composed by Sean Han and Mike Pandolfo, Wonderful
Produced by Mike Pandolfo, Wonderful
Executive Producer: Keith London, Defined Mind

© Pearson Education, Inc. All rights reserved.

Unit 4: Poetry
Big Question Vocabulary—1

 The Big Question: How does communication change us?

Honest and frequent communication is important to keep relationships healthy. When you are in doubt about the meaning of somebody's words or actions, the best thing to do is open a dialogue with him or her and ask.

discuss: to talk about something and exchange ideas

empathy: understanding and identifying with another's feelings

interpretation: an explanation or understanding of something

relationship: a connection or association between people

resolution: a final solution to a problem or difficulty

DIRECTIONS: *Leave a message on the answering machine of a close friend or relative, telling them that you want to talk about something he or she did that upset you. Use all of the vocabulary words.*

© Pearson Education, Inc. All rights reserved.

Unit 4: Poetry
Big Question Vocabulary—2

The Big Question: How does communication change us?

When we read a newspaper or watch television, we receive information, but we do not usually contribute information. In some cases, though, it is possible to take some action that communicates a message in response to news.

communication: the act of speaking or writing to share ideas

comprehension: the ability to understand something

informed: having knowledge gained through study, communication, research, and so on

respond: to reply; to react favorably

understanding: *n.* a grasp of the meaning of something;

          adj. having compassion or showing sympathy

DIRECTIONS: *Think about a news story or issue that you care about, and then answer the questions below. Use the vocabulary words in parentheses in each of your answers.*

1. Where did you hear about the news story or issue? (*communication*)

_____

_____

_____

2. What new knowledge did you gain when you heard the story or issue? (*informed*)

_____

_____

_____

3. What are you confused about related to the story or issue? (*understanding*)

_____

_____

_____

4. What would clarify the story for you? (*comprehension*)

_____

_____

_____

5. Is there any action you can take to improve or change this issue? (*respond*)

_____

_____

_____

© Pearson Education, Inc. All rights reserved.

Name _____ Date _____

Unit 4: Poetry
Big Question Vocabulary—3

The Big Question: How does communication change us?

Sometimes a conversation with someone can cause you to understand things in a new way and, as a result, take action.

aware: informed; knowledgeable

exchange: to give something for something else, as in an exchange of ideas

illuminate: to make clear; to give light to

meaning: what is expressed or what is intended to be expressed; the purpose or significance of something

react: to act in response to an agent or influence

DIRECTIONS: *Use the vocabulary words to help Douglas understand the newspaper strike.*

Douglas had no idea why his paper was not delivered this morning. It had ruined his morning. On his way to work, he stopped at a newsstand and was told about a strike at the newspaper office. Sure enough, as he passed the newspaper office, there were picketers, holding signs.

One of the picketers stopped Douglas and asked him to sign a petition to help the newspaper staff get a raise in pay.

They had the following conversation:

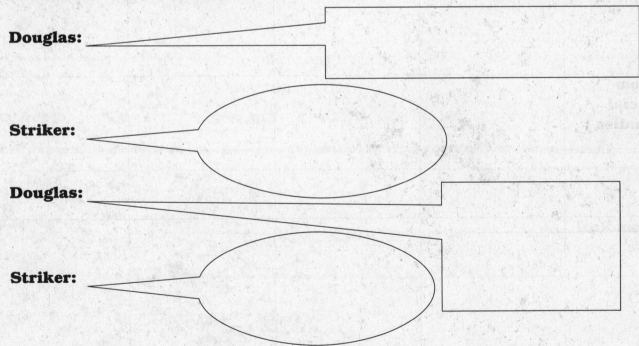

Douglas:

Striker:

Douglas:

Striker:

© Pearson Education, Inc. All rights reserved.

Name _____ Date _____

Unit 4: Poetry
Applying the Big Question

The Big Question: How does communication change us?

DIRECTIONS: *Complete the chart below to apply what you have learned about communication. One row has been completed for you.*

Example	The subject	What happens	The writer's response	How my ideas changed
From Literature	Making decisions in "The Road Not Taken"	The speaker makes a decision about a small matter.	The decision may change his life forever.	I realize that small decisions may affect my entire life.
From Literature				
From Science				
From Social Studies				
From Real Life				

© Pearson Education, Inc. All rights reserved.

Name _____ Starting Date _____ Ending Date _____

Unit 4: Poetry Skills Concept Map—1

How does communication change us?

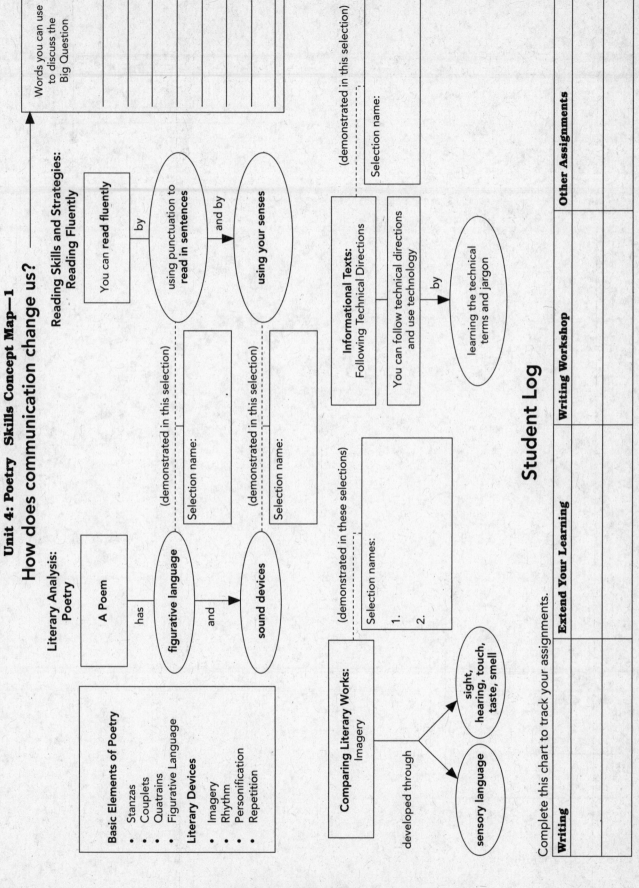

Literary Analysis:
Poetry

A Poem — has → figurative language — and → sound devices

(demonstrated in this selection)
Selection name:

(demonstrated in this selection)
Selection name:

Basic Elements of Poetry
- Stanzas
- Couplets
- Quatrains
- Figurative Language

Literary Devices
- Imagery
- Rhythm
- Personification
- Repetition

Reading Skills and Strategies:
Reading Fluently

You can read fluently — by → using punctuation to read in sentences — and by → using your senses

Informational Texts:
Following Technical Directions

You can follow technical directions and use technology — by → learning the technical terms and jargon

(demonstrated in this selection)
Selection name:

Comparing Literary Works:
Imagery

developed through → sight, hearing, touch, taste, smell / sensory language

(demonstrated in these selections)
Selection names:
1.
2.

Student Log

Complete this chart to track your assignments.

Writing	Extend Your Learning	Writing Workshop	Other Assignments

Words you can use to discuss the Big Question

© Pearson Education, Inc. All rights reserved.

Vocabulary Warm-up Word Lists

Study these words from the poetry of Pat Mora. Then, apply your knowledge to the activities that follow.

Word List A

pale [PAYL] *adj.* of a whitish or grayish color
   The <u>pale</u> flowers contrasted nicely with the bright green leaves.

retreat [ri TREET] *v.* move away from one place back to another
   The girls <u>retreat</u> to their rooms after dinner.

scratches [SKRACH iz] *v.* rubs with a grating or rasping noise
   Pushed by the wind, the branch <u>scratches</u> at the window.

sighs [SYZ] *v.* draws in and lets out a deep, loud breath, as when sad, weary, or relieved
   Gloria <u>sighs</u> and whispers, "That was close!"

tangles [TAN guhlz] *n.* confused masses; snarls
   It takes Jean 15 minutes to brush the <u>tangles</u> out of her hair.

thorns [THORNZ] *n.* sharp, leafless spines growing from a plant
   The <u>thorns</u> have been removed from these long-stemmed roses.

Word List B

boulders [BOHL derz] *n.* large rocks or stones, worn or rounded as by water
   Several large <u>boulders</u> fell from the mountain and blocked the road.

gusts [GUSTS] *n.* sudden, violent rushes of wind
   Strong <u>gusts</u> turned Peter's umbrella inside out.

lightning [LYT ning] *n.* sudden flashes of light in the sky caused by electricity running between a cloud and the earth or between two clouds
   The thunder frightened the baby, but the <u>lightning</u> fascinated her.

scurry [SKER ee] *v.* run quickly or in haste; scamper
   Some birds <u>scurry</u> along the shore dodging the waves.

tosses [TAWS iz] *v.* throws or flings about
   The stormy sea <u>tosses</u> the little fishing boat wildly among the waves.

tumbleweed [TUM buhl weed] *adj.* of the tumbleweed, a desert plant that breaks from its roots when dried out and is blown about by the wind
   We pitched our tent in a <u>tumbleweed</u> area.

Unit 4 Resources: Poetry
© Pearson Education, Inc. All rights reserved.
7

The Poetry of Pat Mora
Vocabulary Warm-up Exercises

Exercise A *Fill in each blank in the following paragraph with an appropriate word from Word List A. Use each word only once.*

Miranda [1] _____ with satisfaction as she prunes the roses. As usual, her roses are gorgeous. Her favorites are the [2] _____ pink ones, but her friend Suzie prefers the bright red ones. Miranda cuts a dozen for Suzie. Then, she removes the [3] _____ from each stem. As Miranda works, her dog Strider [4] _____ at the ground, looking for who knows what. "Strider!" calls Miranda, "stop that! You will dig up my bulbs!" After taking care of the roses and getting Strider to leave the bulb area alone, Miranda turns to the climbing vine on her back fence. Its wild [5] _____ need some sorting out and trimming. At last, Miranda is done. She and Strider [6] _____ to the patio, where they rest contentedly, admiring the garden.

Exercise B *Answer the questions with complete sentences or explanations.*

1. What might make a rabbit <u>scurry</u> out of a farmer's vegetable garden?
   _____

2. What kind of weather is likely to accompany <u>lightning</u>?
   _____

3. What might <u>gusts</u> of wind do to laundry hanging on a clothesline?
   _____

4. Would a rain forest or a desert be more likely to be a <u>tumbleweed</u> area?
   _____

5. Can small children pick up <u>boulders</u>?
   _____

6. Anna <u>tosses</u> her hair from side to side as she talks to Billy. Why might she be doing this?
   _____

© Pearson Education, Inc. All rights reserved.

The Poetry of Pat Mora
Reading Warm-up A

Read the following passage. Pay special attention to the underlined words. Then, read it again, and complete the activities. Use a separate sheet of paper for your written answers.

Mrs. Vanderspek sighs with dismay as she brushes her daughter Marsha's hair. "How do you get all these tangles?" she asks. Before her daughter can answer, Mrs. Vanderspek catches her breath in alarm. Looking out the window, she sees that the pale blue sky is suddenly turning dark. Hail unexpectedly starts to fall. A loud roar fills the air. The television program they had been watching is suddenly interrupted with a tornado warning.

"Tornado!" shouts Mrs. Vanderspek. "To the storm cellar! I will get baby Jimmy, and you get the dog!"

The next 2 minutes are filled with a frenzy of activity. As Mrs. Vanderspek rushes to get Jimmy from the crib, Marsha calls for the dog. "Max! Max! Come here, boy!" she yells, hoping the dog can hear her over the sounds of the hail and the wind. As Marsha calls from the front door, Max scratches at the back door, trying to get in. Mrs. Vanderspek hears him as she runs through the house with the baby. She opens the door to let him in.

They all rush out the front door, across the porch, down the stairs, and through the rose garden, heading toward the storm shelter. Along the way, branches with thorns, tossed violently about by the wind, grab at their clothes, slowing them down.

At last, they reach the storm cellar. Mrs. Vanderspek hands the baby to Marsha so she can use both hands to open the door. With some effort, she manages to get it open, and the frightened family members retreat to the safety of the cellar. Getting the door closed is one more challenge, but with both Marsha and her mother working on it, they manage to get it closed tight and locked down. Safe at last from the fury of the approaching tornado, Mrs. Vanderspek turns to Marsha and says, "Now just look at your hair! I hope you remembered to bring that brush!"

1. Circle the words that tell how Mrs. Vanderspek sighs. Write a sentence using the word *sighs*.

2. Underline the words in a nearby sentence that tell where the tangles are. What are *tangles*?

3. Circle the word that means the opposite of pale. Define *pale*.

4. Underline the words that tell where the dog scratches. Use the word *scratches* in a sentence.

5. Underline the words that tell what the thorns do. How do people working in rose gardens protect themselves from *thorns*?

6. Circle the words that tell the place to which the family members retreat. Describe a place to which you like to *retreat* sometimes.

Name _____ Date _____

The Poetry of Pat Mora
Reading Warm-up B

Read the following passage. Pay special attention to the underlined words. Then, read it again, and complete the activities. Use a separate sheet of paper for your written answers.

Warren Faidley has an unusual job. He is a professional storm chaser. While other people <u>scurry</u> away from such extreme weather conditions as tornadoes, hurricanes, and lightning storms, he gets up close, capturing the excitement on film and video. The pictures he takes have made him famous. You have probably seen some of his photographs of tornadoes, hurricanes, and jagged bolts of <u>lightning</u>. They have appeared in newspapers, magazines, books, films, and advertisements in almost every country of the world.

Faidley's interest in tornadoes began when he was about 13 years old. He noticed <u>gusts</u> of wind forming into whirlwinds in the dusty vacant lots in his neighborhood in Tucson, Arizona. These spinning columns of dust resembled small tornadoes. He had recently seen the movie *The Wizard of Oz*, which gave him the idea of riding his bike into the middle of one of these so-called "dust devils." He wore an old jacket and safety goggles to protect himself. He says that he was able to get into the middle of a dust devil several times. There, the air was still and almost dust free. A wall of dirt full of newspaper and <u>tumbleweed</u> debris spun around him. As he looked up, he could see the blue sky.

In 1991, Faidley pursued his first real tornado. It was rated an F5, the most violent of all tornadoes. Only about 1 percent of tornadoes get such a rating. The F5 rating means that the winds are between 261 and 318 miles per hour. Such a storm picks up <u>boulders</u> as if they were pebbles and <u>tosses</u> them with ease through the air. As Faidley shot the video of this violent storm, his emotions ran from excitement to terror. Since then, he has had many terrifying moments, but these have not stopped him from chasing tornadoes. Sometimes, he has even had to outrun tornadoes that have started to chase him, but the thrill of the adventure is what keeps him going.

1. Underline the words that mean the opposite of "scurry away from." Describe a situation that might cause a mouse to *scurry* away.

2. Circle the words that give further information about <u>lightning</u>. Write a sentence using the word *lightning*.

3. Underline the words that tell what the <u>gusts</u> of wind were doing. What might *gusts* of wind do to the water on a lake?

4. Circle the word that *tumbleweed* describes. Are you likely to find *tumbleweed* debris in a big city? Explain.

5. Underline the words that tell how the storm picks up <u>boulders</u>. What is the difference between *boulders* and pebbles?

6. Circle the words that tell where the storm <u>tosses</u> the boulders. Use *tosses* in a sentence.

© Pearson Education, Inc. All rights reserved.

Pat Mora
Listening and Viewing

Segment 1: Meet Pat Mora
- According to Pat Mora, why is it important to use one's "home" language when writing?
- What two languages does Mora use when writing? Why?

_____

_____

_____

_____

Segment 2: Poetry
- How does the shape of "Uncoiling" help you visualize the poem?
- How does the poem's shape add to its intensity?

_____

_____

_____

_____

Segment 3: The Writing Process
- What does Pat Mora do when she revises a poem?
- Do you agree with Pat Mora that revising is an important part of the writing process? Why or why not?

_____

_____

_____

_____

Segment 4: The Rewards of Writing
- Pat Mora believes that writing should be viewed as an exploration. What can you gain from using writing as a tool to explore?

_____

_____

_____

_____

© Pearson Education, Inc. All rights reserved.

Learning About Poetry

Poetry is a literary form that relies on the precise meanings of words, their emotional associations, their sounds, and the rhythms they create. **Figurative language,** or language that is not intended to be interpreted literally, helps poets to express ideas and feelings in a fresh way.

- A **metaphor** compares two apparently unlike things without using the words *like, as, than,* or *resembles:* "My love is a red, red rose."
- A **simile** uses a connecting word to make such comparisons.
- In **personification,** human qualities are given to nonhuman or inanimate things.
- **Imagery** is descriptive language poets use to create word pictures, or **images.** Images appeal to one or more of the five senses: sight, hearing, touch, taste, and smell.

Poets also use various **sound devices** to give their works a musical quality.

- **Rhythm** is the pattern created by the stressed and unstressed syllables of words.
- **Rhyme** is the repetition of identical or similar sounds in stressed syllables of words.
- **Alliteration** is the repetition of the initial consonant sounds of words. **Assonance** is the repetition of vowel sounds in nearby words. **Consonance** is the repetition of consonants within nearby words in which the separating vowels differ.
- **Onomatopoeia** is the use of a word whose sound imitates its meaning, such as *clank, crackle,* and *sputter.*

The following are some major types and forms of poetry.
Narrative poetry tells a story in verse.

- **Ballad:** a relatively brief, songlike narrative about an adventure or a romance
- **Epic:** a long narrative poem about gods or heroes

Dramatic poetry tells a story using a character's own thoughts or statements.
Lyric poetry expresses the feelings of a single speaker, creating a single effect.

- **Haiku:** a poem containing three lines and seventeen syllables and using imagery to convey a single, vivid emotion
- **Sonnet:** a fourteen-line lyric poem with formal patterns of rhyme, rhythm, and line structure

DIRECTIONS: *Circle the letter of the answer that best matches each numbered item.*

1. words not meant literally
   A. figurative language
   B. onomatopoeia
   C. quatrain

2. sonnet
   A. narrative poem
   B. dramatic poem
   C. lyric poem

3. pattern of stressed and unstressed syllables
   A. rhythm
   B. free verse
   C. tercets

4. "their eyes are lasers"
   A. simile
   B. metaphor
   C. personification

5. "fear of a frightful fiend"
   A. assonance
   B. consonance
   C. alliteration

Name _____ Date _____

The Poetry of Pat Mora
Model Selection: Poetry

Poets use **sound devices**—such as rhyme, rhythm, alliteration, assonance, and onomatopoeia—to create musical, appealing effects with words. Poets also create unexpected insights and perspectives by using words in fresh ways. **Figurative language**—such as simile, metaphor, and personification—goes beyond the literal meanings of words to express ideas and feelings in a fresh way. A poem also becomes vivid and memorable through the use of **imagery,** sensory language that appeals to one or more of the five senses (sight, hearing, smell, taste, and touch). '

DIRECTIONS: *Read the passages from "Uncoiling" and "A Voice." Then, answer the questions that follow each passage.*

1. With thorns, she scratches
    on my window, tosses her hair dark with rain . . . ("Uncoiling")

    A. What figure of speech do these lines contain?

    _____

    B. To which sense(s) does the imagery in these lines appeal?

    _____

2. She spews gusts and thunder,
    spooks pale women who scurry to
      lock doors, windows
        when her tumbleweed skirt starts its spin. ("Uncoiling")

    A. Identify one example of alliteration in these lines.

    _____

    B. Identify one example of assonance in the passage.

    _____

3.   In your house that smelled like
    rose powder, you spoke Spanish formal
    as your father, the judge without a courtroom
    in the country he floated to in the dark
    on a flatbed truck. ("A Voice")

    A. Which lines in the passage illustrate the use of simile? (Hint: There are two similes.)

    _____

    B. Explain the metaphor contained in the words "the judge without a courtroom."

    _____

    _____

© Pearson Education, Inc. All rights reserved.

"Uncoiling" and "A Voice" by Pat Mora
Open-Book Test

Short Answer *Write your responses to the questions in this section on the lines provided.*

1. You are reading a poem that tells a story about a family whose home is damaged in a fire. What type of poem is it? Why?

   _____

   _____

2. You are reading a poem in which owls *screech* and trees *rustle*. What kind of figurative language is the poet using? Explain.

   _____

   _____

   _____

3. You are reading a poem that begins with this line: *The babbling brook, a child at play, tumbles on its merry way.* Name and explain one kind of figurative language used in this line.

   _____

   _____

   _____

   _____

4. Most poems have structure. What is the grouping of lines within a poem called?

5. In "Uncoiling," why do the "pale women" sing "lace lullabies" to their children?

   _____

   _____

   _____

6. How does poet Pat Mora use alliteration in the last three lines of "Uncoiling"?

   _____

   _____

   _____

   _____

© Pearson Education, Inc. All rights reserved.

7. What meaning do you attribute to the title "Uncoiling"?

_____

_____

_____

8. In Pat Mora's poem "A Voice," the speaker describes something her mother found "undoable" as a child. What is this "undoable" thing? According to the poet, how was this thing finally done?

_____

_____

_____

_____

9. Could the next generation referred to in "A Voice" be described as spunky? Explain using the meaning of *spunky* in your answer.

_____

_____

_____

10. In the chart below, write a phrase from each poem by Pat Mora that appeals to the sense of hearing. Then answer the question that follows.

"Uncoiling"	"A Voice"

How are the sounds you chose similar or different?

_____

_____

Essay

Write an extended response to the question of your choice or to the question or questions your teacher assigns you.

11. When poets use personification, they give human qualities to nonhuman things. In an essay, explain how Pat Mora uses personification in "Uncoiling." What nonhuman thing is described? What human qualities or actions does the poet give it? Use examples from the poem to support your ideas.

12. Pat Mora has said that in "A Voice," one of her goals was to "explore Mom's power in the life of our family." In an essay, compare and contrast the powerful woman in "A Voice" with the one in "Uncoiling." What qualities do they share? How are their brands of power different?

13. Pat Mora says that "Poetry is a word journey." Sometimes a journey can be fast and direct, focused mainly on the destination. Other times, a journey can be slow and meandering, focused mainly on the sights, sounds, and smells of the landscape. Choose either "Uncoiling" or "A Voice" and write an essay describing the "journey" on which the poem takes you. What is the speed and focus of the journey? What is its destination? Support your ideas with references to the poem.

14. **Thinking About the Big Question: How does communication change us?** In a sense, "A Voice" is the story of how a new form of communication—the English language—changed not only a single person, but an entire family. Write an essay in which you explain how this is true. In your view, are the changes you describe positive ones or negative ones? Explain.

Oral Response

15. Go back to question 7, 8, or 10 or to the question your teacher assigns to you. Take a few minutes to expand your answer and prepare an oral response. Find additional details in either "Uncoiling" or "A Voice" that support your points. If necessary, make notes to guide your oral response.

Name _____ Date _____

The Poetry of Pat Mora
Selection Test A

Learning About Poetry *Identify the letter of the choice that best answers the question.*

____ 1. In poetry, a *quatrain* may be defined as which of the following?
A. a poem consisting of fourteen lines
B. a poem consisting of seventeen syllables
C. a stanza consisting of four lines
D. the prologue to an epic

____ 2. Which of the following best defines the term *rhyme scheme* in poetry?
A. the repetition of initial consonant sounds
B. the pattern of end rhymes
C. the pattern created by stressed and unstressed syllables
D. the use of a connecting word to make a comparison

____ 3. What is the term for a word whose sound imitates its meaning, as in *buzz* and *hiss*?
A. couplet
B. assonance
C. consonance
D. onomatopoeia

____ 4. A poem with no set meter or rhyme scheme is an example of which of the following?
A. epic
B. lyric
C. free verse
D. ballad

____ 5. Which of the following is defined as a songlike narrative about an adventure or a romance?
A. lyric
B. stanza
C. ballad
D. haiku

© Pearson Education, Inc. All rights reserved.

Critical Reading

____ 6. Which of the following devices do these lines from "Uncoiling" illustrate?

> She sighs clouds. / head thrown back, eyes closed . . .

    A. simile

    B. personification

    C. alliteration

    D. rhyme

____ 7. Which of the following techniques do these lines from "Uncoiling" illustrate?

> She spews gusts and thunder, / spooks pale women who scurry to / lock doors, windows / when her tumbleweed skirt starts its spin.

    A. alliteration

    B. end rhyme

    C. simile

    D. regular meter

____ 8. Which of the following is the main subject of "Uncoiling"?

    A. the sweetness of the women's lullabies

    B. the power of the storm

    C. human beings' struggles with nature

    D. the danger to the children

____ 9. To which sense(s) do the images in these lines mostly appeal?

> until she becomes / sound, spins herself / to sleep, sand stinging her ankles, / whirring into her raw skin like stars.

    A. sight only

    B. sight and hearing

    C. smell and taste

    D. hearing and touch

____ 10. What seems to be the speaker's attitude or tone in "Uncoiling"?

    A. fear and anger

    B. respect and awe

    C. amusement

    D. indifference

____ 11. Who or what is the main subject of "A Voice"?

    A. the speaker's inner conflicts

    B. the squabbles among Mom's four children

    C. Mom's achievements and example

    D. the father's journey from Mexico

© Pearson Education, Inc. All rights reserved.

_____ **12.** Which literary device from "A Voice" do these lines illustrate?

> Their eyes were pinpricks, and you faked hoarseness.

A. simile   C. personification

B. metaphor   D. assonance

_____ **13.** Judging by what you can infer from details in "A Voice," which of the following best describes Mom's life when she was in school?

A. Her life was full of challenges.

B. She had trouble learning English.

C. The other kids picked on her.

D. Her teachers were role models for her.

_____ **14.** Which emotion does the speaker in "A Voice" most likely feel about Mom?

A. anger   C. gratitude

B. jealousy   D. resignation

_____ **15.** These lines contain an example of which of the following?

> Your breath moves
> through the family like the wind
> moves through the trees.

A. personification   C. simile

B. alliteration   D. rhyme

Essay

16. Imagery is descriptive language that creates vivid word pictures. Images become vivid and powerful when they appeal to one or more of the five senses: sight, hearing, smell, touch, and taste. Choose either "Uncoiling" or "A Voice." Then, write an essay in which you identify and discuss two of the images in the poem. Tell what each image contributes to the poem as a whole.

17. A poem's theme is its central message or insight about human life or behavior. Some poets state the theme directly. More often, however, the theme is implied. In an essay, identify and discuss the theme of one of Pat Mora's poems—"Uncoiled" or "A Voice." Support your main ideas with specific references to the text.

18. **Thinking About the Big Question: How does communication change us?** In a sense, Pat Mora's poem "A Voice" is the story of a new form of communication—the English language. Speaking English changed her mother and an entire family. In your view, was the change to speaking English good or bad for the mother and her family? Explain your answer in a brief essay.

© Pearson Education, Inc. All rights reserved.

The Poetry of Pat Mora
Selection Test B

Learning About Poetry *Identify the letter of the choice that best completes the statement or answers the question.*

____ 1. In poetry, *stanzas* are which of the following?
A. sensory images
B. lyrics
C. metaphors
D. groups of lines

____ 2. What is the term for a fourteen-line lyric poem with formal patterns of line, rhythm, and line structure?
A. dramatic monologue
B. epic
C. sonnet
D. ballad

____ 3. Which of the following types of figurative language do these lines illustrate?
With thorns, she scratches / on my window, tosses her hair dark with rain . . .
A. simile
B. metaphor
C. personification
D. symbol

____ 4. Which of the following is the repetition of consonants as in *hip* and *hop*?
A. assonance
B. consonance
C. alliteration
D. onomatopoeia

____ 5. Which of the following best defines *meter*?
A. a controlled pattern of rhythm
B. descriptive language used to create word pictures
C. a comparison of two apparently unlike things
D. the repetition of identical or similar sounds in stressed syllables of words

____ 6. What is a poem containing three unrhymed lines of five, seven, and five syllables?
A. sonnet
B. haiku
C. ballad
D. epic

____ 7. In the phrase "the murmuring of innumerable bees," which two literary devices do you recognize?
A. sonnet form and imagery
B. onomatopoeia and assonance
C. rhyme and assonance
D. consonance and imagery

Critical Reading

____ 8. On which of the following does the speaker in "Uncoiling" focus?
A. a festive meal   C. a peaceful sunset
B. a hectic journey   D. a powerful storm

____ 9. Which device does the poet use here?
boulders retreat like crabs / into themselves.
A. simile   C. personification
B. metaphor   D. alliteration

____ 10. In "Uncoiling," why do the "pale women" sing "lace lullabies"?
A. to pray
B. to pass the time
C. to calm their children
D. to practice for a recital

____ 11. At the end of "Uncoiling," which of the following happens?
A. The women's children fall asleep.
B. The women's songs end.
C. The storm intensifies.
D. The storm wears itself out.

____ 12. The *tone* of a work is the author's attitude toward the subject matter, the characters, or the audience. In "Uncoiling," the speaker's tone is best described as which of the following?
A. angry   C. pessimistic
B. humorous   D. awed

____ 13. Which of the following best explains the significance of the title of "Uncoiling"?
A. The title conjures up the image of a snake.
B. The title suggests tension and energy.
C. The title is intended to puzzle the reader.
D. The title contains personification.

____ 14. Who is the speaker in "A Voice"?
A. one of Mom's four children
B. one of the poet's classmates
C. Mom
D. Dad

____ 15. To which sense(s) does the imagery in these lines appeal?
In your house that smelled like / rose powder, you spoke Spanish formal / as your father . . .
A. sight   C. touch
B. smell and hearing   D. smell and taste

____ 16. In "A Voice," why did Mom travel to the state capitol when she was in school?
   A. to attend the governor's inauguration
   B. to file a petition
   C. to participate in a speaking contest
   D. to visit a museum

____ 17. Which literary technique appears in this passage?
   The family story says your voice is the voice / of an aunt in Mexico, spunky as a peacock.
   A. metaphor
   B. personification
   C. alliteration
   D. simile

____ 18. In "A Voice," why does the speaker feel grateful to Mom?
   A. Through her courage and determination, Mom has been an admirable role model.
   B. Mom has encouraged the speaker to learn English.
   C. The speaker has benefited from Mom's strict discipline.
   D. Mom is always the source of wise advice.

____ 19. Which of the following best describes the speaker's tone in "A Voice"?
   A. affectionate and admiring
   B. disillusioned and sad
   C. angry and resentful
   D. mysterious and suspenseful

Essay

20. Imagery is descriptive language used to create word pictures, or images. Images are enhanced by sensory language, which provides details related to the five senses. Choose either "Uncoiling" or "A Voice," and write an essay in which you discuss and evaluate Pat Mora's use of imagery. When you think about the poem, what images do you recall? Be sure to identify the sense appealed to in each image that you discuss.

21. Pat Mora uses sound devices to create word music. When you think about "Uncoiling" and "A Voice," what sound devices do you recall? In an essay, discuss Mora's use of sound effects such as rhythm, alliteration, assonance, and onomatopoeia. As much as possible, support your main ideas with specific references to the poems.

22. Three principal types of figurative language are simile, metaphor, and personification. Carefully note Mora's use of figurative language in "Uncoiling" and "A Voice." Then, in an essay, discuss Pat Mora's use of these three types of figures of speech. As you consider each individual example, evaluate its effectiveness.

23. **Thinking About the Big Question: How does communication change us?** In a sense, "A Voice" is the story of how a new form of communication—the English language—changed not only a single person, but an entire family. Write an essay in which you explain how this is true. In your view, are the changes you describe positive ones, or negative ones? How so?

Vocabulary Warm-up Word Lists

Study these words from the poetry of Langston Hughes, William Wordsworth, Gabriela Mistral, and Jean de Sponde. Then, apply your knowledge to the activities that follow.

Word List A

battered [BAT erd] *adj.* beaten up by physical or emotional forces
   The old house looked <u>battered</u> by years of weather and neglect.

deferred [dee FERD] *adj.* put off until a future time
   Our vacation is <u>deferred</u> until my mother is well.

fast [FAST] *adv.* firmly and tightly
   The boat is tied <u>fast</u> and cannot drift away.

soundlessly [SOWND lis lee] *adv.* happening without any noise
   I opened the door <u>soundlessly</u> so I would not wake anyone inside.

sparkling [SPAHRK ling] *adj.* shining brightly with points of light
   The water was <u>sparkling</u> with the light of the sun.

sprightly [SPRYT lee] *adj.* in a light and lively way
   My grandmother may be older, but she has a <u>sprightly</u> walk.

Word List B

academic [AK uh dem ik] *adj.* relating to education
   My school has a good <u>academic</u> program and most students graduate.

immovable [im MOO vuh buhl] *adj.* impossible to move or change
   Although we beg, our father is <u>immovable</u> and will not let us in the boat unless we are wearing life jackets.

inward [IN werd] *adj.* of or on the inside, such as a person's private thoughts and feelings
   Although she looked confident, an <u>inward</u> doubt nagged at her.

margin [MAHR jin] *n.* edge of something
   He was on the <u>margin</u> of their group and never really a member.

solitude [SAHL i tood] *n.* state of being alone
   Many authors require <u>solitude</u> and go to quiet places to write.

theory [THEER ee] *n.* idea that has not been proven to be true
   The police have a <u>theory</u> about the crime and are looking for proof.

© Pearson Education, Inc. All rights reserved.

Poetry Collection: Langston Hughes, William Wordsworth, Gabriela Mistral, Jean de Sponde
Vocabulary Warm-up Exercises

Exercise A *Fill in each blank in the following paragraph with an appropriate word from Word List A. Use each word only once.*

The ducks move [1] _____ on the surface of the lake. Often, their quacking conversation makes quite a racket, but not tonight. A full moon is rising, promising to provide the lake with the same [2] _____ dress, dotted with light crystals, it has worn all day courtesy of the sun. The bats are arriving, despite their dark mystique a surprisingly [3] _____ group, flying ever-so-lightly over the lake. The day's water sports are done and both the motor boat and the fishing boat are secured [4] _____ for the night. The edge of the dock is scuffed and [5] _____ where the boats knock against it when a big wave rolls in. Fixing the dock is one of many repairs [6] _____ until the lovely days of summer are past.

Exercise B *Decide whether each of the following statements is true or false. Explain your answers.*

1. An <u>academic</u> scholarship would be given to a good student.
   T / F _____

2. People usually share their <u>inward</u> thoughts with just about anyone.
   T / F _____

3. An <u>immovable</u> object is one that might stay permanently in one place.
   T / F _____

4. It can be risky to believe in a <u>theory</u> without proof.
   T / F _____

5. A person who is enjoying <u>solitude</u> is most likely at a party.
   T / F _____

6. A beach is sometimes found on the <u>margin</u> of a lake.
   T / F _____

© Pearson Education, Inc. All rights reserved.

Poetry Collection: Langston Hughes, William Wordsworth, Gabriela Mistral, Jean de Sponde
Reading Warm-up A

Read the following passage. Pay special attention to the underlined words. Then, read it again, and complete the activities. Use a separate sheet of paper for your written answers.

Molly had a problem. She had a poem to write, but her mind was empty of ideas. She had avoided writing the poem, so the problem was <u>deferred</u>. Now the poem was due and she needed inspiration.

Molly wandered outdoors to sit on her favorite rock. It was big and flat. She daydreamed that it was held <u>fast</u> to the ground by miles of granite extending to the earth's core. The rock was a firm and secure place for observing. Now all she had to do was watch, listen, think, and feel.

A robin appeared, bouncing <u>soundlessly</u> around the yard. Its silence would help it surprise juicy worms as it picked between blades of grass for a meal. One wing drooped a bit, and Molly thought of a poem with the words *broken-winged bird*. Seeing the robin hobbling along gave those words new meaning.

The ground was wet from a light rain. The sun broke free of the disappearing clouds and suddenly there were <u>sparkling</u> beads of water on the grass, like generously sprinkled diamonds. The wind came up, and a bed of tulips and daffodils waved and bobbed in the breeze. Molly thought of another poem she had read about dancing daffodils. These had the lively and <u>sprightly</u> attitude of the ballet dancers her mother loved, and seeing the flowers in motion gave the poet's words new meaning.

Then, she saw a quick movement near the <u>battered</u> tree on the edge of the yard. Recently, the tree had been knocked down by a storm. It now lay on the ground. Molly held her breath as a spotted fawn came near and then, silently, followed by its protective mother. Molly watched her lick the fawn and nudge it along and thought of a poem about a mother and her baby. She even thought of a poem about love.

The deer moved away and Molly felt ready to find her notebook and write. Watching and listening, thinking and feeling, she had found her inspiration.

1. Circle the words that are clues to the meaning of <u>deferred</u>. Explain what is being *deferred* in the passage.

2. Circle the words that are clues to the meaning of <u>fast</u>. Underline what the girl imagines to be the reason that the rock stays *fast* in place.

3. Circle a word that is a clue to the meaning of <u>soundlessly</u>. Give an antonym, or word with the opposite meaning, for *soundlessly*.

4. Underline the phrase that describes how something might look when it is <u>sparkling</u>. Give a synonym, or word with the same meaning, for *sparkling*.

5. Circle the word that is a clue to the meaning of <u>sprightly</u>. Underline what the girl compares to the *sprightly* flowers.

6. Circle the words that are a clue to the meaning of <u>battered</u>. Describe what this *battered* tree might look like.

© Pearson Education, Inc. All rights reserved.

Name _____ Date _____

Poetry Collection: Langston Hughes, William Wordsworth, Gabriela Mistral, Jean de Sponde
Reading Warm-up B

Read the following passage. Pay special attention to the underlined words. Then, read it again, and complete the activities. Use a separate sheet of paper for your written answers.

Nature, love, and the power of dreams have long inspired poets. What may not be as obvious is that these same forces also influence <u>academic</u> thinkers, such as scientists. They even inspire practical researchers, such as inventors. One example is Alexander Graham Bell. His invention of the telephone grew out of a life of observing nature and out of his love for his mother and wife, both of whom were deaf.

Bell was born in Scotland but moved to Canada with his family. There, they settled in Brantford, Ontario, near the Grand River. Young Bell called this his "dreaming place." He spent many hours at the <u>margin</u> of the river, standing on the edge of a cliff and looking at the water below. Throughout his life, he enjoyed being alone in nature and having opportunities to think while separated from the rest of the world. In the <u>solitude</u> of his visits to the cliff, he studied the properties of wind and water.

Growing up, the needs of the deaf were part of his everyday life. His father taught deaf students and his mother was herself deaf. Most people tried to speak to her through a tube in her ear. Bell had a <u>theory</u> that vibrations from his voice traveling through her bones would be a better way to communicate with her. He tested his idea by getting close to her forehead and speaking to her in low, deep tones. It is not clear how successful he was. However, each experience strengthened his inner passion and his <u>inward</u> resolve to understand sound transmission, whether or not he found outward success.

By the time he was an adult, Bell was living in Boston and teaching at a school for the deaf. There, he met Mabel Hubbard, a student whom he would later marry. He was determined to achieve his goals, and he was <u>immovable</u> in his decision. He continued his experiments with sound. In 1875, he successfully transmitted the first sounds over a wire. In 1876, he invented the telephone— born from his investigations of a world of silence.

1. Circle a word that is a clue to the meaning of <u>academic</u>. In what way is an *academic* thinker different from a practical researcher?

2. Circle a word that is a clue to the meaning of <u>margin</u>. From the information in the passage, describe what standing on the *margin* of the land above a river might be like.

3. Underline words and phrases that together provide a definition for <u>solitude</u>. Why is nature a good place to find *solitude*?

4. Circle the word that is a clue to the meaning of <u>theory</u>. From the example in the passage, explain whether a *theory* is the same as a fact.

5. Circle a word that is a clue to the meaning of <u>inward</u>. In your own words, contrast an *inward* resolve with outward success.

6. Circle the word that is a clue to the meaning of <u>immovable</u>. Give a synonym, or word with the same meaning, for *immovable*.

© Pearson Education, Inc. All rights reserved.

Poetry Collection: Langston Hughes, William Wordsworth, Gabriela Mistral, Jean de Sponde

Writing About the Big Question

How does communication change us?

Big Question Vocabulary

aware	communication	comprehension	discuss	empathy
exchange	illuminate	informed	interpretation	meaning
react	relationship	resolution	respond	understanding

A. *Use one or more words from the list above to complete each sentence.*

1. Two people who do not speak the same language may find _____ difficult.

2. Because we shared their feelings deeply, we wanted to communicate our _____ to them.

3. A good dictionary is a valuable resource for determining the _____ of an unfamiliar word.

4. Sometimes you need courage and patience when you _____ a difficult issue or conflict with others.

5. To communicate with others effectively, you need to remain _____ of their point of view.

B. *Follow the directions in responding to each of the items below.*

1. List two different times when you have found **communication** with another person difficult.

   _____

   _____

2. Write two sentences to explain one of these experiences, and describe how it made you feel. Use at least two of the Big Question vocabulary words.

   _____

   _____

C. *Complete the sentence below. Then, write a short paragraph in which you connect the sentence to the Big Question.*

When the speaker of a poem asks the audience to **respond** to a question, the audience is encouraged to _____

_____

_____

_____

Poetry Collection: Langston Hughes, William Wordsworth,
Gabriela Mistral, Jean de Sponde

Literary Analysis: Figurative Language

Figurative language is language that is used imaginatively rather than literally. Figurative language includes one or more **figures of speech,** literary devices that make unexpected comparisons or change the usual meanings of words. The following are figures of speech:

- **Simile:** a comparison of two apparently unlike things using *like, as, than,* or *resembles*
- **Metaphor:** a comparison of two apparently unlike things without using *like, as, than,* or *resembles*
- **Personification:** giving human characteristics to a nonhuman subject
- **Paradox:** a statement, an idea, or a situation that seems contradictory but actually expresses a truth

DIRECTIONS: *Read the following passages and then use the lines provided to identify each example of figurative language. Briefly indicate the reason for your answer.*

1. "Does it stink like rotten meat?" ("Dream Deferred")

   _____

   _____

2. "Life is a broken-winged bird / That cannot fly." ("Dreams")

   _____

   _____

3. "Ten thousand saw I at a glance,
   Tossing their heads in sprightly dance." ("I Wandered Lonely as a Cloud")

   _____

   _____

4. "They flash upon that inward eye
   Which is the bliss of solitude." ("I Wandered Lonely as a Cloud")

   _____

   _____

5. "The wind wandering by night
   rocks the wheat.
   Hearing the loving wind,
   I rock my son." ("Meciendo")

   _____

   _____

6. "What becomes more and more secure, the longer
   it is battered by inconstancy . . .?" ("Sonnets on Love XIII")

   _____

   _____

Poetry Collection: Langston Hughes, William Wordsworth,
Gabriela Mistral, Jean de Sponde

Reading: Read Fluently

Reading fluently is reading smoothly and continuously while also comprehending the text and appreciating the writer's artistry. To improve your fluency when reading poetry, **read in sentences.** Use punctuation—periods, commas, colons, semicolons, and dashes—rather than the ends of lines to determine where to pause or stop reading.

DIRECTIONS: *Read the following passages and then answer the questions on the lines provided.*

1. "God, the Father, soundlessly rocks
   his thousands of worlds.
   Feeling His hand in the shadow,
   I rock my son." ("Meciendo")

   At the ends of which lines would you make major pauses in reading? Minor pauses? No pause at all?

   _____

   _____

2. "But if that dead
   sage could return to life, he would find a clear
   demonstration of his idea, which is not
   pure theory after all. That putative spot
   exists in the love I feel for you, my dear." ("Sonnets on Love XIII")

   After which words would you make a minor pause? After which words would you make a major pause?

   _____

   _____

3. "The waves beside them danced; but they
   Outdid the sparkling waves in glee;
   A poet could not but be gay,
   In such a jocund company;
   I gazed—and gazed—but little thought
   What wealth the show to me had brought:" ("I Wandered Lonely as a Cloud")

   After which words at the end of lines should you not make any pause at all?

   _____

   _____

Name _____ Date _____

Poetry Collection: Langston Hughes, William Wordsworth,
Gabriela Mistral, Jean de Sponde
Vocabulary Builder

Word List

barren   deferred   fester   paradoxical   pensive   solitude

A. DIRECTIONS: *Answer each of the following questions.*

____ 1. Which of the following is the best synonym for *deferred*?

    A. postponed   **B.** analyzed   **C.** replaced   **D.** completed

____ 2. Which of the following most nearly means the opposite of *pensive*?

    A. deliberate   **B.** thoughtless   **C.** envious   **D.** cautious

____ 3. Which of the following is the best synonym for *barren*?

    A. plentiful   **B.** sterile   **C.** elegant   **D.** wealthy

____ 4. Which of the following most nearly means the opposite of *solitude*?

    A. linkage   **B.** loneliness   **C.** sadness   **D.** relaxation

B. DIRECTIONS: *For each of the following items, think about the meaning of the italicized word and then answer the question.*

1. Would most of the people at a lively party be likely to be in a *pensive* mood? Why or why not?

_____

2. Would you be happy if your salary or the fee for a job you had completed was unexpectedly *deferred*? Why or why not?

_____

3. Would a *paradoxical* statement be easy to understand at first? Why or why not?

_____

4. If a wound is allowed to *fester*, will it heal quickly? Why or why not?

_____

C. WORD STUDY: *Match the word in Column A with its meaning in Column B by writing the correct letter on the line provided.*

____ 1. transfer   **A.** meet with

____ 2. conifer   **B.** carry across

____ 3. confer   **C.** greater liking

____ 4. preference   **D.** pine or spruce tree

Poetry Collection: Langston Hughes, William Wordsworth,
Gabriela Mistral, Jean de Sponde

Enrichment: Nature in Art

In "I Wandered Lonely as a Cloud," William Wordsworth writes about "A host, of golden daffodils, / Beside the lake, beneath the trees, / Fluttering and dancing in the breeze." He also describes how the flowers he sees are "Continuous as the stars that shine / And twinkle on the milky way." Through such memorable images, Wordsworth not only gives his readers a detailed description of the daffodils, but he also shares his feelings about the flowers and the natural world.

Nature has attracted poets, writers, painters, musicians, and sculptors for thousands of years, and it has inspired many fascinating works of art. What other images of nature have you seen in books and at museums? What different feelings about nature do these works express and evoke in you?

A. DIRECTIONS: *Identify Wordsworth's response to the natural world by answering each of the following questions.*

1. What are some of the most memorable images of nature from Wordsworth's poem "I Wandered Lonely as a Cloud"?

   _____

   _____

   _____

2. What attitude toward the natural world does Wordsworth express in this poem? What feelings do his images of nature evoke in you? Do his images attract you to nature? Why or why not?

   _____

   _____

   _____

   _____

B. DIRECTIONS: *Just as writers such as Wordsworth have captured the beauty of the natural world in their poetry, visual artists have presented their perspectives on nature in paintings, sculptures, and photographs. Create a visual anthology of three works of fine art from a variety of time periods. These works should express a variety of artistic responses to the natural world. To get started, look through prints and art books in your school or local library. If possible, you might make a trip to a local art museum. You can also find many reproductions online. Choose three works of fine art, and study them carefully. Record details about each work. Describe each work briefly, and tell what the artist's attitude toward nature is. Also, describe your emotional response to the work—the feelings it evoked in you. Then, write a brief report in which you compare and contrast your three works of art and discuss your emotional response to each of them. Be prepared to present your report to the rest of your class.*

Name _____ Date _____

Poetry Collection: Langston Hughes, William Wordsworth, Gabriela Mistral, Jean de Sponde

Open-Book Test

Short Answer *Write your responses to the questions in this section on the lines provided.*

1. Explain what Langston Hughes means by a "dream deferred" in his poem of that name. Base your answer on the meaning of *deferred*.

   _____

   _____

   _____

2. Cite a simile from the poem "Dream Deferred." Explain the way in which it describes a deferred dream.

   _____

   _____

   _____

   _____

3. How is Langston Hughes's poem "Dreams" both a hopeful and a hopeless poem? Support your answer with quotes from the poem.

   _____

   _____

   _____

   _____

4. Cite a metaphor from the poem "Dreams." Explain the metaphor in your own words.

   _____

   _____

   _____

5. How many sentences would you read when reading aloud the first six lines of William Wordsworth's poem "I Wandered Lonely as a Cloud"?

   _____

   _____

6. In "I Wandered Lonely as a Cloud," the poet describes the way sights and memories cause changes in the speaker's emotions. Fill in the timeline below with the events and the speaker's moods throughout the poem. Then answer the question that follows.

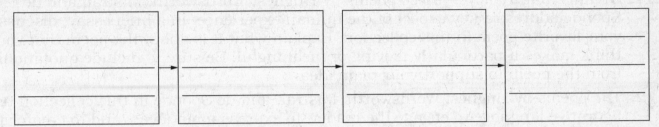

Which word from the timeline best describes the speaker's overall mood?

_____

7. Poets often personify nature by giving it human traits or having it take human actions. Give an example of personification from Gabriela Mistral's poem "Rocking."

_____

_____

_____

8. In "Rocking," what two different things might the poet mean when she writes that "The sea is divine"?

_____

_____

_____

9. In "Sonnets on Love XIII," how are Archimedes' words in the first two lines paradoxical?

_____

_____

_____

_____

10. In "Sonnets on Love XIII," the poet Jean de Sponde compares love to a lever. A lever works by reducing the amount of force needed to move something. How is love similar?

_____

_____

_____

© Pearson Education, Inc. All rights reserved.

Essay

Write an extended response to the question of your choice or to the question or questions your teacher assigns you.

11. Dreams, nature, love—these poems by Hughes, Wordsworth, Mistral, and de Sponde address a key aspect of the human experience. In a brief essay, discuss your favorite poem in this collection. Explain what it is about the poem that you think makes it particularly moving or meaningful. Be sure to include quotations from the poem to support your main idea.

12. The poems by Hughes, Wordsworth, Mistral, and de Sponde in this collection use figurative language to engage the reader, to express main ideas, and to create vivid images. Write an essay in which you analyze the figurative language in one of these poems. Be sure to define and give examples of the types of figurative language you identify. Then explain how the figurative language reflects or deepens the poem's meaning.

13. Reread the final stanza of William Wordsworth's poem "I Wandered Lonely as a Cloud." Then, in an essay, explain the meaning of this passage. How does this stanza differ from the first two? Who or what are "they" in line 21? What is the speaker's "inward eye"? Why are the daffodils significant to the speaker? Use evidence from the poem to support your analysis.

14. **Thinking About the Big Question: How does communication change us?** Each of the poems by Hughes, Wordsworth, Mistral, and de Sponde in this collection communicates a main idea that might be understood as a piece of advice. Choose one poem from the collection and express the advice it seems to be giving. If a reader took this advice to heart, how might it change the remainder of his or her day—or life?

Oral Response

15. Go back to question 3, 6, or 10 or to the question your teacher assigns you. Take a few minutes to expand your answer and prepare an oral response. Find additional details in the relevant poem that support your points. If necessary, make notes to guide your oral response.

© Pearson Education, Inc. All rights reserved.

Poetry Collection: Langston Hughes, William Wordsworth,
Gabriela Mistral, Jean de Sponde
Selection Test A

Critical Reading *Identify the letter of the choice that best answers the question.*

____ 1. In "Dream Deferred," the lines "Or crust and sugar over—/ like a syrupy sweet?" are an example of which kind of figurative language?
  A. simile
  B. metaphor
  C. personification
  D. paradox

____ 2. Which of the following is the best paraphrase of the line, "What happens to a dream deferred?"
  A. Putting off a dream can be disappointing, even dangerous.
  B. Some dreams must be put off.
  C. What happens when a dream is not realized?
  D. What happens when people dream?

____ 3. In "Dreams," Langston Hughes compares life without dreams to which of the following?
  A. an eagle on a cliff
  B. a bird with a broken wing
  C. a heavy, sagging load
  D. a raging storm

____ 4. In "Dreams," Langston Hughes's theme, or central message, concerns which of the following?
  A. the way to make your dreams come true
  B. the vital link between dreams and hope
  C. the foolishness of unrealistic dreams
  D. the false appeal of dreams of wealth

____ 5. What figure of speech do these lines from "I Wandered Lonely as a Cloud" illustrate?
      The waves beside them danced: but they
      Outdid the sparkling waves in glee. . . .
  A. simile
  B. metaphor
  C. personification
  D. paradox

____ 6. In Wordsworth's poem, what is the speaker doing when he says that the daffodils "flash upon that inward eye"?
  A. He is looking at a photograph of daffodils taken with a flash.
  B. He is recalling the visual memory of the daffodils.
  C. He is looking at a bunch of daffodils in a vase.
  D. He is making plans to revisit the place where he saw the daffodils.

_____ 7. By the end of Wordsworth's poem "I Wandered Lonely as a Cloud," how has the speaker's outlook on life changed?

  A. He no longer enjoys his daily life and wants to go back to where he saw the daffodils.

  B. He longs to find another person with whom to share the beauties of nature.

  C. He is able to find contentment by writing about his everyday experiences.

  D. He is always able to find contentment by simply remembering the daffodils.

_____ 8. What is the speaker in Gabriela Mistral's poem "Meciendo" doing?

  A. listening to the ocean's waves crash

  B. rocking her child

  C. praying by the sea

  D. sitting at the edge of a wheat field

_____ 9. Which of the following is the best brief expression of the theme of "Meciendo"?

  A. the love of a mother for her child

  B. the calming effect of the sea

  C. the chilly night breezes

  D. the influence of nature on our lives

_____ 10. In order to read a poem fluently, which of the following should you do?

  A. read as rapidly as you can

  B. look up unfamiliar words in a dictionary

  C. read the footnotes and definitions

  D. read in sentences and use punctuation

_____ 11. In "Sonnets on Love XIII," the speaker makes a connection between the ancient Greek scientist Archimedes and which of the following?

  A. the circumference of the Earth

  B. the structure of the solar system

  C. the power of love

  D. the beauty of nature

_____ 12. Which of the following best defines *paradox*?

  A. the use of deliberate exaggeration for effect

  B. the use of parallel structure for a series of similar grammatical elements

  C. an imitation of a literary or musical work

  D. an apparent contradiction that actually expresses a truth

Vocabulary and Grammar

___ 13. If you were in a *pensive* mood, how might a friend describe you?

    A. foolish

    B. practical

    C. merry

    D. thoughtful

___ 14. Identify the prepositions in these lines from "Dreams" by Langston Hughes:

    Hold fast to dreams

    For when dreams go

    Life is a barren field

    Frozen with snow.

    A. *fast, barren, frozen*

    B. *hold, go*

    C. *to, with*

    D. *for, when*

Essay

15. Which of these poems speaks to you most powerfully? In a brief essay, discuss your favorite poem in this collection. Explain what it is about the poem that you think makes it particularly moving or meaningful. Be sure to comment on the poet's use of figurative language.

16. Your assignment is to prepare an oral interpretation of one of these poems. Which poem best lends itself to an oral reading, and why? In an essay, explain why you chose the poem you have selected. Then, discuss the ways in which you would prepare for your performance. In your discussion, include specific references to elements such as sound effects, imagery, and figurative language in the poem. Tell how you would vary the tone of your voice and where you would pause for effect.

17. **Thinking About the Big Question: How does communication change us?** Each of the poems in this collection by Hughes, Wordsworth, Mistral, and de Sponde communicates a main idea. This idea might be seen as advice, or a suggestion, on how to live your life. Choose one poem from the collection and tell the advice it seems to give you.

Poetry Collection: Langston Hughes, William Wordsworth, Gabriela Mistral, Jean de Sponde

Selection Test B

Critical Reading *Identify the letter of the choice that best completes the statement or answers the question.*

____ 1. Which sentence best summarizes the message of "Dream Deferred"?
A. Dreams get more and more confusing the longer they are postponed.
B. People always wonder what happens to the dreams they never fulfill.
C. People lose interest in dreams that are not fulfilled.
D. Postponing dreams can lead to frustration and even violence.

____ 2. What figure of speech does Langston Hughes use in the following lines?
   Does it dry up
   like a raisin in the sun?
A. personification
B. paradox
C. simile
D. metaphor

____ 3. In "Dreams," when the speaker says that "Life is a broken-winged bird / That cannot fly," the figure of speech is an example of
A. simile.
B. paradox.
C. personification.
D. metaphor.

____ 4. Which of the following best states the theme, or underlying message, of "Dreams"?
A. Dreams can make life seem empty.
B. Dreams allow people to live forever.
C. People can be crippled by their dreams.
D. A life without dreams is no life at all.

____ 5. In "I Wandered Lonely as a Cloud," what is the best description of what the daffodils are doing when the speaker sees them?
A. They are wilting in the afternoon sun.
B. They are twinkling.
C. They are fluttering in the breeze.
D. They are closing their petals.

____ 6. What effect does the sight of the daffodils seem to have on the speaker as he views the scene?
A. Knowing that the flowers will not last, he experiences frustration.
B. He longs to be with friends who will share the sight.
C. He is no longer calm, but anxious.
D. He is no longer lonely and troubled, but joyful.

____ 7. In "I Wandered Lonely as a Cloud," what is the "wealth" that the speaker believes the daffodils have brought him?
   A. money earned by his growing and selling flowers
   B. his increased knowledge of flowers, lakes, and clouds
   C. his ability to find strength and happiness in the beauty of nature
   D. his ability to write about nature and then sell his writing for money

____ 8. Read the following lines from "I Wandered Lonely as a Cloud":
   7 Continuous as the stars that shine
   8 And twinkle on the milky way,
   9 They stretched in never-ending line
   10 Along the margin of a bay:
   11 Ten thousand saw I at a glance,
   12 Tossing their heads in sprightly dance.

   When reading these lines, you should *not* pause at the end of
   A. lines 7 and 8.   C. lines 8 and 10.
   B. lines 7 and 9.   D. lines 10 and 11.

____ 9. What figure of speech does Gabriela Mistral use in these lines from "Meciendo"?
   The sea rocks her thousands of waves.
   The sea is divine.
   Hearing the loving sea,
   I rock my son.

   A. simile   C. personification
   B. metaphor   D. paradox

____ 10. In "Meciendo," which of the following best describes the speaker's tone, or attitude toward the subject?
   A. agitated   C. loving
   B. aggressive   D. despairing

____ 11. A paradox is a figure of speech that
   A. uses a comparative word such as *like* or *as*.
   B. gives human qualities to something nonhuman.
   C. seems contradictory but actually expresses a truth.
   D. stands for itself and also something outside or beyond itself.

____ 12. In "Sonnet on Love XIII," the statement of Archimedes "Give me a place to stand . . . and I can move the world" exemplifies which of the following?
   A. simile
   B. metaphor
   C. personification
   D. paradox

_____ 13. Which of the following best expresses the poet's message in "Sonnet on Love XIII"?
   A. Love is fleeting and often deceptive.
   B. All too often, love is not reciprocated.
   C. Love cheers the heart and makes lovers merry.
   D. The power of love is virtually immeasurable.

Vocabulary and Grammar

_____ 14. Which of the following is the best synonym for *pensive*?
   A. temporary   C. carefree
   B. thoughtful   D. anxious

_____ 15. If Elaine *deferred* her trip to India, what did she do?
   A. She planned her trip carefully.   C. She postponed her trip.
   B. She paid for her trip in installments.   D. She canceled her trip abruptly.

_____ 16. In the sentence "William Wordsworth lived most of his life in the Lake District," which words are prepositions?
   A. *most* and *life*   C. *of* and *in*
   B. *lived* and *life*   D. *his* and *Lake*

Essay

17. The poems by Langston Hughes both relate to the nature of dreams. In an essay, compare and contrast "Dream Deferred" and "Dreams." Comment on Hughes's use of such elements as figurative language, tone, and theme, or overall message. Be sure to support your ideas with references to the text.

18. The poems in this collection use figurative language to express ideas and create vivid images. Write an essay in which you analyze the figurative language in one of these poems. Define the type or types of figurative language, and give an example of each type. Then, explain how the figurative language affects the poem's meaning.

19. The final lines of William Wordsworth's poem "I Wandered Lonely as a Cloud" read as follows:
   They flash upon that inward eye / Which is the bliss of solitude; / And then my heart with pleasure fills, / And dances with the daffodils.

   What is the meaning of this passage? What is the speaker's "inward eye"? Why are the daffodils significant to the speaker? Explain your answers in an essay.

20. **Thinking About the Big Question: How does communication change us?** Each of the poems by Hughes, Wordsworth, Mistral, and de Sponde in this collection communicates a main idea that might be understood as a piece of advice. Choose one poem from the collection and express the advice it seems to be giving. If a reader took this advice to heart, how might it change the remainder of his or her day—or life?

Vocabulary Warm-up Word Lists

Study these words from the poetry of Richard Brautigan, Emily Dickinson, and Stanley Kunitz. Then, apply your knowledge to the activities that follow.

Word List A

assent [uh SENT] *v.* agree or express agreement
   We will <u>assent</u> to their wishes and have the party at their house.

demur [di MER] *v.* hesitate or protest because of doubts or objections
   If he asks me to go along with his scheme, I will have to <u>demur</u>.

ecology [ee CAHL uh jee] *n.* relationship between living creatures and their environment
   Cleaning up the river improved the <u>ecology</u> of the region.

grace [GRAYS] *n.* quality of showing goodwill or beauty and charm
   She is full of <u>grace</u> and a joy to know for all who befriend her.

hireling [HYR ling] *adj.* doing or done only for the money
   That is a <u>hireling</u> job and not one to choose as a career.

virtue [VER choo] *n.* quality of being morally good or of having a special power
   One <u>virtue</u> of aspirin is its ability to stop a headache.

Word List B

discerning [di SERN ing] *adj.* having good judgment or understanding
   She is a <u>discerning</u> friend and often helps me do the right thing.

extremity [ik STREM i tee] *n.* outer edge; farthest point
   The popular kids were the group's center, and the less popular kids were at its <u>extremity</u>.

grievous [GREE vuhs] *adj.* very serious and likely to be harmful
   He had a <u>grievous</u> wound and was lucky to survive at all.

maimed [MAYMD] *adj.* injured seriously and often permanently
   In the Civil War, thousands of men were <u>maimed</u> after losing limbs.

mutually [MYOO choo uhl lee] *adv.* done or felt toward or for each other
   The sisters were <u>mutually</u> frustrated by one another's behavior.

prevail [pree VAYL] *v.* achieve success after a struggle
   With hard work, he was able to <u>prevail</u> and improve his grades.

Poetry Collection: Richard Brautigan, Emily Dickinson, Stanley Kunitz
Vocabulary Warm-up Exercises

Exercise A *Fill in each blank in the following paragraph with an appropriate word from Word List A. Use each word only once.*

A naturalist will tell you that there is goodness and moral [1] _____ in enjoying the plants and animals found in wild places. For nature-lovers, no job in the outdoors is a [2] _____ position. Money is only one of the benefits. These people would also feel rewarded by the chance to observe the [3] _____ of a place and even contribute to the positive interaction between humans and nature. Other people may [4] _____ to the idea that nature is good, but they may not be comfortable being in the wild. Then, there are those who, if offered the chance to explore nature, would [5] _____. What is important is to approach different views with [6] _____, trying to understand them all.

Exercise B *Decide whether each of the following statements is true or false. Explain your answers.*

1. The planets that are closest to the sun are found on the <u>extremity</u> of our solar system.
   T / F _____

2. You can be <u>mutually</u> happy with yourself.
   T / F _____

3. A person who was <u>maimed</u> might need medical attention for life.
   T / F _____

4. People should never believe what a <u>discerning</u> person has to say.
   T / F _____

5. If you give up when faced with hardships, you will <u>prevail</u>.
   T / F _____

6. Someone with a <u>grievous</u> concern would probably be very worried or upset.
   T / F _____

Poetry Collection: Richard Brautigan, Emily Dickinson, Stanley Kunitz

Reading Warm-up A

Read the following passage. Pay special attention to the underlined words. Then, read it again, and complete the activities. Use a separate sheet of paper for your written answers.

John Muir is honored for his far-reaching influence on modern conservation—the protection of natural places, animals, and plants. Muir was ahead of his time. He called for the protection of natural places long before most people would <u>assent</u> to the idea and agree that there was a need.

Muir's enjoyment of the outdoors began as a boy in Scotland. He came to America with his family in 1849, at age eleven. They settled in Wisconsin. During breaks from farm work, Muir explored the countryside. He developed a curiosity about <u>ecology</u>, the interaction of creatures and their environment.

Even as a young man, Muir saw things differently. Most people would object strongly, or at least <u>demur</u>, at the idea of rising at one o'clock in the morning to study. Not Muir. He had a lifelong love of learning and an inventive mind.

In 1860, he entered the University of Wisconsin, but he left before graduating. He traveled in the wilderness of the northern U.S. and Canada. He marveled at the landscape and saw a moral goodness and <u>virtue</u> in nature.

To earn money, Muir worked as a mechanic at <u>hireling</u> jobs. In 1867, a work accident temporarily blinded him. When he recovered, he pledged to spend the rest of his life in nature. He did, for almost 50 years.

Muir eventually settled near the Sierra Nevada Mountains and Yosemite Valley in California. He wrote hundreds of articles and over a dozen books on his experiences and philosophy. Muir believed nature offered a kind of <u>grace</u> and decency that benefited people. He encouraged everyone to "climb the mountains and get their good tidings."

In 1892, he founded the Sierra Club: "To do something for wilderness and make the mountains glad." Today, it is the largest environmental organization in the country. Muir is also remembered for the many national parks that were created through his influence.

1. Circle the word that is a clue to the meaning of <u>assent</u>. Give a word that means the opposite of *assent*.

2. Circle the phrase that helps explain the meaning of <u>ecology</u>. Underline the sentence that explains how Muir developed an interest in *ecology*.

3. Circle the word that is a clue to the meaning of <u>demur</u>. Give a synonym, or word with a similar meaning, for *demur*.

4. Underline the words that are a clue to the meaning of <u>virtue</u>. Circle what Muir saw as having *virtue*.

5. Underline the phrase that is a clue to the meaning of <u>hireling</u>. What would a *hireling* worker care most about when taking a job? Explain.

6. Circle the word that is a clue to the meaning of <u>grace</u>. Underline Muir's idea of how people could experience the *grace* found in nature.

Poetry Collection: Richard Brautigan, Emily Dickinson, Stanley Kunitz

Reading Warm-up B

Read the following passage. Pay special attention to the underlined words. Then, read it again, and complete the activities. Use a separate sheet of paper for your written answers.

In 1782, the Second Continental Congress chose the bald eagle, found only in North America, as the symbol of the United States. It was <u>mutually</u> agreed upon by most members. Benjamin Franklin, however, preferred the wild turkey, calling the bald eagle "too lazy to fish for himself."

Franklin, a usually <u>discerning</u> thinker, was wrong in his understanding of the bald eagle. It, indeed, feeds on fish—and on water birds and small mammals. When a bald eagle feeds, it dives from the sky at speeds up to 100 miles per hour. However, it can lift only about 5 pounds with its sharp talon claws. A determined bald eagle will swim to shore while dragging its prey, using its wings as paddles.

The bald eagle's ferocious feeding habits gave it a bad reputation. Early settlers believed it attacked their livestock. The threat of having their farm animals killed or <u>maimed</u> with permanent injuries led settlers to hunt eagles.

The greatest danger to the bird developed in the mid-1900s. Pesticides used at the time got into the food chain. Bald eagles were seriously harmed. The most <u>grievous</u> damage was done to their eggs, which did not mature. By the 1960s, there were only about 400 breeding pairs—fewer than 1,000 eagles—in the lower forty-eight U.S. states.

The eagle is among the creatures on the top <u>extremity</u>, or farthest edge, of the food chain. The eagle's loss had an impact on the other plants and animals in the chain. Scientists realized that something had to be done.

In 1973, President Richard Nixon signed The Endangered Species Act into law. It led to reforms in pesticide use and to other measures that helped save the eagles.

Today, the bald eagle population has soared to more than 6,000 breeding pairs in the lower forty-eight states. Around 50,000 birds flourish in Alaska. If those numbers continue to rise, the bald eagle will <u>prevail</u>. After its long struggle, it can be declared fully recovered.

1. Explain who <u>mutually</u> agreed to make the bald eagle the national symbol of the United States. Use your own words to explain the meaning of *mutually* in the passage.

2. Circle a word that is a clue to the meaning of <u>discerning</u>. Why was Franklin not a *discerning* thinker when it came to the bald eagle?

3. Circle the phrase that is a clue to the meaning of <u>maimed</u>. Why might an eagle attack result in a cow or sheep being *maimed*?

4. Circle the phrase that is a clue to the meaning of <u>grievous</u>. Why would something that destroyed a bald eagle's eggs do *grievous* damage to the bird?

5. Circle the phrase that gives the meaning of <u>extremity</u>. Underline the phrase that explains the significance of the bald eagle's place on the *extremity* of the food chain.

6. Underline a phrase and a word that give a clue to the meaning of <u>prevail</u>. Give a synonym for *prevail*.

© Pearson Education, Inc. All rights reserved.

Poetry Collection: Richard Brautigan, Emily Dickinson, Stanley Kunitz

Writing About the Big Question

How does communication change us?

Big Question Vocabulary

aware	communication	comprehension	discuss	empathy
exchange	illuminate	informed	interpretation	meaning
react	relationship	resolution	respond	understanding

A. *Use one or more words from the list above to complete each sentence.*

1. Experienced public speakers know that repeating an important point improves their audience's _____ of it.

2. In small discussion groups, you can _____ ideas with your classmates.

3. In any _____ with another person, good _____ is very valuable.

4. We read newspapers and magazines to stay _____ about current events.

5. It often happens that no two readers have exactly the same _____ of a poem.

B. *Follow the directions in responding to each of the items below.*

1. List two different times when your **understanding** of another person's point of view helped improve your **relationship** with him or her.

_____

_____

2. Write two sentences to explain one of these experiences, and describe how it made you feel. Use at least two of the Big Question vocabulary words.

_____

_____

C. *Complete the sentence below. Then, write a short paragraph in which you connect the sentence to the Big Question.*

As a result of advances in computer technology, **communication** between people has become _____

_____

_____

_____

© Pearson Education, Inc. All rights reserved.

Name _____ Date _____

Poetry Collection: Richard Brautigan, Emily Dickinson, Stanley Kunitz
Literary Analysis: Figurative Language

Figurative language is language that is used imaginatively rather than literally. Figurative language includes one or more **figures of speech,** literary devices that make unexpected comparisons or change the usual meanings of words. The following are figures of speech:

- **Simile:** a comparison of two apparently unlike things using *like, as, than,* or *resembles*
- **Metaphor:** a comparison of two apparently unlike things without using *like, as, than,* or *resembles*
- **Personification:** giving human characteristics to a nonhuman subject
- **Paradox:** a statement, an idea, or a situation that seems contradictory but actually expresses a truth

DIRECTIONS: *Read the following passages and then use the lines provided to identify each example of figurative language. Briefly indicate the reason for your answer. Note that some passages may exemplify more than one figure of speech.*

1. "Where mammals and computers
   live together in mutually
   programming harmony
   like pure water
   touching pure sky" ("All Watched Over by Machines of Loving Grace")

   _____

   _____

2. "I've heard it in the chillest land—
   And on the strangest Sea—
   Yet, never, in Extremity,
   It asked a crumb—of Me." ("'Hope is the thing with feathers—")

   _____

   _____

3. "The man who sold his lawn to standard oil
   Joked with his neighbors come to watch the show
   While the bulldozers, drunk with gasoline,
   Tested the virtue of the soil
   Under the branchy sky
   By overthrowing first the privet-row." ("The War Against the Trees")

   _____

   _____

4. "Much madness is divinest Sense—
   To a discerning Eye—
   Much Sense—the starkest Madness—" ("Much Madness is divinest Sense")

   _____

   _____

Name _____ Date _____

Poetry Collection: Richard Brautigan, Emily Dickinson, Stanley Kunitz
Reading: Read Fluently

Reading fluently is reading smoothly and continuously while also comprehending the text and appreciating the writer's artistry. To improve your fluency when reading poetry, **read in sentences.** Use punctuation—periods, commas, colons, semicolons, and dashes—rather than the ends of lines to determine where to pause or stop reading.

DIRECTIONS: *Read the following passages and then answer the questions on the lines provided.*

1. "I like to think
   (it has to be!)
   of a cybernetic ecology
   where we are free of our labors
   and joined back to nature,
   returned to our mammal
   brothers and sisters,
   and all watched over
   by machines of loving grace." ("All Watched Over by Machines of Loving Grace")

   At the ends of which lines would you make major pauses in reading? Minor pauses? No pauses at all?

   _____

   _____

   _____

2. "All day the hireling engines charged the trees,
   Subverting them by hacking underground
   In grub-dominions, where dark summer's mole
   Rampages through his halls,
   Till a northern seizure shook
   Those crowns, forcing the giants to their knees." ("The War Against the Trees")

   After which words would you make a minor pause? After which words would you make no pause at all?

   _____

   _____

   _____

© Pearson Education, Inc. All rights reserved.

Poetry Collection: Richard Brautigan, Emily Dickinson, Stanley Kunitz
Vocabulary Builder

Word List

abash   discerning   preliminaries   prevail   seizure   subverting

A. DIRECTIONS: *Answer each of the following questions.*

____ 1. Which of the following is the best synonym for *discerning*?
   A. differentiating
   B. insightful
   C. despising
   D. prepared

____ 2. Which of the following most nearly means the opposite of *preliminaries*?
   A. consequences
   B. circumstances
   C. details
   D. considerations

____ 3. Which of the following is the best synonym for *subverting*?
   A. expanding   B. reducing   C. encouraging   D. undermining

____ 4. Which of the following most nearly means the opposite of *prevail*?
   A. be defeated   B. praise   C. endure   D. analyze

B. DIRECTIONS: *In each of the following items, think about the meaning of the italicized word and then answer the question.*

1. Would you want the pilot of an airplane flight to possess a *discerning* eye? Why or why not?
   _____

2. Do *preliminaries* take place before, during, or after the main event?
   _____

3. Would a warm, gentle breeze be likely to *abash* a person? Why or why not?
   _____

4. Does a *seizure* suggest a violent or a gentle action or event? Explain your answer.
   _____

C. WORD STUDY: Use the context of the sentences and what you know about the Latin root *-vert-* to explain your answer to each question.

1. If people *subvert* the government, do they support it or undermine it?
   _____
   _____

2. If you have an *aversion* to turnips, do you like them or dislike them?
   _____
   _____

3. If a statement is *incontrovertible*, can it be disproved or refuted?
   _____
   _____

© Pearson Education, Inc. All rights reserved.

Name _____ Date _____

Enrichment: Computers in the Workplace

In the poem "All Watched Over by Machines of Loving Grace," Richard Brautigan predicts a future society in which computers make us "free of our labors." Although Brautigan's imaginary world might still be viewed as extreme, today's computers have indeed changed and revolutionized a variety of workplaces.

Computers are used in offices and laboratories throughout the world for typing, gathering, organizing, and exchanging information. People working in business and finance use computers to store large amounts of business data and to analyze changes in the world's uneasy markets 24 hours a day. In schools, computers assist students in their learning, and in libraries, computers help people as they research topics and locate books and articles. Different kinds of computer programs are also used regularly by architects and designers, who can modify their designs on computer screens; by manufacturers and scientists, who can use computers to design machine tools and complex hospital and laboratory instruments; and by air-traffic controllers, who can guide planes using a computer screen. You might be surprised to know that today's computers are even used to control robots working on automobile assembly lines—completing tasks previously performed by people.

A. DIRECTIONS: *Answer the following questions on the lines provided.*

1. What basic computer skills are needed for many of today's jobs?

   _____

   _____

2. In what ways do you think the computer has made many of today's workplaces less dangerous, more interesting, and more efficient?

   _____

   _____

3. Do you think computers have actually made some jobs more tedious? Explain.

   _____

   _____

4. Based on what you have learned about computer technology, do you think the imaginary world described by Brautigan has become something of a reality in the early twenty-first century? Why or why not?

   _____

   _____

   _____

B. DIRECTIONS: *Choose a job or field that interests you, and then carry out research to discover what computer skills, if any, are needed for this job. You may do your research at a library, or you may contact a company or a person employed in your field of choice. Find out how computers and other kinds of technology have changed that particular field over the past several years. Write a brief report on your findings.*

© Pearson Education, Inc. All rights reserved.

Poetry Collection: Langston Hughes, William Wordsworth, Gabriela Mistral,
Jean de Sponde, Richard Brautigan, Emily Dickinson, Stanley Kunitz

Integrated Language Skills: Grammar

Prepositions and Prepositional Phrases

A **preposition** is a word that relates a noun or pronoun that appears with it to another word in the sentence. Although most prepositions, such as *at, by, in,* and *with,* are single words, some prepositions, such as *because of* and *in addition to,* are compound. In the following example from "The War Against the Trees," the prepositions are in italics.

> "Ripped *from* the craters much too big *for* hearts
>
> The club-roots bared their amputated coils"

The **object of a preposition** is the noun or pronoun at the end of a prepositional phrase. In the following example, the prepositional phrase is underlined and the object of the preposition is in italics.

> Gabriela Mistral wrote many poems <u>about *children*</u>.

A. PRACTICE: *Read the following passages from the poems in these collections. On the lines provided, write each prepositional phrase. Then, circle the object of the preposition.*

1. "'Hope is the thing with feathers—
   That perches in the soul—'"

   _____

2. "Where we are free of our labors
   and joined back to nature . . .'"

   _____

3. "That putative spot
   exists in the love I feel for you, my dear."

   _____

B. Writing Application: *Write a brief paragraph in which you describe the way you get to school in the morning. Use at least five prepositional phrases in your writing, and underline each prepositional phrase you use.*

_____

_____

_____

_____

_____

_____

_____

Poetry Collection: Langston Hughes, William Wordsworth, Gabriela Mistral, Jean de Sponde, Richard Brautigan, Emily Dickinson, Stanley Kunitz

Support for Writing a Description of a Scene

Use the following lines to make prewriting notes for your description of a scene in nature.

Choice of Scene: _____

_____

Sensory Details:

1. **Sight:** _____

_____

_____

2. **Sound:** _____

_____

_____

3. **Touch:** _____

_____

_____

4. **Smell:** _____

_____

_____

5. **Taste:** _____

_____

_____

Unified Impression: _____

_____

Now, use your notes to write a few paragraphs or a poem describing a scene in nature.

Unit 4 Resources: Poetry
© Pearson Education, Inc. All rights reserved.
51

Poetry Collection: Langston Hughes, William Wordsworth, Gabriela Mistral, Jean de Sponde, Richard Brautigan, Emily Dickinson, Stanley Kunitz

Support for Extend Your Learning

Listening and Speaking: Poetry Collection: Richard Brautigan, Emily Dickinson, Stanley Kunitz

Use the following lines to make prewriting notes for your inspirational speech about dreams, nature, or love.

My Speech Topic: _____

My Central Idea: _____

_____

Ideas for Body Language and Eye Contact: _____

_____

_____

My Conclusion: _____

_____

Listening and Speaking: Poetry Collection: Langston Hughes, William Wordsworth, Gabriela Mistral, Jean de Sponde

Use the following lines to make prewriting notes for your inspirational speech about dreams, nature, or love.

My Speech Topic: _____

My Central Idea: _____

_____

Ideas for Body Language and Eye Contact: _____

_____

_____

My Conclusion: _____

_____

© Pearson Education, Inc. All rights reserved.

Poetry Collection: Richard Brautigan, Emily Dickinson, Stanley Kunitz
Open-Book Test

Short Answer *Write your responses to the questions in this section on the lines provided.*

1. What two things are compared in the simile in the second stanza of "All Watched Over by Machines of Loving Grace" by Richard Brautigan?

   _____

   _____

2. In "All Watched Over by Machines of Loving Grace," Richard Brautigan, the poet, begins each stanza with "I like to think of. . . ." Explain why you think the poet really does or does not like to think of the things he describes.

   _____

   _____

   _____

   _____

3. In "'Hope' is the thing with feathers—," Emily Dickinson compares hope to a bird. What birdlike qualities does she assign to hope?

   _____

   _____

   _____

4. In the second stanza of "'Hope' is the thing with feathers," what does Emily Dickinson, the poet, mean when she says that the little bird "kept so many warm"?

   _____

   _____

   _____

5. Would you read aloud the last two lines of Emily Dickinson's "'Hope' is the thing with feathers—" as one or two sentences? Explain your answer.

   _____

   _____

   _____

6. According to Emily Dickinson's poem "Much Madness is divinest Sense—," who decides what is madness and what is sense? Why is this a paradox?

   _____

   _____

   _____

   _____

© Pearson Education, Inc. All rights reserved.

7. In Emily Dickinson's "Much Madness is divinest Sense—," what does the speaker believe a "discerning eye" can see? Base your response on the meaning of *discerning*.

    _____

    _____

    _____

8. Cite an example of personification in Stanley Kunitz's poem "The War Against the Trees."

    _____

    _____

    _____

9. What does the poet Stanley Kunitz imagine in the fourth stanza of "The War Against the Trees"?

    _____

    _____

    _____

10. In the chart below, list two preliminaries to "The War Against the Trees." Then list two events that occurred during the "war."

Preliminary 1	Preliminary 2	War Event 1	War Event 2

Essay

Write an extended response to the question of your choice or to the question or questions your teacher assigns you.

11. Four types of figurative language can be found in this poetry collection: simile, metaphor, personification, and paradox. Find examples of these figures of speech in the poems of Brautigan, Dickinson, and Kunitz. Then discuss each example in an essay. Include a definition of the figure of speech with each example.

12. In an essay, choose either "All Watched Over by Machines of Loving Grace" by Richard Brautigan or "The War Against the Trees" by Stanley Kunitz and discuss the ideas and attitudes about technology and the natural world that the poem expresses. Do you consider the poem a critique, a warning, an expression of hope—or something else? How does the poet use figurative language to express his ideas?

Name _____ Date _____

13. In this poetry collection, the poets Brautigan, Dickinson, and Kunitz use figurative language to convey ideas and create vivid images. Write an essay in which you analyze the figurative language in one of the poems. Define at least two types of figurative language, and explain how these types are at work in the poem. Finally, evaluate the poet's use of each type of figurative language. In what ways does it deepen the poem's meaning? Tell how effective it is and why it is effective.

14. **Thinking About the Big Question: How does communication change us?** In Richard Brautigan's vision of the future in "All Watched Over by Machines of Loving Grace," does computer technology seem to have strengthened humans' ability to communicate or weakened it? Explain your response in an essay.

Oral Response

15. Go back to question 4, 6, or 9 or to the question your teacher assigns to you. Take a few minutes to expand your answer and prepare an oral response. Find additional details in the poems by Brautigan, Dickinson, and Kunitz that support your points. If necessary, make notes to guide your oral response.

Poetry Collection: Richard Brautigan, Emily Dickinson, Stanley Kunitz

Selection Test A

Critical Reading *Identify the letter of the choice that best answers the question.*

____ 1. According to the speaker in "All Watched Over by Machines of Loving Grace," what two things should exist together in harmony?
   A. deer and people
   B. water and sky
   C. mammals and computers
   D. computers and machines

____ 2. Which of the following best defines a *simile*?
   A. an apparent contradiction
   B. a type of literal speech
   C. a comparison using *like* or *as*
   D. an exaggeration

____ 3. According to the speaker in "All Watched Over by Machines of Loving Grace," how can computer technology bring people closer to nature?
   A. by making travel easier
   B. by freeing people of their labors
   C. by improving communication
   D. by cleaning the environment

____ 4. In "Hope is the thing with feathers—," Emily Dickinson compares hope to which of the following?
   A. a bird
   B. a star
   C. a wave
   D. a dream

____ 5. When reading poetry, you can improve your fluency by doing which of the following?
   A. researching the poet's life
   B. pausing at the ends of lines
   C. reading in sentences and using punctuation
   D. thinking about the poem's title

_____ 6. Tone is the attitude toward the characters or the subject matter of a literary work. Which of the following best describes the speaker's tone in "'Hope is the thing with feathers—'"?
  A. despairing   C. critical
  B. angry   D. enthusiastic

_____ 7. Which of the following best expresses the central conflict in "The War Against the Trees"?
  A. parents vs. children
  B. cities vs. countryside
  C. nature vs. modern technology
  D. love vs. hate

_____ 8. The words *like, as, than,* or *resembles* commonly appear in which of the following figures of speech?
  A. metaphor   C. simile
  B. hyperbole   D. paradox

_____ 9. Read the following excerpt from "The War Against the Trees":
      13 All day the hireling engines charged the trees,
      14 Subverting them by hacking underground
      15 In grub-dominions, where dark summer's mole
      16 Rampages through his halls,
      17 Till a northern seizure shook
      18 Those crowns, forcing the giants to their knees.

  In reading these lines, where would you *not* pause?
  A. after lines 13 and 16
  B. after lines 14, 15, and 17
  C. after lines 16 and 18
  D. after lines 13 and 15

_____ 10. In "The War Against the Trees," when the speaker refers to "the bulldozers, drunk with gasoline," which figure of speech is involved?
  A. paradox   C. personification
  B. metaphor   D. simile

_____ 11. The theme, or underlying message, of "The War Against the Trees" concerns which of the following?
  A. damage to nature
  B. the return of hope
  C. dangers of violence
  D. respect for technology

_____ **12.** In "Much Madness is divinest Sense," what point is the speaker making?

    A. Everyone is a little mad at one time or another.

    B. Madness and sense are often not what they seem.

    C. The majority is always right.

    D. It is difficult to be sensible.

Vocabulary and Grammar

_____ **13.** Which of the following is the best synonym for *discerning* in these lines?

    Much Madness is divinest Sense
    To a discerning Eye—

    A. predicting   **C.** estimating

    B. recalling   **D.** understanding

_____ **14.** In the sentence "Brautigan was older than the hippies and a product of the Beat generation that preceded them," which of the following is the prepositional phrase?

    A. than the hippies   **C.** of the Beat generation

    B. and a product   **D.** that preceded them

Essay

15. Four common types of figurative language are simile, metaphor, personification, and paradox. Choose one of these figures of speech and discuss it in a brief essay. Be sure to include an accurate definition of the figure of speech. Then, support your main ideas with specific examples of this type of figurative language drawn from the poems in this collection.

16. The theme of a literary work is its central idea, or underlying message, about human life or behavior. Writers sometimes spell out the theme explicitly. Most of the time, though, the reader has to infer a work's theme, using clues from the work itself. Choose one of the poems in this collection and write a brief essay discussing the work's theme. Begin your essay by identifying the work and stating the theme. Then, support your interpretation of the theme with specific details from the work. Finally, tell whether or not you agree with the theme, and why.

17. Thinking About the Big Question: How does communication change us? Poet Richard Brautigan has a vision of the future in "All Watched Over by Machines of Loving Grace." He sees mammals and computers living together. He sees mammals watched over by machines. Does Brautigan say that computer technology has strengthened humans' ability to communicate or has it weakened it? Explain your response in an essay.

© Pearson Education, Inc. All rights reserved.

Poetry Collection: Richard Brautigan, Emily Dickinson, Stanley Kunitz
Selection Test B

Critical Reading *Identify the letter of the choice that best completes the statement or answers the question.*

____ 1. Which figure of speech do these lines illustrate?

Where deer stroll peacefully
past computers
as if they were flowers
with spinning blossoms.

    A. simile
    B. metaphor
    C. personification
    D. paradox

____ 2. In "All Watched Over by Machines of Loving Grace," the future environment that the poet imagines is best described by which of the following?
    A. peaceful
    B. nightmarish
    C. anxious
    D. boring

____ 3. In "'Hope is the thing with feathers—," Emily Dickinson implies that hope
    A. comes to people whether they seek it or not.
    B. remains ever elusive and nearly impossible to achieve.
    C. irritates people with its cheerfulness.
    D. is easily discouraged from entering people's lives.

____ 4. Which of the following sentences is the best paraphrase of the line "'Hope is the thing with feathers—"?
    A. A bird represents hope.
    B. Hope is a bird.
    C. Hope wears feathers.
    D. Hope can seem small and unassuming, like a bird.

____ 5. The speaker of "'Hope is the thing with feathers—" evidently believes that hope
    A. helps people through difficult times.
    B. defies definition.
    C. and dreams are closely linked.
    D. can be lost in extreme situations.

____ 6. In "The War Against the Trees," the line "All day long the hireling engines charged the trees" illustrates which figure of speech?
    A. simile
    B. metaphor
    C. paradox
    D. personification

© Pearson Education, Inc. All rights reserved.

____ 7. Read the following excerpt from "The War Against the Trees":

   7 Forsythia-forays and hydrangea-raids
   8 Were but preliminaries to a war
   9 Against the great-grandfathers of the town,
   10 So freshly lopped and maimed.
   11 They struck and struck again,
   12 And with each elm a century went down.

   Where should you *not* pause when reading these lines?
   A. after lines 7 and 8
   B. after lines 8 and 9
   C. after lines 10 and 11
   D. after lines 11 and 12

____ 8. In "The War Against the Trees," who or what are "the great-grandfathers of the town" in the lines "Were but preliminaries to a war / Against the great-grandfathers of the town"?
   A. the members of the city council
   B. the town's historical buildings
   C. the town's elm trees
   D. the town's Civil War veterans

____ 9. In "The War Against the Trees," which of the following best describes the speaker's tone, or attitude toward his subject?
   A. uncaring and indifferent
   B. optimistic and agitated
   C. melancholy and sympathetic
   D. cheerful and carefree

____ 10. When the speaker in Emily Dickinson's poem declares in the opening lines that "Much Madness is divinest Sense— / To a discerning Eye," what figure of speech does the poet use?
   A. metaphor
   B. paradox
   C. personification
   D. simile

____ 11. At the end of "Much Madness is divinest Sense," the speaker's tone might best be described as
   A. cheerful.
   B. nostalgic.
   C. ominous.
   D. gentle.

____ 12. Metaphor differs chiefly from simile in that metaphor
   A. is used for nonhuman objects in the natural world.
   B. contains many layers of significance.
   C. does not use an explicit comparative word such as *like* or *as*.
   D. may be extended over many lines of verse.

© Pearson Education, Inc. All rights reserved.

Vocabulary and Grammar

____ 13. Which of the following best defines *preliminaries*?
    A. minor events
    B. rare events
    C. events occurring before the main event
    D. events occurring after the main event

____ 14. Which of the following is most nearly the opposite of *discerning*?
    A. understanding
    B. analyzing
    C. blind
    D. greedy

____ 15. A preposition never appears alone. With which part of speech does a preposition always appear?
    A. an adjective
    B. a noun or pronoun
    C. a conjunction
    D. a verb

____ 16. Identify the objects of prepositions in these lines from "The War Against the Trees."
    The man who sold his lawn to standard oil
    Joked with his neighbors come to watch the show
    A. *standard oil, neighbors*
    B. *sold, lawn*
    C. *standard oil, show*
    D. *come, watch*

Essay

17. In an essay, compare and contrast "All Watched Over by Machines of Loving Grace" with "The War Against the Trees." What ideas and attitudes about technology and the natural world are expressed in each poem? How do Richard Brautigan and Stanley Kunitz use vivid imagery and figurative language to express their ideas?

18. The poets in these selections use figurative language to express ideas and create vivid images. Write an essay in which you analyze the figurative language in one of these poems. Define the type or types of figurative language, and explain how such language affects the poem's meaning.

19. **Thinking About the Big Question: How does communication change us?** In Richard Brautigan's vision of the future in "All Watched Over by Machines of Loving Grace," does computer technology seem to have strengthened humans' ability to communicate or weakened it? Explain your response in an essay.

© Pearson Education, Inc. All rights reserved.

Vocabulary Warm-up Word Lists

Study these words from the poetry of Walter Dean Myers; Alfred, Lord Tennyson; and May Swenson. Then, apply your knowledge to the activities that follow.

Word List A

bait [BAYT] *n.* something offered to persuade someone to do something
When Snow White was offered the delicious apple, she could not resist taking the <u>bait</u>.

beaming [BEEM ing] *n.* act of smiling or sending out rays of light
The children were so happy, they were <u>beaming</u> with joy.

crawls [KRAWLZ] *v.* moves slowly
Time <u>crawls</u> when you are watching a boring movie.

disgrace [dis GRAYS] *n.* shame; loss of others' respect
It is no <u>disgrace</u> to fail if you tried your best.

dripping [DRIP ing] *v.* falling in drops
Water was <u>dripping</u> slowly from the leaking faucet.

peeping [PEEP ing] *v.* making brief, high-pitched noises
The chick was <u>peeping</u> right after it emerged from the egg.

Word List B

exploded [ik SPLOHD ed] *v.* burst; suddenly showed strong emotions
The audience <u>exploded</u> with laughter at the comic's slapstick humor.

flirts [FLERTS] *v.* shows attraction to or an interest in, in a playful way
My brother <u>flirts</u> with the waitress at the diner, but it is all in the spirit of fun.

loaded [LOHD ed] *adj.* filled with; in baseball, said of the bases when there are runners on all three bases
With the bases <u>loaded</u>, one hit would win the game.

ripping [RIP ing] *v.* slang for "rushing quickly"
The shoppers were <u>ripping</u> through the store to grab the bargains before they were gone.

thunderbolt [THUHN der bohlt] *n.* flash of lightning accompanied by thunder
Our dog hid under the table when he heard the <u>thunderbolt</u> strike.

wrinkled [RING kuhld] *adj.* having small folds or ridges
I ironed the <u>wrinkled</u> blouse before putting it on.

© Pearson Education, Inc. All rights reserved.

Poetry Collection: Walter Dean Myers; Alfred, Lord Tennyson; May Swenson
Vocabulary Warm-up Exercises

Exercise A *Fill in each blank in the following paragraph with an appropriate word from Word List A. Use each word only once.*

My friend Juan loves to take me fishing. He gets down on his hands and knees and

[1] _____ around on the ground to find the worms we use as

[2] _____ to attract the fish. Then, we stand in the stream for hours.

Cold water is [3] _____ from our clothes. It is so quiet at the stream! The

only sounds we hear all morning are from the baby birds [4] _____ in

the trees. You should see Juan's face [5] _____ with joy when he catches

a fish. Sometimes, when the fish are not biting, I have to remind him that it is no

[6] _____ to go home empty-handed. Fishing can be fun even if you

never catch a thing!

Exercise B *Decide whether each of the following statements is true or false. Explain your answers.*

1. If the audience <u>exploded</u> with laughter, the comedian was probably a success.
   T / F _____

2. Someone who <u>flirts</u> with danger is probably very foolish.
   T / F _____

3. If the bases on a baseball diamond are <u>loaded</u>, it means that no one is on them.
   T / F _____

4. If you are <u>ripping</u> through a football field, you are more likely to be a player than
   the referee.
   T / F _____

5. A <u>thunderbolt</u> is not dangerous if you are standing under a tree.
   T / F _____

6. A <u>wrinkled</u> forehead could show that you are confused.
   T / F _____

© Pearson Education, Inc. All rights reserved.

Poetry Collection: Walter Dean Myers; Alfred, Lord Tennyson; May Swenson

Reading Warm-up A

Read the following passage. Pay special attention to the underlined words. Then, read it again, and complete the activities. Use a separate sheet of paper for your written answers.

I was fifteen the summer my cousin Stuart came from Chicago to visit us on the farm. Stuart had never lived anywhere but Chicago, and the country was a big mystery to him. It is no <u>disgrace</u> to feel a little unsettled when you are in a brand new place. I am sure I would have felt just as confused if someone had plunked me down in the middle of a big, bustling city.

If you are expecting a story about how Stuart and I had some exciting adventure together that summer, you are going to be disappointed. The truth is, not much happened. Mostly, we just walked along the crooked stream that winds its way through the woods and talked about our lives. One day, Stuart tripped over a vine and fell right into the stream. He was soaked to the skin, and water was <u>dripping</u> out of the expensive sneakers he always wore. We both thought this was hilarious.

Sometimes, we would go fishing, but Stuart did not much care for handling the live <u>bait</u>. I did not mind putting the worm on his hook for him, but he was still kind of squeamish about the whole thing. Be that as it may, the boy did catch some mighty fine trout that summer.

What Stuart liked best was listening to the birds that were always <u>peeping</u> early in the morning. He said he almost never hears birds back home, which seemed kind of sad to me. Stuart liked having animals around. He has a big dog in his apartment back in Chicago, but that is not the same as having a yard full of chickens and a cow in the barn just outside your house. One day, our neighbor's cat snuck under the fence and almost made off with one of our hens. Stuart thought that this was quite a wonderful event, but my father was not so amused. Still, he had to laugh when he saw Stuart's face <u>beaming</u> with delight over the marvel of it all.

It was a quiet summer, and time usually <u>crawls</u> when nothing much happens. This peaceful summer, however, was one of the best of my young life.

1. Underline the words that tell what is not a <u>disgrace</u>. Write a sentence about something that would be a *disgrace*.

2. Circle the word that tells what was <u>dripping</u>. Write a sentence about something else that might be *dripping*.

3. Circle the word that tells what the boys were using as <u>bait</u> for the fish. Name something that might be *bait* for you.

4. Circle the words that hint at the meaning of <u>peeping</u>. Describe something that could be *peeping*.

5. Circle the word that gives a clue to the meaning of <u>beaming</u>. Under what circumstances might your face be *beaming*?

6. Underline the word that tells what usually <u>crawls</u> when nothing happens. Write a sentence using this meaning of *crawls*.

Poetry Collection: Walter Dean Myers; Alfred, Lord Tennyson; May Swenson
Reading Warm-up B

Read the following passage. Pay special attention to the underlined words. Then, read it again, and complete the activities. Use a separate sheet of paper for your written answers.

The school poetry contest was only a week away, and Tess was determined to be the winner. Now, all she had to do was think of a topic, write a brilliant poem, and submit it before the contest deadline.

Tearing a blank sheet of paper out of her math notebook, Tess sat down to think. Her mind, usually <u>loaded</u> with good ideas, now felt as blank as the blindingly white paper she was staring at. Where were all those ideas that usually were <u>ripping</u> nonstop through her head? With a <u>wrinkled</u> forehead, Tess struggled to come up with a topic.

Mr. Lee, her English teacher, had taught the class about pattern poems. In a pattern poem, the lines of the poem form a picture on the page. She liked the idea of writing a poem in the shape of a diamond, with a long line in the middle and shorter lines tapering off at the beginning and end. A good form for a poem about baseball or precious gems, she thought, but not quite right for this contest.

Mr. Lee said it was important to choose a subject you really care about, but how were you supposed to know what that was? Tess closed her eyes and let her mind drift to that special quiet place where poems seemed to dwell. Then, suddenly and without warning, an idea struck her like a <u>thunderbolt</u> out of the blue: She would write a poem about writing poetry!

"What exactly does a poet do?" Tess asked herself. A poet is someone who <u>flirts</u> with language, playfully teasing words and ideas into a literary form—a word sculpture of sound and meaning. She thought for a few seconds more, and then she began to write.

The job of a poet?
Using rhythm and rhyme
To make sound mate with sense
And make words dance in time.

Not bad for a start, she thought, already picturing the audience at the poetry festival as it <u>exploded</u> in applause after hearing her poem. Not bad at all.

1. Underline the words that tell what Tess's mind is usually <u>loaded</u> with. Explain what someone whose mind is *loaded* in this way is likely to do.

2. Circle the word that hints at the meaning of <u>ripping</u>. Rewrite the sentence, replacing *ripping* with a word that has a similar meaning.

3. Circle the word that tells what was <u>wrinkled</u>. List two other kinds of things that can be *wrinkled*.

4. Circle the word that tells what struck Tess like a <u>thunderbolt</u>. Describe a striking *thunderbolt*.

5. Underline the phrase that gives a clue to the meaning of <u>flirts</u>. Explain what *flirts* means.

6. Underline the words that tell who <u>exploded</u> in applause. Give another example of a time someone or something *exploded*.

© Pearson Education, Inc. All rights reserved.

Poetry Collection: Walter Dean Myers; Alfred, Lord Tennyson; May Swenson

Writing About the Big Question

How does communication change us?

Big Question Vocabulary

aware	communication	comprehension	discuss	empathy
exchange	illuminate	informed	interpretation	meaning
react	relationship	resolution	respond	understanding

A. *Use one or more words from the list above to complete each sentence.*

1. Discussing a difficult poem with friends can often help _____ the poet's purpose.

2. My _____ of a poem is often improved if I read the poem aloud.

3. Sal made a New Year's _____ to start learning a foreign language this year.

4. People's facial expressions often signal how they _____ to a statement or question.

5. If you _____ to a question too abruptly, people may think you are being rude.

B. *Follow the directions in responding to each of the items below.*

1. List two different times when your senses—sight, hearing, touch, taste, and smell— played an important part in your **relationship** with the world around you.

_____

_____

2. Write two sentences to explain one of these experiences, and describe how it made you feel. Use at least two of the Big Question vocabulary words.

_____

_____

C. *Complete the sentence below. Then, write a short paragraph in which you connect the sentence to the Big Question.*

By reading someone else's **interpretation** of a common experience, a reader can learn to _____

_____

_____

_____

Name _____ Date _____

Poetry Collection: Walter Dean Myers; Alfred, Lord Tennyson; May Swenson
Literary Analysis: Sound Devices

Poets use **sound devices** to emphasize the sound relationships among words. These devices include the following:

- **Alliteration:** the repetition of initial consonant sounds in stressed syllables: "*running and ripping*"
- **Consonance:** the repetition of final consonant sounds in stressed syllables with different vowel sounds, as in *bat* and *met*
- **Assonance:** the repetition of similar vowel sounds in stressed syllables that end with different consonant sounds, as in *please* and *steam*
- **Onomatopoeia:** the use of a word whose sound imitates its meaning, as in *hiss* and *buzz*

DIRECTIONS: *Analyze each poem. For each poem, give one or more examples of each of the following sound devices. If a poem does not use a particular sound device, write* None.

Sound Device	"Summer"	"The Eagle"	"Analysis of Baseball"
Alliteration			
Assonance			
Consonance			
Onomatopoeia			

© Pearson Education, Inc. All rights reserved.

Name _____ Date _____

Reading: Read Fluently

Reading fluently is reading smoothly and continuously while also comprehending the text and appreciating the writer's artistry. To avoid being tripped up by the meaning as you read, **use your senses.** To do so, notice language that appeals to the five senses:

- sight
- hearing
- smell
- taste
- touch

Using your senses will help you connect with a poem and appreciate the effects that the poet creates.

DIRECTIONS: *As you read each poem in this collection, note words and phrases that appeal to your senses. On the following chart, write sensory details in the appropriate section. (Copy the words or phrases exactly.) Because an image can appeal to more than one sense, you may enter a word or phrase more than once.*

Senses	"Summer"	"The Eagle"	"Analysis of Baseball"
Sight			
Hearing			
Smell			
Taste			
Touch			

© Pearson Education, Inc. All rights reserved.

Name _____ Date _____

Poetry Collection: Walter Dean Myers; Alfred, Lord Tennyson; May Swenson
Vocabulary Builder

Word List

analysis   azure   clasps

A. DIRECTIONS: *Answer each of the following questions.*

_____ 1. Which of the following is the best synonym for *clasps* as Tennyson uses it in the line "He clasps the crag with crooked hands"?
    A. handles   C. punches
    B. grips   D. connects

_____ 2. Which of the following might be described as *azure*?
    A. a tiger   C. the sky
    B. autumn leaves   D. a diamond

_____ 3. Which of the following is the best synonym for *analysis*?
    A. thorough examination   C. temporary suspension
    B. superficial argument   D. reflective speech

B. DIRECTIONS: *For each of the following items, think about the meaning of the italicized word and then answer the question.*

1. Which of the following colors is closest to *azure*: gold, brown, blue-green, or gray? Explain.

_____

_____

2. If you *clasp* someone's hand in greeting or farewell, is your gesture likely to be friendly or hostile? Explain.

_____

_____

3. Would an *analysis* of an issue help you to understand it better? Why or why not?

_____

C. WORD STUDY: Use the context of each sentence and what you know about the Greek prefix *ana-* to rewrite the sentence so that it makes sense. Be careful not to change the word in italics.

1. Because she felt the two theories were *analogous*, and she couldn't wait to point out the differences between them.

_____

_____

2. The *anachronisms* in that novel showed that the author was keenly aware of the historical setting.

_____

_____

3. The *Analects* are a single teaching by the ancient Chinese philosopher Confucius.

_____

_____

© Pearson Education, Inc. All rights reserved.

Poetry Collection: Walter Dean Myers; Alfred, Lord Tennyson; May Swenson
Enrichment: Seasons in Literature

In his poem "Summer," Walter Dean Myers vividly evokes some of the activities and moods associated with that season. Although May Swenson does not specifically describe the seasons when baseball is played, many people associate the game with spring and summertime.

Nature's seasons and their connections to the cycles of life are the subjects of many works of literature. Work with a partner or small group of students to create an anthology of seasons in literature. You can start your search by looking for keywords, such as the names of seasons or words associated with the senses.

A. DIRECTIONS: *Use the following chart to organize selections for your anthology. List at least two selections for each season. Write the selections title and author in the corresponding part of the chart. (Note that you can include short stories, plays, and nonfiction, as well as poetry.)*

Type of Selection	Title and Author	Spring	Summer	Autumn	Winter
Poem					
Short story					
Play, essay					
Other					

B. DIRECTIONS: *Decide which selections you want to use and how to organize them. Work together with your group to compile and design your anthology. Share your finished anthology with the rest of the class.*

© Pearson Education, Inc. All rights reserved.

Poetry Collection: Walter Dean Myers; Alfred, Lord Tennyson; May Swenson
Open-Book Test

Short Answer *Write your responses to the questions in this section on the lines provided.*

1. Identify an example of onomatopoeia in "Summer" by Walter Dean Myers. Explain your choice, defining *onomatopoeia.*

   _____

   _____

   _____

2. What two different sides of summer do the two stanzas in "Summer" illustrate?

   _____

   _____

   _____

   _____

3. Alliteration is the repetition of initial consonant sounds. Cite an example of alliteration in "Summer."

   _____

   _____

4. In "The Eagle," Alfred, Lord Tennyson describes the bird as fierce and powerful. Cite a phrase from the poem that expresses this idea.

   _____

   _____

   _____

5. In "The Eagle," what is the "azure world" that surrounds the bird? Base your response on the meaning of the word *azure.*

   _____

   _____

6. In "The Eagle," which of the five senses most helps the reader understand what he or she is reading? Explain and give an example of the imagery you choose.

   _____

   _____

   _____

© Pearson Education, Inc. All rights reserved.

7. Which line in the first stanza of "The Eagle" contains consonance? What words create the consonance?

_____

_____

_____

8. Does "Analysis of Baseball" by May Swenson lead you to think the speaker enjoys baseball or considers it a silly, mindless game?

_____

_____

_____

_____

9. How many sentences are in lines 35–48 of "Analysis of Baseball"?

_____

_____

10. In the chart, list an example of a word or series of words that are the sound devices found in "Analysis of Baseball." Then, answer the question that follows the chart.

Alliteration	Consonance	Assonance	Onomatopoeia

What do these sound devices help the reader hear?

_____

_____

Essay

Write an extended response to the question of your choice or to the question or questions your teacher assigns you.

11. What feelings or attitudes do the poets Myers, Lord Tennyson, and Swenson have toward their subject matter? Do you share these feelings? Answer these questions in an essay. First, identify each poem's main subject. (Hint: Look at the poem's title.) Next, describe how the poet seems to feel about that subject. Use examples and details from the poem to support your ideas. Finally, tell whether you have similar feelings about the subject and why.

© Pearson Education, Inc. All rights reserved.

12. The poets Myers, Lord Tennyson, and Swenson use sound devices to give their works a musical quality. As in music, the sounds of a poem can suggest a variety of moods and tones, from joyful to melancholy to fearful. Choose one poem in this collection and write an essay in which you identify the poem's sound devices. Explain the effect of these devices on the poem's mood and meaning.

13. The poems in this collection, "Summer," "The Eagle," and "Analysis of Baseball," illustrate some of the ways poets can use sound devices to create musical effects. In an essay, describe a musical soundtrack that would provide appropriate background music for an oral reading of each of the three poems. Be sure that the selections on your soundtrack suit the poem's subject matter and mood. If you cannot suggest a particular piece of music, describe the type of music that you think should go with each poem.

14. **Thinking About the Big Question: How does communication change us?** Poems are a form of communication: They send a set of ideas or insights from the poet to the reader. A good poem often has the effect of changing the way the reader thinks or feels about the subject. Which poem in this collection changed the way you regard an everyday object or experience? Explain your choice in an essay, citing specific details from the poem to support what you say.

Oral Response

15. Go back to question 2, 4, or 8 or to the question your teacher assigns to you. Take a few minutes to expand your answer and prepare an oral response. Find additional details in "Summer," "The Eagle," or "Analysis of Baseball" that support your points. If necessary, make notes to guide your oral response.

Poetry Collection: Walter Dean Myers; Alfred, Lord Tennyson; May Swenson
Selection Test A

Critical Reading *Identify the letter of the choice that best answers the question.*

____ 1. In "Summer," which of the following best describes the speaker's attitude toward the season of summer?

    A. dread   C. respect

    B. enjoyment   D. tolerance

____ 2. In "Summer," the word *buzzin* is an example of which of the following sound devices?

    A. alliteration   C. onomatopoeia

    B. assonance   D. consonance

____ 3. When you read a poem, which of the following will help you connect with the poem?

    A. read the end of the poem first

    B. notice words that appeal to your senses

    C. ignore the punctuation

    D. analyze the rhyme scheme

____ 4. In "Summer," why does the poet repeat "hot days" and "days" in these lines?

    I like hot days, hot days

    Sweat is what you got days

    A. He repeats them for musical effect.

    B. He cannot think of a different word.

    C. He is communicating a serious message.

    D. He is communicating a humorous idea.

____ 5. Which of the following is the best description of Tennyson's poem "The Eagle"?

    A. a vivid description of a bird of prey

    B. a celebration of nature's beauty

    C. a simile comparing life to a diving eagle

    D. a contrast between an eagle at rest and a person at rest

____ 6. In Tennyson's poem, why does the eagle fall?

    A. It loses its grip on the crag.   C. It is diving for a fish.

    B. It is hit by a bolt of lightning.   D. It symbolizes the loss of hope.

____ 7. In "The Eagle," the line "He clasps the crag with crooked hands" illustrates which of these sound devices?

    A. alliteration

    B. end rhyme

    C. consonance

    D. onomatopoeia

____ 8. In "Analysis of Baseball," which of the following does the speaker focus on?

    A. the suspense felt by the fans

    B. the conflicts between players and umpires

    C. hitting and catching the ball

    D. the thrills of World Series competition

____ 9. In the following lines from "Analysis of Baseball," which sound device do the words *thud* and *dud* illustrate?

    Ball bounces

    off bat, flies

    air, or thuds

    ground (dud). . . .

    A. alliteration   C. consonance

    B. onomatopoeia   D. personification

____ 10. In "Analysis of Baseball," which of the following best describes the speaker's attitude toward the sport?

    A. bored   C. reserved

    B. enthusiastic   D. detached

____ 11. Read these lines from "Analysis of Baseball":

    Ball goes in

    (thwack) to mitt,

    and goes out

    (thwack) back

    to mitt.

    To which sense do the lines primarily appeal?

    A. taste   C. sight

    B. smell   D. hearing

© Pearson Education, Inc. All rights reserved.

Vocabulary and Grammar

____ **12.** What does the word *azure* mean in this line from Tennyson's poem?

Close to the sun in lonely lands,
Ring'd with the azure world, he stands.

A. the color blue
B. the color gray
C. a rough texture
D. a smooth surface

____ **13.** A prepositional phrase that functions as an adjective can modify which of the following?

A. a verb
B. an adverb
C. a noun or pronoun
D. another preposition

____ **14.** In the sentence "Alfred, Lord Tennyson rose from humble beginnings to become England's most popular poet," how does the prepositional phrase "from humble beginnings" function?

A. as an adjective
B. as an appositive
C. as an adverb
D. as a conjunction

Essay

15. Onomatopoeia is the use of a word whose sound imitates its meaning. This sound device often produces humorous effects. In an essay, discuss the use of onomatopoeia in either "Summer" or "Analysis of Baseball." Be sure to comment on how onomatopoeia contributes to the tone and mood of the poem you select.

16. Which poem in this group did you enjoy the most? In an essay, identify your favorite poem in this collection and give two reasons why it appeals to you most. Be sure to comment on how the poet's use of sound devices affects your response to the poem.

17. **Thinking About the Big Question: How does communication change us?** A poem can have the effect of changing the way the reader thinks or feels about the subject. For example, "Summer" can help the reader better appreciate the fun and relaxation of summer. Which of the poems by Alfred, Lord Tennyson or May Swenson in this collection changed the way you regard an everyday object or experience? Explain your choice in an essay. Use details from the poem to support what you say.

© Pearson Education, Inc. All rights reserved.

Poetry Collection: Walter Dean Myers; Alfred, Lord Tennyson; May Swenson
Selection Test B

Critical Reading *Identify the letter of the choice that best completes the statement or answers the question.*

_____ 1. What kind of weather does the speaker describe in "Summer"?
   A. stormy
   B. hot
   C. clear
   D. foggy

_____ 2. In "Summer," the line "Bugs buzzin from cousin to cousin" illustrates which sound device?
   A. alliteration
   B. assonance
   C. onomatopoeia
   D. all of the above

_____ 3. As a sound device in poetry, *consonance* may be defined as which of the following?
   A. the repetition of a vowel sound in words that are close together
   B. the pattern of rhyme at the end of lines
   C. the use of a word whose sound imitates its meaning
   D. the repetition of final consonant sounds in stressed syllables

_____ 4. For the speaker in "Summer," one of the most appealing features of the season is that
   A. the whole family can go to the beach.
   B. it seldom rains.
   C. the days are lazy.
   D. the children can ride their bikes.

_____ 5. In "Summer," on the whole, the speaker's tone, or attitude toward the subject, might best be described as which of the following?
   A. ironic
   B. outraged
   C. indifferent
   D. approving

_____ 6. The line "Bugs buzzin from cousin to cousin" is an example of which figure of speech?
   A. simile
   B. metaphor
   C. personification
   D. paradox

_____ 7. At the beginning of "The Eagle," where does the bird find itself?
   A. flying over water
   B. perched on a tree branch
   C. perched on a crag
   D. soaring high in the air

____ 8. The line "Ring'd with the azure world, he stands," appeals to which sense?
   A. sound
   B. touch
   C. sight
   D. smell

____ 9. Which of the following can you infer from the end of "The Eagle"?
   A. The bird folds its wings and falls into a deep sleep.
   B. The eagle recognizes its mate.
   C. The eagle plummets to the sea and grasps its prey.
   D. The eagle begins to build a nest.

____ 10. In "The Eagle," the line "The wrinkled sea beneath him crawls" illustrates which of the following sound devices?
   A. alliteration
   B. assonance
   C. consonance
   D. onomatopoeia

____ 11. The description of the eagle in Tennyson's poem primarily emphasizes which of the following aspects of the bird?
   A. its grace
   B. its power
   C. its instinct
   D. its size

____ 12. What three things or people are repeatedly emphasized in "Analysis of Baseball"?
   A. the pitcher, the catcher, and the umpire
   B. the fans, the players, and the managers
   C. the ball, the bat, and the mitt
   D. the bat, the helmet, and the backstop

____ 13. In "Analysis of Baseball," the words *dud, thwack,* and *pow* are an example of which sound device?
   A. alliteration
   B. assonance
   C. consonance
   D. onomatopoeia

____ 14. When you read, using your senses can help you do which of the following?
   A. identify a poem's speaker
   B. evaluate the assumptions of the poet
   C. connect with a poem and appreciate its effects
   D. enlarge your vocabulary

____ 15. Read the following lines from "Analysis of Baseball":
   Ball hits
   bat, or it
   hits mitt.

   Which of the following sound devices do the lines illustrate?
   A. alliteration only
   B. alliteration and assonance
   C. onomatopoeia only
   D. onomatopoeia and consonance

____ 16. On the whole, the speaker's tone in "Analysis of Baseball" might best be described as
   A. intellectual.
   B. analytical.
   C. playful.
   D. detached.

Vocabulary and Grammar

____ 17. Which of the following is the best synonym for *azure* in Tennyson's line "Ring'd with the azure world, he stands"?
   A. blue
   B. dark
   C. transparent
   D. golden

____ 18. Which word most nearly means the opposite of *clasps* as it is used in Tennyson's line, "He clasps the crag with crooked hands"?
   A. squeezes
   B. twists
   C. releases
   D. grabs

____ 19. In the sentence "The claws of the eagle were sharp," the prepositional phrase functions as which of the following?
   A. pronoun
   B. adjective
   C. adverb
   D. infinitive

Essay

20. Sound devices in poetry combine to give words a musical quality. Choose one of the poems in this collection and write an essay in which you identify the poem's sound devices. Explain the effect of these devices on the poem's mood and meaning.

21. The poems in this group illustrate some of the ways in which poets can use sound devices for musical effects. In an essay, identify and discuss a musical soundtrack that would furnish appropriate background for an oral reading of each of the three poems. Be sure that your soundtrack suits the subject matter, mood, and tone of each selection. If you cannot suggest a specific piece of music, describe the type of music that you think should accompany each poem.

22. **Thinking About the Big Question: How does communication change us?** Poems are a form of communication: They send a set of ideas or insights from the poet to the reader. A good poem often has the effect of changing the way the reader thinks or feels about the subject. Which poem in this collection changed the way you regard an everyday object or experience? Explain your choice in an essay, citing specific details from the poem to support what you say.

Vocabulary Warm-up Word Lists

Study these words from the poetry of Yusef Komunyakaa, Lewis Carroll, and Edgar Allan Poe. Then, apply your knowledge to the activities that follow.

Word List A

balmy [BAHL mee] *adj.* warm and pleasant
   I like going to the beach on a balmy summer day.

dunk [DUNK] *v.* in basketball, jump toward the basket and throw the ball through the hoop from above
   He was able to jump high above the basket and dunk.

glistening [GLIS uh ning] *adj.* shiny and looking wet
   The glistening morning dew was a beautiful sight.

hook [HOOK] *v.* in basketball, shoot the ball over the head with the hand that is farther from the basket
   Players hook the ball to avoid being blocked.

lanky [LANG kee] *adj.* very tall and thin
   By the time he started high school, he had grown too lanky for the football team.

slam [SLAM] *v.* throw or strike against something with great force
   The basketball player tried to slam the ball through the hoop.

Word List B

clamor [KLAM er] *n.* loud continuous noise; noisy shouting
   We could hardly hear ourselves talk over the clamor in the street.

endeavor [en DEV er] *n.* attempt to do something difficult or new
   Our endeavor to raise money for the charity was a great success.

intention [in TEN shuhn] *n.* a plan to do something
   Is it your intention to attend the meeting?

menace [MEN is] *n.* threatening quality; something dangerous or threatening
   I heard the menace in the dog's growl.

outmaneuvered [owt muh NOO verd] *v.* gained an advantage by using skillful or well-planned movements
   We outmaneuvered the other team and won the game.

slain [SLAYN] *v.* killed violently
   The soldiers who were slain were buried on the battlefield.

Poetry Collection: Yusef Komunyakaa, Lewis Carroll, Edgar Allan Poe
Vocabulary Warm-up Exercises

Exercise A *Fill in each blank in the following paragraph with an appropriate word from Word List A. Use each word only once.*

It was a beautiful [1] _____ afternoon, and my friends and I could hardly wait for school to be over. It was not that we disliked school, but we liked playing basketball much more. As soon as the bell rang, we headed straight for the playground.

[2] _____ with sweat, we played hard. My friend Jim, a great jumper,

is lean and [3] _____. He likes to sail high over the basket and

[4] _____ the ball from above. It is always thrilling to watch him

[5] _____ the ball through the hoop with such power. I am not tall

enough to play Jim's style of basketball, but I practice my shots every chance I get. I can

even [6] _____ the ball so that it soars over Jim's head when he is

guarding me. We have a great time together playing basketball!

Exercise B *Write a complete sentence to answer each question. In each answer, use the word from Word List B that has the same meaning as the underlined word or group of underlined words in the question.*

1. How would you feel if your opponent <u>gained an advantage over you</u> in a game of checkers?

   _____

2. What do you think is the greatest <u>threat</u> to peace in the world today?

   _____

3. What is your <u>plan</u> regarding a future career?

   _____

4. What might an employer do to cause his or her employees to create a <u>loud noise</u>?

   _____

5. What would you do if you read that people in another country were being <u>killed</u> for voicing their opposition to their government?

   _____

6. What <u>project</u> have you recently completed that you were especially proud of?

   _____

Poetry Collection: Yusef Komunyakaa, Lewis Carroll, Edgar Allan Poe

Reading Warm-up A

Read the following passage. Pay special attention to the underlined words. Then, read it again, and complete the activities. Use a separate sheet of paper for your written answers.

James Naismith, a physical education teacher in Springfield, Massachusetts, invented basketball in 1891. The first game was played in Springfield the following year. In 1936, basketball became an Olympic event. Women's basketball was added to the Olympics in 1976. In 2004, Argentina and Italy won the gold and silver medals, respectively, in women's basketball, with the United States capturing the bronze.

The basic idea of the game is very simple. Each team tries to throw the ball through its opponent's basket while stopping the other team from scoring. Running with the ball without bouncing it is illegal. The ball must be dribbled, shot, or passed to another player.

Being tall is a big advantage when playing basketball. A lean and <u>lanky</u> player can generally reach farther and jump higher than a smaller opponent. Most professional male players are well over 6 feet tall. The average height of the women who won the U.S. Olympic gold was 6 feet.

The ability to shoot accurately is one of the most important skills in basketball. The lay-up shot is used when a player can charge in under the basket. To <u>hook</u> the ball, a player shoots over the shoulder. This shot allows players to keep their body between the opponent and the ball. Very tall players like to <u>dunk</u> the ball by leaping high over the basket. They can then <u>slam</u> the ball through the hoop to score two points. Fans love to see their favorite players hanging off the rim with the stadium lights <u>glistening</u> off the backboard. This action looks great on television, but it can be very dangerous if the player falls.

Watching athletes play basketball is fun, but playing it is even more fun. Whether it is cold and wet outside or a beautiful <u>balmy</u> day, you can probably find an indoor or outdoor court to play on. Even if no one is around to play with, you can have a good time practicing different shots all by yourself. Why not give it a try?

1. Circle the word that gives a clue to the meaning of <u>lanky</u>. Why is it an advantage for a basketball player to be *lanky*?

2. Underline the words that explain what it means to <u>hook</u> the ball. Why do you think the word *hook* is used for this action?

3. Underline the words that tell who is likely to <u>dunk</u>. Why do you think a player has to leap high to *dunk* a ball?

4. Circle the words that tell what players <u>slam</u>. Explain what basketball players do when they *slam*.

5. Circle the words that tell what is <u>glistening</u>. Write a sentence about something else you might describe as *glistening*.

6. Circle the words that mean the opposite of <u>balmy</u>. What do you like to do on a *balmy* day?

Poetry Collection: Yusef Komunyakaa, Lewis Carroll, Edgar Allan Poe
Reading Warm-up B

Read the following passage. Pay special attention to the underlined words. Then, read it again, and complete the activities. Use a separate sheet of paper for your written answers.

Almost every country in the world tells stories about dragons. Dragon myths have been passed on for thousands of years in various cultures throughout the world.

Most of us are familiar with the fire-breathing dragon of European folklore. This huge, snakelike monster is almost always portrayed as a <u>menace</u> to society. Eventually, the outraged citizenry raise a <u>clamor</u>, and some valiant individual must step forward and battle the dreadful beast.

In medieval tales, it is usually a brave knight who volunteers to slay the dragon and free the maiden it holds captive. Of course, the dragon has no <u>intention</u> of giving up without a fight. In the end, however, the knight's <u>endeavor</u> to vanquish his opponent is always successful. Despite its cunning and great physical strength, the wicked dragon is eventually <u>outmaneuvered</u> by the clever and fearless knight. The dragon is <u>slain</u>, and his killer walks away with the treasure and the heart of the rescued maiden.

Unlike their European cousins, the dragons of Asia are usually portrayed as wise and friendly creatures. This kinder and gentler dragon seldom has wings and rarely breathes fire. Asian dragons can be distinguished by the number of toes they have. A three-toed dragon is Japanese, a four-toed dragon is Indonesian or Korean, and a five-toed dragon, or Lung, is Chinese.

Some say that the Chinese dragon is made up of many types of animals. It has the body of a snake, the head of a camel, the scales of a fish, the horns of a stag, the eyes of a hare, the paws of a tiger, and the claws of an eagle. Chinese dragons generally bring good luck; however, they can be dangerous if not treated with the proper respect. Chinese dragons that feel insulted may express their displeasure by causing storms or floods. Fortunately, they are less likely than European dragons to start fires as the result of a careless sneeze.

1. Underline the words that tell what is a <u>menace</u> to society. Explain what a *menace* is.

2. Circle the words that tell who raises a <u>clamor</u>. Describe what they would do when raising a *clamor*.

3. Underline the words that tell what the dragon has no <u>intention</u> of doing. Write a sentence about an *intention* of your own.

4. Underline the words that identify the knight's <u>endeavor</u>. What might happen if he failed in this *endeavor*?

5. Circle the words that tell who is <u>outmaneuvered</u>. Underline the words that tell by whom. Explain what *outmaneuvered* means in this passage.

6. Circle the word that gives a clue to the meaning of <u>slain</u>. Write a sentence using *slain*.

© Pearson Education, Inc. All rights reserved.

Poetry Collection: Yusef Komunyakaa, Lewis Carroll, Edgar Allan Poe
Writing About the Big Question

How does communication change us?

Big Question Vocabulary

aware	communication	comprehension	discuss	empathy
exchange	illuminate	informed	interpretation	meaning
react	relationship	resolution	respond	understanding

A. *Use one or more words from the list above to complete each sentence.*

1. Most of us _____ favorably when someone invites us to a party.

2. For good _____ in a foreign country, some knowledge of the language is helpful.

3. The committee met several times to _____ that issue before it made a final decision.

4. Otto was a man of few words, and it was sometimes hard to figure out his real _____.

5. Thelma's _____ of the poem had never occurred to me, but I had to admit that it made sense.

B. *Follow the directions in responding to each of the items below.*

1. List two different times when you had a disagreement with a friend.

   _____

   _____

2. Write two sentences to explain one of these experiences, and describe how it made you feel. Use at least two of the Big Question vocabulary words.

   _____

   _____

C. *Complete the sentence below. Then, write a short paragraph in which you connect the sentence to the Big Question.*

By reading about the **meaning** that someone finds in certain sounds, a reader can learn to _____

_____

_____

_____

© Pearson Education, Inc. All rights reserved.

Name _____ Date _____

Poetry Collection: Yusef Komunyakaa, Lewis Carroll, Edgar Allan Poe
Literary Analysis: Sound Devices

Poets use **sound devices** to emphasize the sound relationships among words. These devices include the following:

- **Alliteration:** the repetition of initial consonant sounds in stressed syllables: "*muffled monotone*"
- **Consonance:** the repetition of final consonant sounds in stressed syllables with different vowel sounds, as in *toll* and *bell*
- **Assonance:** the repetition of similar vowel sounds in stressed syllables that end with different consonant sounds, as in "*mellow wedding bells*"
- **Onomatopoeia:** the use of a word whose sound imitates its meaning, as in *jangle* and *knells*

DIRECTIONS: *Analyze each poem. For each poem, give one or more examples of each of the following sound devices. If a poem does not use a particular sound device, write* None.

Sound Device	"Slam, Dunk, & Hook"	"Jabberwocky"	"The Bells"
Alliteration			
Assonance			
Consonance			
Onomatopoeia			

© Pearson Education, Inc. All rights reserved.

Name _____ Date _____

Reading: Read Fluently

Reading fluently is reading smoothly and continuously while also comprehending the text and appreciating the writer's artistry. To avoid being tripped up by the meaning of words as you read, **use your senses.** To do so, notice language that appeals to the five senses:

- sight
- hearing
- smell
- taste
- touch

Using your senses will help you connect with a poem and appreciate the effects that the poet creates.

DIRECTIONS: *As you read each poem in this collection, note words and phrases that appeal to your senses. On the following chart, write sensory details in the appropriate section. (Copy the words or phrases exactly.) Because an image can appeal to more than one sense, you may enter a word or phrase more than once.*

Senses	"Slam, Dunk, & Hook"	"Jabberwocky"	"The Bells"
Sight			
Hearing			
Smell			
Taste			
Touch			

© Pearson Education, Inc. All rights reserved.

Name _____ Date _____

Poetry Collection: Yusef Komunyakaa, Lewis Carroll, Edgar Allan Poe
Vocabulary Builder

Word List

endeavor   feint   jibed   metaphysical
monotone   palpitating   voluminously

A. DIRECTIONS: *Match each word in Column A with the correct definition in Column B.*

Column A	Column B
___ 1. metaphysical	A. fully
___ 2. palpitating	B. spiritual
___ 3. voluminously	C. changed direction
___ 4. jibed	D. throbbing

B. DIRECTIONS: *Revise each sentence so that the underlined vocabulary word is used logically. Be sure not to change the vocabulary word.*

1. He spoke in a *monotone*, full of delightful and surprising shifts in tone and mood.

   _____

2. Making a *feint* to her right, the soccer player plunged headlong in that direction.

   _____

3. He was determined to make an *endeavor* at finishing the assignment that evening, and so he went to bed early.

   _____

C. WORD STUDY: Use the context of the sentences and what you know about the Greek prefix *mono-* to explain your answer to each question.

1. If the animals of a certain species are *monogamous*, do they have one mate or many?

   _____

   _____

2. Is a person with *monomania* interested in one subject or in many?

   _____

   _____

3. In a play, is a *monologue* spoken by one character or by many?

   _____

   _____

© Pearson Education, Inc. All rights reserved.

Name _____   Date _____

Enrichment: Physical Education

Sports and Games

Whether you play basketball, like the boys in "Slam, Dunk, & Hook," or whether you play checkers, chess, or soccer, there are rules you must follow as you play. Rules or instructions for playing usually help make the game fair, and some make the game more fun or challenging. For most games and sports, the rules make the most sense if they are presented in a certain order. For example, it would not help a new tennis player to learn about serving the ball before learning how to hold the racquet.

DIRECTIONS: *Think of a game or sport with which you are familiar. You are going to introduce some portion of this game—a certain play or move, for example—to someone who does not know the game at all. First, list some terms and expressions connected with the game. Then, add specific details, and organize the facts to create complete instructions for the play. To organize your instructions, you may want to use headings such as these: Object of the Game, Equipment Required, Order of Action or Order of Play, and so on.*

Game or Sport: _____

Portion of Game I Am Introducing: _____

Terms and Expressions (with definitions if necessary): _____

_____

_____

_____

Instructions: _____

_____

_____

_____

_____

_____

_____

_____

_____

_____

_____

_____

_____

© Pearson Education, Inc. All rights reserved.

Poetry Collections: Walter Dean Myers; Alfred, Lord Tennyson; May Swenson; and Yusef Komunyakaa, Lewis Carroll, Edgar Allan Poe

Integrated Language Skills: Grammar

Prepositional Phrases as Modifiers

A **prepositional phrase,** such as *on the court* or *of the bells*, is made up of a preposition and a noun or pronoun, called the object of the preposition, with all of its modifiers. Prepositional phrases may function either as adjectives by modifying nouns or pronouns or as adverbs by modifying verbs, adjectives, and adverbs.

When acting as an adjective, a prepositional phrase is called an *adjective phrase.* **Adjective phrases** modify a noun or pronoun by telling *what kind* or *which one.*

    Example: We enjoy the sounds *of summer.* (*of summer* modifies the noun *sounds*)

When functioning as an adverb, a prepositional phrase is called an *adverb phrase.* **Adverb phrases** modify a verb, an adjective, or an adverb by telling *where, when, in what way,* or *to what extent.*

    Examples: In summer, we enjoy outdoor activities. (*in summer* modifies the verb *enjoy*)

           The forest was quiet *before dawn.* (*before dawn* modifies the adjective *quiet*)

A. PRACTICE: *For each of the following sentences, use the space provided to write all the prepositional phrases. Classify each one as an adjective phrase or an adverb phrase. Then, write the word that each phrase modifies.*

1. Basketball is popular with many sports fans.

    _____

2. The game was invented in the late nineteenth century.

    _____

3. The inventor of basketball was a physical education instructor named James Naismith.

    _____

4. Naismith's new game originally involved two teams of nine players.

    _____

B. Writing Application: *Write a brief paragraph describing your favorite sport or game. In your paragraph, use at least two adjective phrases and two adverb phrases. Underline each prepositional phrase and label it as an adjective phrase or adverb phrase.*

_____

_____

_____

_____

Name _____ Date _____

Poetry Collection: Walter Dean Myers; Alfred, Lord Tennyson; May Swenson; Yusef Komunyakaa; Lewis Carroll; Edgar Allan Poe

Support for Writing an Editorial

Use the following chart to develop prewriting notes for an editorial that will be related to a poem in this collection.

Title of Poem: _____

Issue or Topic Related to Poem: _____

_____

_____

My Opinion Statement: _____

_____

_____

Supporting Details:

1. _____

_____

2. _____

_____

3. _____

_____

4. _____

_____

5. _____

_____

Opposing Arguments / Counterarguments:

_____

_____

_____

_____

Now, use your notes to write an editorial about the issue you have chosen.

© Pearson Education, Inc. All rights reserved.

Name _____ Date _____

Poetry Collection: Walter Dean Myers; Alfred, Lord Tennyson; May Swenson; Yusef Komunyakaa; Lewis Carroll; Edgar Allan Poe

Support for Extend Your Learning

Research and Technology

Together with your group, use a format such as the one shown to develop an illustrated version of one of the poems in this collection.

Title of Poem: _____

Images That Capture Poem's Mood: _____

_____

_____

_____

_____

_____

Ideas for Photographs/Artwork: _____

_____

_____

_____

_____

_____

Now use your notes to develop an illustrated version of a poem in this collection.

Poetry Collection: Edgar Allan Poe, Yusef Komunyakaa, Lewis Carroll
Open-Book Test

Short Answer *Write your responses to the questions in this section on the lines provided.*

1. What sound device is present in line 38 of Edgar Allan Poe's poem "The Bells"? Explain your answer.

   _____

   _____

2. In "The Bells," each set of bells has a different purpose. This purpose reflects a certain human emotion. For example, the sleigh bells show merriment. Identify the other bells, and name the emotion reflected by each set.

   _____

   _____

   _____

   _____

3. How are the four stanzas of "The Bells" similar in the use of sound devices?

   _____

   _____

   _____

4. Which set of bells in "The Bells" would most likely cause your heart to begin "palpitating"? Base your answer on the meaning of *palpitating*.

   _____

   _____

5. In Yusef Komunyakaa's poem "Slam, Dunk, & Hook," the boys have "Mercury's Insignia" on their shoes. Mercury was a winged Roman god. What does this suggest about the boys' ability to play basketball?

   _____

   _____

6. Assonance is the repetition of similar vowel sounds in stressed syllables. How is assonance used in line 30 of "Slam, Dunk, & Hook"? How do the sounds help bring the action to life?

   _____

   _____

   _____

7. Komunyakaa often combines abstract ideas with concrete images. The concrete images in the chart are in the last five lines of "Slam, Dunk, & Hook." Fill in the chart with the abstract idea that each concrete image is paired with. Then answer the question that follows the chart.

Concrete Image	Abstract Idea
bone	
slipknot	
we (the players)	

What do these pairings suggest about the game of basketball?

_____

_____

8. In the second stanza of Lewis Carroll's "Jabberwocky," the boy's father gives him a warning. Summarize the warning in standard English. Does the boy heed it? Explain.

_____

_____

_____

9. What happens in the fifth stanza of "Jabberwocky" (lines 17–20)? Which of your five senses help you picture the action? Cite words in the stanza that appeal to these senses.

_____

_____

_____

10. Even though "Jabberwocky" contains dozens of nonsense words, it is still understandable. How do you explain this?

_____

_____

_____

_____

Essay

Write an extended response to the question of your choice or to the question or questions your teacher assigns you.

11. Each of the poems in this collection—"The Bells," "Slam, Dunk, & Hook," and "Jabberwocky"—are meant to entertain the reader. Choose two of the poems, and write an essay comparing and contrasting their entertainment value. Which is more fun to read? Which is more pleasing to the reader's ear? Which tells a better story? Which would make a better lullaby, performance piece, or movie? Answer these questions, or explain in your own terms what makes each poem entertaining. Be sure to cite details from the poems to support your ideas.

12. The poem "Slam, Dunk, & Hook" shows how basketball was a central part of the poet's early life. The poem is not just about basketball. It is also about relationships, hardships, and aspirations. In an essay, explain how the game of basketball is used in the poem to reveal something larger about the lives of the players. How does the game make them feel? How does it help them cope? How might basketball symbolize a certain kind of response to life's challenges?

13. In an essay, discuss how Lewis Carroll creates humor in "Jabberwocky" by contrasting serious details and events with amusing and ridiculous ones. In addition, indicate how the poet's use of sound devices contributes both to the poem's seriousness and its humor.

14. **Thinking About the Big Question: How does communication change us?** In "Jabberwocky," the father speaks to the boy on two different occasions. In your view, do the father's words influence the boy's actions in any way? What might the poet be trying to say about communication between parents and children, especially as a young person matures and seeks independence? Explain, using details from the poem to support your ideas.

Oral Response

15. Go back to question 2, 6, or 10 or to the question your teacher assigns to you. Take a few minutes to expand your answer and prepare an oral response. Find additional details in the relevant poem that support your points. If necessary, make notes to guide your oral response.

Name _____ Date _____

Poetry Collection: Yusef Komunyakaa, Lewis Carroll, Edgar Allan Poe

Selection Test A

Critical Reading *Identify the letter of the choice that best answers the question.*

____ 1. Which of the following best describes the subject matter of Yusef Komunyakaa's poem "Slam, Dunk, & Hook"?

    A. the speaker's playing on his high school's championship basketball team

    B. a street fight when the speaker was growing up

    C. the speaker's interest in college and professional basketball during the 1950s

    D. the speaker's playing basketball with his friends when he was young

____ 2. In "Slam, Dunk, & Hook," when Komunyakaa says that the boys were "Glistening with sweat," which of the following does the image suggest?

    A. The game took place on a hot day.

    B. The court was unusually large.

    C. The boys were nervous playing in front of the girls.

    D. Trouble always lurked around the corner in the boys' neighborhood.

____ 3. In "Slam, Dunk, & Hook," the line "A high note hung there" illustrates which of the following sound devices?

    A. alliteration

    B. assonance

    C. consonance

    D. onomatopoeia

____ 4. If you want to understand a poem's text and appreciate the poet's artistry, which of the following would be most helpful?

    A. Use a dictionary when you read.

    B. Analyze the symbolism of a poem.

    C. Find out about the poet's life.

    D. Notice words that appeal to your senses.

____ 5. The sound device of alliteration involves repetition of which of the following?

    A. vowel sounds

    B. consonant sounds

    C. both vowels and consonants

    D. whole lines of poetry

_____ 6. In Lewis Carroll's poem "Jabberwocky," what warning is given to the boy?
   A. Beware of the borogoves and the slithy toves.
   B. Beware of the Jabberwock, the Jubjub bird, and the Bandersnatch.
   C. Be careful when you use the vorpal sword to fight a foe.
   D. Do not be late in getting home.

_____ 7. In "Jabberwocky," how is the boy feeling when he returns to his father after meeting the Jabberwock?
   A. discouraged   C. frightened
   B. triumphant   D. angry

_____ 8. Read the following lines from "Jabberwocky":
   One, two! One, two! And through and through
   The vorpal blade went snicker-snack!

   Which of the following devices is illustrated by *snicker-snack*?
   A. assonance   C. metaphor
   B. alliteration   D. parallelism

_____ 9. In "Jabberwocky," to which of the five senses does the line "He chortled in his joy" appeal?
   A. sight   C. taste
   B. hearing   D. touch

_____ 10. Read the following lines from Edgar Allan Poe's "The Bells":
   What a tale their terror tells
      Of Despair!

   Which sound device do these lines illustrate?
   A. alliteration
   B. parallelism
   C. end rhyme
   D. onomatopoeia

_____ 11. Which of the following best describes the atmosphere, or mood, at the end of "The Bells"?
   A. joyful   C. frightening
   B. anxious   D. soothing

Vocabulary and Grammar

____ 12. If a book treats a topic *voluminously*, how would you best describe the book's coverage?

A. scanty   C. amusing

B. superficial   D. thorough

____ 13. Which of the following is the best synonym for *palpitating* in this line from Poe's "The Bells"?

What a horror they outpour
On the bosom of the palpitating air!

A. soaring   C. throbbing

B. sagging   D. darting

____ 14. In the sentence "Edgar Allan Poe's health failed during his final years," the prepositional phrase *during his final years* acts as which of the following?

A. adverb   C. appositive

B. adjective   D. infinitive

Essay

15. All three poems in this collection are notable for the skillful use of sound devices. Choose your favorite poem from the collection. In an essay, discuss how such elements as alliteration, assonance, consonance, and onomatopoeia contribute to the poem's total effect. Be sure to give specific examples from the poem for each device that you discuss.

16. Entertainment plays a major role in the poems in this collection. Write an essay comparing and contrasting two of the poems from the point of view of entertainment. In your essay, be sure to mention how sound effects contribute to the entertainment and enjoyment the poems offer.

17. **Thinking About the Big Question: How does communication change us?** In "Jabberwocky," the speaker warns the boy about the Jabberwock. "Beware the Jabberwock, my son!" he says. Do the father's words change the boy's actions in any way? Explain your answer in an essay. Use details from the poem to support your ideas.

© Pearson Education, Inc. All rights reserved.

Poetry Collection: Yusef Komunyakaa, Lewis Carroll, Edgar Allan Poe
Selection Test B

Critical Reading *Identify the letter of the choice that best completes the statement or answers the question.*

____ 1. The sound device known as alliteration involves which of the following?
  A. rhyme at the end of lines of verse
  B. repetition of initial consonant sounds in stressed syllables
  C. repetition of final consonant sounds in stressed syllables with different vowel sounds
  D. the use of a word whose sound imitates its meaning

____ 2. The line "Swish of strings like silk" illustrates which of the following?
  A. alliteration and assonance
  B. alliteration and consonance
  C. assonance and consonance
  D. alliteration only

____ 3. In "Slam, Dunk, & Hook," the lines "We outmaneuvered the footwork / Of bad angels" mean that
  A. the game distracted them from getting into trouble.
  B. they outwitted their neighborhood enemies.
  C. they were too quick to be defeated.
  D. the playing surface was extremely rough.

____ 4. In "Slam, Dunk, & Hook," Komunyakaa writes that when "Sonny Boy's mama died / He played nonstop all day, so hard / Our backboard splintered." Why did it splinter?
  A. They were too poor to afford a backboard that could stand constant use.
  B. By tragic coincidence, the backboard broke on the same sad day.
  C. Griefstricken, Sonny Boy repeatedly slammed the board with the ball or his hand.
  D. After his mother's death, Sonny Boy began a life of violence.

____ 5. Which of the following is the best way to understand a poem's text and appreciate the poet's artistry?
  A. Reread each poem at least five times.
  B. Research the poet's biography.
  C. Use your five senses when you read.
  D. Consider how the end of a poem relates to the opening lines.

____ 6. In "Jabberwocky" by Lewis Carroll, what draws the boy into the "tulgey wood"?
  A. the mimsy borogoves
  B. the need to hunt and gather food
  C. the wish to slay his longtime foe
  D. the need to find his missing sword

____ 7. Which of the following makes "Jabberwocky" a humorous poem?
  A. the descriptions of the boy and his father
  B. the poem's complex and suspenseful plot
  C. the descriptions of the boy's fighting techniques
  D. nonsense words and descriptions of unusual creatures

_____ 8. In "Jabberwocky," the word *galumphing* is an example of which of the following?
   A. alliteration   C. consonance
   B. assonance   D. onomatopoeia

_____ 9. In "Jabberwocky," which of the following sound devices is exemplified in the line, "Come to my arms, my beamish boy"?
   A. alliteration   C. onomatopoeia
   B. assonance   D. consonance

_____ 10. What is the best description of Lewis Carroll's "Jabberwocky"?
   A. a nonsense poem
   B. an adventure story
   C. an ironic criticism
   D. a sentimental ballad

_____ 11. In "The Bells," which of the following emotions does Edgar Allan Poe focus on?
   A. anger and envy
   B. joy, fear, and grief
   C. pity and fear
   D. love and unselfishness

_____ 12. In "The Bells," the line "How they clang and clash and roar!" illustrates which sound device?
   A. repetition   C. onomatopoeia
   B. consonance   D. parallelism

_____ 13. To which of the five senses do these lines from "The Bells" appeal?

   How they tinkle, tinkle, tinkle
      In the icy air of night!
   While the stars, that oversprinkle
   All the heavens, seem to twinkle
      With a crystalline delight

   A. sight and smell
   B. taste and touch
   C. sight, hearing, and touch
   D. hearing and taste

_____ 14. Which of the following statements about "The Bells" is accurate?
   A. Poe uses very few onomatopoetic words.
   B. There is no repetition in the poem.
   C. Poe ignores the topics of war and despair.
   D. The poem's mood changes markedly.

_____ 15. What is Poe's primary purpose in "The Bells"?
   A. to describe the emotions of joy, happiness, fear, and grief
   B. to imitate the sound of several types of bells
   C. to symbolize the stages of a person's life
   D. to warn people of the constant nearness of death

© Pearson Education, Inc. All rights reserved.

Vocabulary and Grammar

____ **16.** What is the best synonym for *metaphysical* in these lines from "Slam, Dunk, & Hook"?
We were metaphysical when girls / Cheered on the sidelines.

A. beyond excited
B. beyond physical
C. beyond distracted
D. beyond nervous

____ **17.** When the players in "Slam, Dunk, & Hook" *jibed*, what did they do?
A. They missed a basket.
B. They scored two points.
C. They changed direction.
D. They ran straight down the court.

____ **18.** In the sentence "Both books feature a young girl named Alice whose curiosity leads her into amazing fantasy worlds," the phrase *into amazing fantasy worlds* acts as which of the following?
A. adjective phrase
B. adverb phrase
C. infinitive phrase
D. participial phrase

____ **19.** Identify the adjective phrase in the following sentence: Sonny Boy, one of the speaker's friends, plays basketball in the playground all day on the day his mother dies.
A. of the speaker's friends
B. in the playground
C. all day
D. on the day

Essay

20. Yusef Komunyakaa's poem "Slam, Dunk, & Hook" depicts the role basketball played in the speaker's neighborhood during his youth. The poem is not just about basketball, however. In what other activities might people involve themselves in the way the players involve themselves in basketball in the poem? Compare the way people pursue these activities to the way Komunyakaa's youths pursue playing basketball. Give specific examples from the poem for your comparisons.

21. Lewis Carroll's "Jabberwocky" is a classic example of nonsense verse. In an essay, discuss how Carroll creates humor by contrasting serious details and events with amusing and ridiculous ones. In your essay, also indicate how the poet's use of sound devices contributes to the poem's humor.

22. Thinking About the Big Question: How does communication change us? In "Jabberwocky," the father speaks to the boy on two different occasions. In your view, do the father's words influence the boy's actions in any way? What might the poet be trying to say about communication between parents and children, especially as a young person matures and seeks independence? Explain, using details from the poem to support your ideas.

Vocabulary Warm-up Word Lists

Study these words from the poetry of Mary Tall Mountain, Naomi Shihab Nye, and Student Writers. Then, apply your knowledge to the activities that follow.

Word List A

flash [FLASH] *v.* shine brightly for a short time
In the sky, I saw a star <u>flash</u> and then become extinguished by a cloud.

icy [EYE see] *adj.* extremely cold
An <u>icy</u> drink is the best way to cool down on a hot summer day.

overripe [OH ver ryp] *adj.* too ripe; past the ideal time for eating
<u>Overripe</u> bananas are too soft to eat but make good banana bread.

prickly [PRIK lee] *adj.* covered with prickles, or long, sharp points
I fell into a <u>prickly</u> bush while hiking and got all scratched up.

rippled [RIP puhld] *v.* moved in small waves
Out on the lake, the water <u>rippled</u> gently in the slight breeze.

splurge [SPLERJ] *v.* spend more than usual to get something enjoyable
Let us <u>splurge</u> on a big dinner in honor of your birthday.

Word List B

peculiar [pi KYOOL yer] *adj.* strange and a little surprising
A warm winter with little snow is <u>peculiar</u> in most cold climates.

penalty [PEN uhl tee] *n.* punishment for not obeying a rule or law
As a <u>penalty</u> for missing practice, I cannot play in today's game.

shade [SHAYD] *n.* a little bit; a hint or touch of something
There is only a <u>shade</u> of difference between those identical twins.

startled [STAHR tuhld] *adj.* suddenly surprised or slightly shocked
He gave me a <u>startled</u> look when I announced that I was moving.

squinch [SKWINCH] *v.* pinch or squeeze
My grandmother likes to <u>squinch</u> my nose, which is very embarrassing.

unbidden [un BID n] *adv.* not asked for or wished for; uninvited
Problems come <u>unbidden</u> to just about everyone in life.

Poetry by Mary Tall Mountain, Naomi Shihab Nye, Student Writers
Vocabulary Warm-up Exercises

Exercise A *Fill in each blank in the following paragraph with an appropriate word from Word List A. Use each word only once.*

A frigid and [1] _____ day after a big winter storm is a perfect time for a walk outdoors. Ice crystals on the thorns of [2] _____ bushes sparkle and [3] _____ in the sunlight. All around me is fresh, clean snow and I can [4] _____ as much as I want, for there is no end to it. I can make as many snowballs as I can roll. If I get thirsty, I might snack on a snowball or two. A snowball that melts might be called [5] _____ and no longer perfect for eating. However, there is no chance of that happening on a freezing day. Occasionally, a cold breeze moves through the trees with a wave of energy. Branches that [6] _____ in the wind might even drop a bundle of snow on my head and down my back. BRR! That is when it is time to go home.

Exercise B *Answer the questions with complete explanations.*

Example: If you squinch your eyes tighter, are you probably in a bright place or a dark one?

You are probably in a bright place. When you squinch something you squeeze it, and a very bright light causes the eyes to squeeze tighter.

1. If you receive a penalty in a sports game, have you made a good or bad play? Explain.

_____

2. If a friend was acting peculiar and asked for your help, what should you do?

_____

3. If an idea comes to you unbidden, have you probably been thinking about it for a long time? Explain.

_____

4. How might a startled animal react to a loud noise, and why?

_____

5. Would having a shade of luck mean that everything is going great for someone? Explain.

_____

Poetry by Mary Tall Mountain, Naomi Shihab Nye, Student Writers
Reading Warm-up A

Read the following passage. Pay special attention to the underlined words. Then, read it again, and complete the activities. Use a separate sheet of paper for your written answers.

The Native American tribes that depended on the buffalo used all parts of the creature for food and other needs. One example is a dried concoction made from berries and buffalo products. Called "pemmican," it was an early form of today's high-nutrition snack bars. Like modern trends, the popularity of pemmican <u>rippled</u> across the frontier and spread as waves of demand came from fur traders and other settlers.

Meat, marrow, and fat from the buffalo were all needed for pemmican. The meat was sliced into thin strips, dried, and then finely shredded with a stone. The buffalo bones were split open and the marrow was removed.

Most kinds of berries could be used. The varieties that grow on <u>prickly</u> or thorny bushes, like blackberries, were frequent choices. The berries were picked before they were <u>overripe</u> and lost their best flavor and vitamins. Then, the berries were dried in the sun.

There were several more steps in making pemmican. First, the dried meat and berries, bone marrow, and fat were combined. Next, this mixture was formed into sheets and dried again. Then, the sheets of dried pemmican were wrapped in bundles in bison skin. Finally, the skins were sealed with more grease. The pemmican could be stored for years.

Pemmican might not sound like a meal that most people now would <u>splurge</u> on or buy in great quantities. However, by the 1840s, the Hudson Bay Company had bought tons of the pemmican bundles. The company's frontier hunters and trappers used pemmican as a survival food. Pemmican was ready to eat and easy to carry. It came in handy during the cold and <u>icy</u> winters in the wild, when other food was hard to find.

Today, people get similar benefits from "fast nutrition" foods. Unlike pemmican, these "power" snacks are packaged so that they <u>flash</u> and catch people's eyes. The basic idea is the same, though—a shortcut to good nutrition.

1. Underline the phrase that is a clue to the meaning of <u>rippled</u>. Explain the meaning of the phrase "the popularity of pemmican *rippled* across the frontier."

2. Circle the word that is a clue to the meaning of <u>prickly</u>. Underline the word for the thing that is described as *prickly*.

3. Underline the phrase that describes a problem when berries are <u>overripe</u>. Explain a way to keep fruit at home from becoming *overripe*.

4. Underline the phrase that gives a clue to the meaning of <u>splurge</u>. Name something that you would *splurge* on if you could.

5. Circle the word that is a clue to the meaning of <u>icy</u>. Give both a synonym (word with a similar meaning) and an antonym (word with an opposite meaning) for *icy*.

6. Underline the phrase that is a clue to the meaning of <u>flash</u> in the passage. Why might advertisers want a box to *flash*?

Poetry by Mary Tall Mountain, Naomi Shihab Nye, Student Writers
Reading Warm-up B

Read the following passage. Pay special attention to the underlined words. Then, read it again, and complete the activities. Use a separate sheet of paper for your written answers.

Athabaskan refers to a number of Native American peoples and to the language that is a common link among them. Today, there are roughly 175,000 North American Indians who are Athabaskan. However, there is far more than a <u>shade</u> of diversity among them. They make their homes in such contrasting places that their differences are not small but great. Athabaskans live in northwest Alaska, along the coast of Oregon and California, in Arizona, in New Mexico, and in Texas. Desert tribes such as the Navajo and sea-going tribes such as the Haida are both part of the Athabaskan family.

It may seem <u>peculiar</u> to call so many different peoples and their languages Athabaskan. The idea is not strange for researchers, though. They see important similarities among the various Athabaskan languages. Long ago, these tongues may have grown out of a single ancient language.

One Athabaskan group is the Alaskan Athabaskans, to whom poet Mary Tallmountain belonged. They were once nomadic peoples. They moved frequently in their quest to gather enough food for the frigid winter. The <u>penalty</u> for failure was starvation, a harsh punishment. So, at the first sign of spring, they began preparing for the summer fishing. They harvested great schools of salmon, which they then smoked and dried.

Picking berries to dry in the sun was also a summer activity, especially for the children. No doubt many berries were eaten, with little fingers giving the juicy fruit a <u>squinch</u> and a pinch and then popping it into the mouth.

In addition to fishing, men hunted caribou and moose, silently stalking their prey. A <u>startled</u> creature would simply run away, so the hunters were careful not to frighten off the animal they were hunting.

The Athabaskans of Alaska were very industrious. They knew winter would come <u>unbidden</u>, like an uninvited guest who stays too long. Today, they also work hard to preserve their native heritage through programs such as language classes and traditional salmon catches.

1. Underline the phrase that explains the meaning of "more than a <u>shade</u> of diversity." Then, write a definition of *shade*.

2. Circle the phrase that identifies what seems <u>peculiar</u>. Give a synonym, or word with a similar meaning, for *peculiar*.

3. Circle the word that is a clue to the meaning of <u>penalty</u>. Describe a serious *penalty* a person might face for speeding.

4. Circle the word that is a clue to the meaning of <u>squinch</u>. If you ate a sour berry, what part of your face might *squinch* up in response?

5. Underline a phrase that is a clue to the meaning of <u>startled</u>. Give a synonym, or word with a similar meaning, for *startled*.

6. Circle the word that is a clue to the meaning of <u>unbidden</u>. Thinking about the meaning of <u>unbidden</u>, explain why every season arrives *unbidden*.

© Pearson Education, Inc. All rights reserved.

Name _____ Date _____

Poetry by Mary Tall Mountain, Naomi Shihab Nye, Student Writers
Writing About the Big Question

How does communication change us?

Big Question Vocabulary

aware	communication	comprehension	discuss	empathy
exchange	illuminate	informed	interpretation	meaning
react	relationship	resolution	respond	understanding

A. *Use one or more words from the list above to complete each sentence.*

1. Because he was _____ that his audience was very young and inexperienced, Josh spoke slowly and carefully.

2. When Gina asked a rapid-fire series of questions, we didn't know how to _____ or _____.

3. Responsible politicians want the public to be _____ about important issues.

4. Although she came from a wealthy family, the major's _____ with the poor was evident in every speech she gave.

B. *Follow the directions in responding to each of the items below.*

1. List two different times when writing or talking about a topic has improved your **understanding** of it.

   _____

   _____

2. Write two sentences to explain one of these experiences, and describe how it made you feel. Use at least two of the Big Question vocabulary words.

   _____

   _____

C. *Complete the sentence below. Then, write a short paragraph in which you connect the sentence to the Big Question.*

When a writer **responds** strongly to an experience, _____

_____

_____

_____

_____

_____

Poetry by Mary Tall Mountain, Naomi Shihab Nye, Student Writers

Literary Analysis: Imagery

Imagery is language that appeals to one or more of the senses—sight, hearing, touch, taste, and smell. The use of imagery allows writers to express their ideas with vividness and immediacy. Images create mental pictures for readers and allow them to make connections between their own experiences and the ideas presented in poems. Some images have a universal appeal and appear in many poems, but most are unique to one poem. Here is an example from Naomi Shihab Nye's poem "Daily": "These T-shirts we fold into / perfect white squares." The words *white* and *squares* appeal to our sense of sight: We can see the folded T-shirts. The word *fold* also appeals to our sense of touch: We can feel the action of folding the shirts.

DIRECTIONS: *Tell which senses (there may be more than one) are appealed to in each of the following passages. Then, describe the complete image that each passage creates in your mind.*

1. "A shade of feeling rippled
   The wind-tanned skin." ("There Is No Word for Goodbye")

   _____

   _____

   _____

2. "Ah, nothing, she said,
   watching the river flash." ("There Is No Word for Goodbye")

   _____

   _____

   _____

3. "These tortillas we slice and fry to crisp strips
   This rich egg scrambled in a gray clay bowl" ("Daily")

   _____

   _____

   _____

4. "This table I dust till the scarred wood shines" ("Daily")

   _____

   _____

   _____

5. "Adam's reply was cut off by the crash of a huge oak tree being ripped out of the dirt and slamming into the ground . . .". ("Hope")

   _____

   _____

   _____

© Pearson Education, Inc. All rights reserved.

Poetry by Mary Tall Mountain, Naomi Shihab Nye, Student Writers
Vocabulary Builder

Word List

| amid | awestruck | emitting | miraculously |
| scarred | shriveled | submerged | succumbed |

A. DIRECTIONS: *Revise each sentence so that the underlined vocabulary word is used logically. Be sure not to change the vocabulary word.*

1. The performance was so dull that we were <u>awestruck</u>.

   _____

2. After the storm had passed over, we were standing <u>amid</u> howling winds.

   _____

3. Because of the fine weather and the good amount of rain, the flowers in our garden look <u>shriveled</u>.

   _____

4. The furniture is so new that it looks <u>scarred</u> and unstable.

   _____

B. DIRECTIONS: *On the line, write the letter of the choice that is the best synonym, or word with a similar meaning, for each numbered word.*

___ 1. miraculously
    A. accidentally
    B. wonderfully
    C. fearfully
    D. horribly

___ 2. emitting
    A. leaving out
    B. returning
    C. sending out
    D. receiving

___ 3. succumbed
    A. yielded
    B. relaxed
    C. restrained
    D. interpreted

___ 4. submerged
    A. substituted
    B. reimbursed
    C. covered with water
    D. displaced

© Pearson Education, Inc. All rights reserved.

Name _____ Date _____

Poetry by Mary Tall Mountain, Naomi Shihab Nye, Student Writers
Support for Writing to Compare

Use a chart like the one shown to make prewriting notes for an essay comparing and contrasting how the writer's use of imagery adds to the meaning of each selection.

"There Is No Word for Goodbye"
Images of Sokoya ⟶
Speaker's feeling for her aunt: _____

_____

_____

_____

_____

_____

"Daily"
Images of objects/tasks ⟶
Speaker's affection for ordinary things: _____

_____

_____

_____

_____

_____

"Hope" and "The Day of the Storm"
Images of sound-and desertion ⟶
Narrator's fear and loneliness: _____

_____

_____

_____

_____

_____

_____

Name _____ Date _____

Open-Book Test

Short Answer *Write your responses to the questions in this section on the lines provided.*

1. Lines 23–26 of Mary TallMountain's "There Is No Word for Goodbye" reflect some important values and beliefs of the speaker's people. Name one of them.

   _____

   _____

2. Could Sokoya's face in "There Is No Word for Goodbye" be described as shriveled? Base your answer on the meaning of *shriveled*.

   _____

   _____

3. In Naomi Shihab Nye's poem "Daily," what is the speaker's attitude toward the objects and activities she mentions? Provide a quote from the poem to support what you say.

   _____

   _____

4. List an image for the sense of touch in "Daily" and one from "There Is No Word for Goodbye." Then answer the question that follows the chart.

Imagery for the sense of touch in "Daily":
Imagery for the sense of touch in "There Is No Word for Goodbye":

   How are these images alike or different?

   _____

5. Which poem—"There Is No Word for Goodbye" or "Daily"—uses the sparest imagery? How does the spare imagery reflect what happens in the poem?

   _____

   _____

   _____

© Pearson Education, Inc. All rights reserved.

6. Cite an image from the poems "There Is No Word for Goodbye" and "Daily" that seems to suggest affection for a person or an object.

"There Is No Word for Goodbye":

_____

"Daily":

_____

7. In "The Day of the Storm," what does the author Ty Booker mean when he says that he vowed "never to take life's simple gifts for granted"? Give an example of one of the author's simple gifts.

_____

_____

8. In "Hope," what does author David Hilbun mean when he says that Adam "bid a mental farewell to his father and a mental hello to his mother"?

_____

_____

9. "There Is No Word for Goodbye," "The Day of the Storm," "Hope," and "Daily" all include images that appeal to the sense of sight. Identify a sight image from each selection.

"There Is No Word for Goodbye":

_____

"The Day of the Storm":

_____

"Hope":

_____

"Daily":

_____

10. In your view, which of these selections appeals most strongly to the sense of touch: "There Is No Word for Goodbye," "The Day of the Storm," or "Daily"? Explain, citing examples from the text.

_____

_____

_____

_____

© Pearson Education, Inc. All rights reserved.

Essay

Write an extended response to the question of your choice or to the question or questions your teacher assigns you.

11. The two poems in this collection—"There Is No Word for Goodbye" and "Daily"—use a variety of images to bring their ideas to life. In an essay, compare and contrast the imagery in these two poems. Which uses unusual or surprising images? Which uses images from everyday life? Which uses a wide variety of images, and which uses just a few? Conclude your essay by explaining what feelings are associated with the images you have discussed.

12. In your view, which of the two stories—"The Day of the Storm" or "Hope"—captures most vividly the chaos and danger of Hurricane Katrina? Which did you find most emotionally moving? Answer and elaborate upon these questions in an essay, using details and information from the essays to support your ideas.

13. Each of the selections in this collection—"There Is No Word for Goodbye," "Daily," "The Day of the Storm," and "Hope"—might be said to express a certain kind of faith or confidence. In an essay, discuss the faith that the speaker or main character in one of these selections declares or implies. Does the poet or author reveal that this faith is shaken or is it strengthened? Finally, evaluate the contribution of the imagery to the message about faith or confidence.

14. **Thinking About the Big Question: How does communication change us?** In "There Is No Word for Goodbye," a conversation changes the way the speaker thinks about parting with a loved one. In "Daily," imagery puts a spotlight on ordinary life. Use the ideas in one of these poems to write a brief essay on how communication can change us or change the way we view our surroundings.

Oral Response

15. Go back to question 1, 5, 7, or to the question your teacher assigns to you. Take a few minutes to expand your answer and prepare an oral response. Find additional details in the relevant selection that support your points. If necessary, make notes to guide your oral response.

Poetry by Mary Tall Mountain, Naomi Shihab Nye, Student Writers
Selection Test A

Critical Reading *Identify the letter of the choice that best answers the question.*

_____ 1. In "There Is No Word for Goodbye," what is the meaning of "Sokoya" in Alaskan Athabaskan?
   A. mother
   B. uncle
   C. aunt
   D. sister

_____ 2. Read the following lines from "There Is No Word for Goodbye":
   A shade of feeling rippled
      the wind-tanned skin.

   To which senses does the imagery in these lines appeal?
   A. sight only
   B. sight and touch
   C. touch and taste
   D. touch only

_____ 3. According to Sokoya in "There Is No Word for Goodbye," what do people say when they leave each other?
   A. I am sorry.
   B. See you.
   C. Thank you.
   D. Peace.

_____ 4. Which of the following best expresses the poet's tone, or attitude toward the subject matter, in "There Is No Word for Goodbye"?
   A. merry
   B. sarcastic
   C. indifferent
   D. emotional

_____ 5. In this line from "Daily," which word adds vividness to the image?
   These tortillas we slice and fry to crisp strips
   A. tortillas
   B. slice
   C. crisp
   D. fry

Name _____   Date _____

___ 6. In "Daily," which of the following does the speaker list and briefly describe?
   A. the rooms in her house
   B. the chores she performs
   C. the school subjects of her children
   D. the flowers in her garden

___ 7. How would you describe the speaker's tone, or attitude toward the subject, in "Daily"?
   A. depressed
   B. sarcastic
   C. favorable
   D. indifferent

___ 8. Which of the following do all four selections in this group have in common?
   A. a dialogue between two speakers
   B. a clever rhyme scheme
   C. vivid images appealing to the senses
   D. a regular meter

___ 9. In the last line of "Hope," what does the image of the single green plant suggest?
   A. revenge   B. memory   C. survival   D. laughter

___ 10. To what senses does this image from "The Day of the Storm" appeal?
   . . . pine trees, emitting their signature smells from the freshly cracked wood,
      lie in the street like barricades.
   A. sight and touch   C. smell, sight, and hearing
   B. smell and touch   D. giving definitions of words

___ 11. Which of the following best describes the narrator's tone, or attitude toward the subject, at the very end of "The Day of the Storm"?
   A. merry   B. resigned   C. indifferent   D. melancholy

Vocabulary

___ 12. In "Daily," the speaker mentions the "shriveled seeds we plant." Which of the following is the best synonym for *shriveled*?
   A. nourishing
   B. tiny
   C. shrunken
   D. round-shaped

____ **13.** In "The Day of the Storm," the narrator says that "the clouds couldn't take the pressure as they succumbed to the rain." What does he mean by *succumbed?*
A. yielded
B. responded
C. corresponded
D. offered themselves

Essay

14. The imagery in these selections is used to suggest or convey the writer's main idea, or theme. In an essay, discuss the connection between imagery and theme of one of these selections. Consider whether the imagery shows a positive or a negative side of the writer's subject. Explain what attitude toward the subject is shown by the imagery—whether respect, delight, or love. Then, show how the imagery contributes to the main idea.

15. In an essay, compare and contrast the imagery in two of these selections. Consider which author uses images that are more concrete—filled with vivid, particular details—and which uses images that are more general. Consider also which author uses a wider variety of images, and which focuses on just a few. Finally, explain what feelings the writer's associate with the images you have discussed.

16. Thinking About the Big Question: How does communication change us? In "There Is No Word for Goodbye," the speaker of the poem has a conversation with an older aunt. How does this conversation change the way the speaker thinks about parting with a loved one? Use ideas from Mary TallMountain's poem to answer the question in a brief essay.

© Pearson Education, Inc. All rights reserved.

Poetry by Mary Tall Mountain, Naomi Shihab Nye, Student Writers
Selection Test B

Critical Reading *Identify the letter of the choice that best completes the statement or answers the question.*

____ 1. In "There Is No Word for Goodbye," whom does the speaker address?
  A. her mother   C. her daughter
  B. her aunt   D. the reader

____ 2. To which sense do these images from "There Is No Word for Goodbye" mainly appeal?
  Looking through
      the net of wrinkles into
      wise black pools
      of her eyes
  A. sight   B. sound   C. touch   D. taste

____ 3. From hints in "There Is No Word for Goodbye," which of the following inferences can you make?
  A. The speaker is a small child.
  B. The speaker is about to become separated from Sokoya.
  C. Sokoya is about to die.
  D. The speaker will spend a long time with Sokoya.

____ 4. Read the following lines from "There Is No Word for Goodbye":
  We always think you're coming back,
      but if you don't,
      we'll see you some place else.

  Which of the following is the message, or theme, in these lines?
  A. good will toward all human beings
  B. an emphasis on self-restraint
  C. faith in community and in a hereafter
  D. pride in one's origins

____ 5. To which senses do these lines from "Daily" appeal?
  These shriveled seeds we plant,
  corn kernel, dried bean,
  poke into loosened soil,
  cover over with measured fingertips
  A. sight only   C. taste and touch
  B. sight and touch   D. touch only

____ 6. In "Daily," which of the following does the poem's theme concern?
  A. the harsh realities of working life
  B. the beauty and dignity of everyday tasks
  C. the pleasures of living in a comfortable home
  D. the cruelty of poverty and oppression

© Pearson Education, Inc. All rights reserved.

_____ 7. To which senses does the imagery in this excerpt from "Hope" appeal?

Screaming, flipping over and over, he bid a mental farewell to his father . . .

A. sight and smell   C. hearing and sight
B. smell and touch   D. hearing and taste

_____ 8. Why do you think the narrator of "Hope" ends the selection with the image of "a single green plant" amid all the destruction?

A. to emphasize how uneventful the storm was
B. to suggest hope and survival, despite the storm's destruction
C. to emphasize his love for his father
D. to arouse the reader's pity

_____ 9. In "The Day of the Storm," after the narrator speaks to the man in Army fatigues, he says that the man's words "formed themselves into two ton bricks." What feeling does this image suggest?

A. pleasure
B. awe
C. surprise
D. fear

_____ 10. In the final paragraph of "The Aftermath of Katrina," what two contrasting emotions or feelings does the narrator highlight upon his return to Baton Rouge?

A. joy and sadness   C. approval and disapproval
B. curiosity and respect   D. interest and indifference

_____ 11. What is the main difference between the following two images?

wise black pools / of her eyes ("There is No Word for Goodbye")
This table I dust till the scarred wood shines ("Daily")

A. The second is more vivid than the first.
B. The first appeals more to touch, while the second appeals more to sight.
C. The second is a realistic description, while the first is not meant literally.
D. The first appeals to the senses, while the second does not.

_____ 12. Which of the following best describes the speakers' tone, or attitude toward the subject, in the four selections?

A. reverent
B. satirical
C. angry
D. melancholy

_____ 13. Which of the following do these four selections have in common?

A. a somber theme   C. regular patterns of end rhyme
B. vivid imagery   D. multiple speakers

Vocabulary

____ 14. Which of the following is the best synonym, or word with a similar meaning, for *miraculously*?
    A. eerily
    B. wonderfully
    C. predictably
    D. meticulously

____ 15. If a plant looks *shriveled*, how would you describe it?
    A. flourishing and healthy
    B. tall with a weak-looking stem
    C. flowering profusely
    D. shrunken and wrinkled

____ 16. Which of the following is most nearly opposite in meaning to the word *awestruck*?
    A. envious
    B. realistic
    C. indifferent
    D. scrupulous

Essay

17. Imagery allows writers to express their ideas with vividness and immediacy. In which of these selections did you find the imagery especially appealing? In an essay, write a detailed analysis of one of the selections, identifying and commenting on the images used by the author to express his or her main ideas.

18. Each of the selections in this group might be said to express a certain kind of faith or confidence. In "There Is No Word for Goodbye," for example, Sokoya affirms to the speaker her belief that, sooner or later, all people will meet again, despite temporary separations. In an essay, discuss the faith that the speaker or narrator of each selection declares or implies. Then, evaluate the message of each selection, comparing and contrasting their themes.

19. **Thinking About the Big Question: How does communication change us?** In "There Is No Word for Goodbye," a conversation changes the way the speaker thinks about parting with a loved one. In "Daily," imagery puts a spotlight on ordinary life. Use the ideas in one of these poems to write a brief essay on how communication can change us or change the way we view our surroundings.

© Pearson Education, Inc. All rights reserved.

Name _____ Date _____

Description: Descriptive Essay

Prewriting: Choosing Your Topic

Use the following chart to list sights, sounds, smells, tastes, and textures that you encounter over the next few days.

	Day 1	Day 2	Day 3
Sights			
Sounds			
Smells			
Tastes			
Textures			

Drafting: Selecting an Organizational Structure

Choose a graphic organizer for your descriptive essay from the ones below. You need to determine if spatial organization or time-order organization would work better.

Spatial Organization from Left to Right or Front to Back

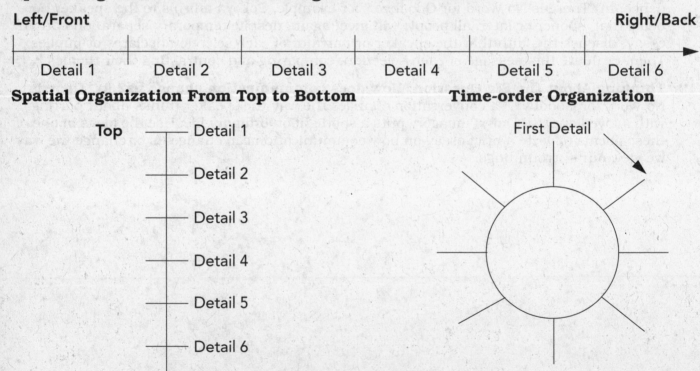

Left/Front   Right/Back

Detail 1   Detail 2   Detail 3   Detail 4   Detail 5   Detail 6

Spatial Organization From Top to Bottom   Time-order Organization

Top —— Detail 1

—— Detail 2

—— Detail 3

—— Detail 4

—— Detail 5

—— Detail 6

First Detail

© Pearson Education, Inc. All rights reserved.

Name _____ Date _____

Writing Workshop
Descriptive Essay: Integrating Grammar Skills

Varying Sentence Patterns

The most basic sentence pattern uses a subject followed by a verb. However, overuse of this pattern can make writing dull and stiff. To add interest, vary your sentences by beginning them in different ways.

Basic Sentence	Begin with . . .	New Sentence
The town recently built a public pool.	Adverb	*Recently*, the town built a public pool.
It is large and rectangular and has a diving board at one end.	Adjective	*Large and rectangular*, it has a diving board at one end.
We often swim in the pool on hot afternoons.	Prepositional Phrase	*On hot afternoons*, we often swim in the pool.
Tom swims late in the day, doing laps around the pool.	Participial Phrase	*Doing laps around the pool*, Tom swims late in the day.
Celia practices her diving when she has a chance.	Adverb Clause	*When she has a chance*, Celia practices her diving.
The lifeguard, a town employee, comes on duty at nine.	Appositive	*A town employee*, the lifeguard comes on duty at nine.

Identifying Sentences Using the Basic Subject-Verb Pattern

A. DIRECTIONS: *Put a check on the line before each sentence that uses the basic subject-verb pattern.*

_____ 1. Santa Fe is one of the oldest cities in America.

_____ 2. It was founded by the Spanish and dates to 1609.

_____ 3. At the center of the town is a plaza, or large square.

_____ 4. The Palace of Governors, one of America's oldest buildings, is on the plaza.

Fixing Sentences to Vary Sentence Patterns

B. DIRECTIONS: *On the line provided, rewrite each sentence so that it varies the subject-verb pattern. Do not use the same type of beginning more than once.*

1. Many towns in New England have a town green.

_____

2. The green, a large square in the town center, is a centuries-old tradition.

_____

3. Our town green is long and attractive and lined with trees.

_____

4. Fine shops facing the green sell a variety of goods.

_____

© Pearson Education, Inc. All rights reserved.

Unit 4: Poetry
Benchmark Test 7

Literary Analysis: Figurative Language *Identify the type of figurative language used in each of the following sentences.*

1. An angry sky loomed overhead.
   - A. simile
   - B. metaphor
   - C. paradox
   - D. personification

2. Her novel was a passport to adventure.
   - A. simile
   - B. metaphor
   - C. paradox
   - D. personification

3. The rumbling storm sounded like a freight train headed our way.
   - A. simile
   - B. metaphor
   - C. paradox
   - D. personification

4. The younger she dresses, the older she looks.
   - A. simile
   - B. metaphor
   - C. paradox
   - D. personification

Literary Analysis: Sound Devices

5. The word *fizz* is an example of which sound device?
   - A. alliteration
   - B. consonance
   - C. assonance
   - D. onomatopoeia

6. Which sound device does this phrase demonstrate?

   cruel cackles of crazed crones
   - A. alliteration
   - B. consonance
   - C. assonance
   - D. onomatopoeia

7. The words *jump* and *stunt* are examples of which sound device?
   - A. alliteration
   - B. consonance
   - C. assonance
   - D. onomatopoeia

8. The words *hum* and *ham* are examples of which sound device?
   - A. alliteration
   - B. consonance
   - C. assonance
   - D. onomatopoeia

© Pearson Education, Inc. All rights reserved.

Literary Analysis: Imagery

9. What is the aim of imagery in poetry?
   A. To create rhyme
   B. To create meter
   C. to add symbolism
   D. to appeal to the senses

10. To which sense does the following image appeal?

    Sara brushed the crumbs from her lap.

    A. touch
    B. sound
    C. smell
    D. sight

11. To which senses does the following image appeal?

    "These tortillas we slice and fry to crisp strips."

    A. smell and touch
    B. touch and sight
    C. sight and smell
    D. sight and sound

Reading Skill: Reading Fluency

12. Which of the following is the best strategy for improving fluency when reading poetry?
    A. Read quickly.
    B. Read expressively.
    C. Read in sentences.
    D. Read slowly.

13. Which of the following words is an example of sensory language?
    A. astonishing
    B. hideous
    C. pleasure
    D. smoky

Read the poem. Then, answer the questions that follow.

Where My Books Go

All the words that I utter,
　　And all the words that I write,
Must spread out their wings untiring,
　　And never rest in their flight,
Till they come where your sad, sad heart is,
　　And sing to you in the night,
Beyond where the waters are moving,
　　Storm-darken'd or starry bright.

William Butler Yeats

14. How many sentences does this poem include?
    A. one
    B. two
    C. four
    D. eight

15. Which of the following words from the poem is a sensory word?
    A. wings
    B. untiring
    C. heart
    D. starry

16. To what are books compared in this poem?
    A. clouds
    B. airplanes
    C. birds
    D. stars

Reading Informational Material: Technical Directions and Use Technology

17. Which of the following documents is most likely to include technical directions?
    A. a novel
    B. a short story
    C. a warranty
    D. a how-to guide

18. Which statement about technical directions is true?
    A. Technical directions often include language specific to a topic.
    B. Technical directions do not need to be read carefully.
    C. Technical directions are usually boring and do not need to be read at all.
    D. Technical directions can be done in any order.

19. What is an MP3?
    A. a way to broadcast visual information over the computer
    B. a computer file format used for audio recordings
    C. a format for delivering frequently changing files
    D. a cord that connects a computer to another device

Vocabulary: Word Roots and Prefixes

20. In the following sentence, what does the word *deferred* mean?

    During the Vietnam War, military service could be deferred by enrolling in college.

    A. avoided   C. substituted
    B. satisfied   D. delayed

21. The root word -vert- means "turn." Using this knowledge, what does the word *inverted* mean?
    A. horizontal
    B. upside down
    C. sideways
    D. advanced

22. In the following sentence, what does the word *subverting* mean?

    Anyone who brings a weapon into a school is subverting the concept of a safe learning environment.
    A. ruining
    B. challenging
    C. revising
    D. ignoring

23. In the following sentence, what does the word *analysis* mean?

    After an analysis of Joe's test results, his doctor determined that he had a rare form of bone cancer.
    A. calculation
    B. review
    C. systematic evaluation
    D. division

24. The prefix mono- means "one, single, or alone." Using this knowledge, what is the meaning of the word *monotone*?
    A. a harmony
    B. an unchanging note or sound
    C. a melody
    D. a chord

25. What is the meaning of the word formed by adding *mono-* to *-pod*?
    A. a single celled organism
    B. a type of plant
    C. a two sided brace
    D. a single-legged support

Grammar

26. In the following sentence, which word is a preposition?

    I am going to the store.
    A. I
    B. am
    C. to
    D. the

27. Which relationships do many prepositions describe?
   A. size relationships
   B. value relationships
   C. personal relationships
   D. spatial relationships

28. What function does the word *fence* serve in the following sentence?

   The fox ran under the fence.

   A. subject
   B. preposition
   C. object of preposition
   D. predicate noun

29. What is the object of the preposition in the following sentence?

   Snorkel dropped his bone right on me.

   A. Snorkel
   B. bone
   C. right
   D. me

30. What must a prepositional phrase include?
   A. a preposition and a noun or pronoun
   B. a preposition and an adjective or article
   C. a preposition and a verb or adverb
   D. a preposition and a conjunction or interjection

31. How many prepositional phrases are in the following sentence?

   Put the pen near the front of the desk under the pad just behind the box.

   A. one
   B. two
   C. three
   D. four

32. Which of the following sentence patterns is often overused?
   A. subject-verb
   B. subject-verb-object
   C. subject-verb-prepositional phrase
   D. subject-verb-adverb

33. What is an introductory prepositional phrase?
   A. a prepositional phrase in an introduction
   B. a prepositional phrase that introduces a character
   C. a prepositional phrase that starts a paragraph
   D. a prepositional phrase that begins a sentence

34. What must you add if an introductory prepositional phrase has four or more words?
   A. a space
   B. a comma
   C. a semicolon
   D. a colon

ESSAY

Writing:

35. Write a paragraph or poem that describes a scene in nature that you have experienced. Remember: nature can be close to home or far away. Try to make the scene so vivid that the reader's experience is nearly as memorable as your experience was. Use sensory words in your description to make the scene come alive for the reader.

36. Write an editorial for your student or local newspaper about an environmental issue that you really care about. Be as clear as possible in presenting your opinion and include facts, examples, and other information to back it up.

37. Write an essay that describes a favorite person, pet, place, or thing. Use figurative language, sensory details, and an organization that makes sense for your topic.

© Pearson Education, Inc. All rights reserved.

Name _____

Starting Date _____ Ending Date _____

Unit 4: Poetry Skills Concept Map—2

How does communication change us?

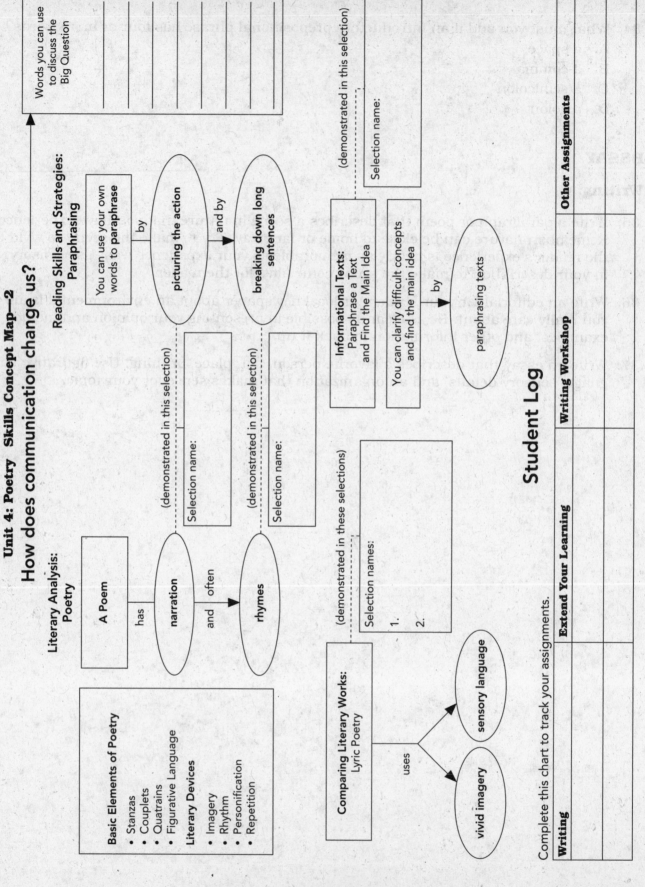

Literary Analysis: Poetry

A Poem — has → narration — and often → rhymes

(demonstrated in this selection)
Selection name: _____

(demonstrated in this selection)
Selection name: _____

Basic Elements of Poetry
- Stanzas
- Couplets
- Quatrains
- Figurative Language

Literary Devices
- Imagery
- Rhythm
- Personification
- Repetition

Reading Skills and Strategies: Paraphrasing

You can use your own words to paraphrase — by → picturing the action — and by → breaking down long sentences

Informational Texts: Paraphrase a Text and Find the Main Idea

You can clarify difficult concepts and find the main idea — by → paraphrasing texts

(demonstrated in this selection)
Selection name: _____

Comparing Literary Works: Lyric Poetry

uses → vivid imagery / sensory language

(demonstrated in these selections)
Selection names:
1. _____
2. _____

Words you can use to discuss the Big Question

Student Log

Complete this chart to track your assignments.

Writing	Extend Your Learning	Writing Workshop	Other Assignments

Vocabulary Warm-up Word Lists

Study these words from the poetry of Ernest Lawrence Thayer, William Stafford, and Sandra Cisneros. Then, apply your knowledge to the activities that follow.

Word List A

cyclone [SI klohn] *n.* a strong storm in which air spins quickly; a hurricane
   The cyclone knocked down this tree.

defiance [dee FY ens] *n.* a hostile or challenging attitude toward authority
   His defiance of the law landed him in jail.

kindling [KIND ling] *n.* small pieces of wood or other materials used to start a fire
   We gathered kindling for the campfire.

occurred [uh KURD] *v.* happened; took place
   The Battle of Gettysburg occurred in 1863.

pulsing [PUHLS ing] *adj.* getting bigger and smaller in a rhythmic way; flashing, as a light
   The pulsing light reflected from the steel building hurt my eyes.

shattered [SHAT erd] *v.* broken suddenly into pieces
   The vase was shattered by the fall.

Word List B

confident [KAHN fi duhnt] *adj.* sure that you can do something; having no doubt
   His quick smile and confident manner made him a natural leader.

grandeur [GRAN jer] *n.* impressive power, beauty, or size; magnificence
   The grandeur of the scenery took my breath away.

haughty [HAW tee] *adj.* scornfully proud; looking down on other people
   The haughty princess would not say hello to the farmer's wife.

indulged [in DULJD] *v.* gave in to; let yourself do something
   During his vacation, he indulged his desire to travel.

rebounded [REE bown did] *v.* bounced back
   His voice rebounded when he shouted across the canyon.

sedan [si DAN] *n.* automobile with seats for at least four people
   The five of us took a ride in our comfortable new sedan.

© Pearson Education, Inc. All rights reserved.

Poetry Collection: Ernest Lawrence Thayer, William Stafford, Sandra Cisneros
Vocabulary Warm-up Exercises

Exercise A *Fill in each blank in the following paragraph with an appropriate word from Word List A. Use each word only once.*

I tackled my first babysitting job last Friday night. Taking care of six-year-old twins is not easy. As soon as their parents left, the boys decided to play catch with a glass pitcher, which [1] _____ into a thousand pieces when it crashed to the floor. While I swept up, the twins chased each other around the living room and knocked over some [2] _____ that had been neatly piled beside the fireplace. When I asked them to calm down, they acted even wilder in direct [3] _____ of my request. The house looked as if an earthquake had [4] _____ or as if it had been struck by a [5] _____! I could feel the blood [6] _____ in my brain. Fortunately, the boys had tired themselves out. The little angels suddenly said goodnight and hurried off to bed!

Exercise B *Answer the questions with complete explanations.*

1. Is a <u>confident</u> person likely to be nervous at a job interview?

   _____

2. Would a person who comments on the <u>grandeur</u> of a sunset probably sound annoyed?

   _____

3. If someone responds to your question with a <u>haughty</u> response, how did that person feel about the question?

   _____

4. Would you be better off if your parents <u>indulged</u> your every wish?

   _____

5. What objects would create sounds that <u>rebounded</u>?

   _____

6. Would your class be more comfortable traveling in a bus or a <u>sedan</u>?

   _____

Poetry Collection: Ernest Lawrence Thayer, William Stafford, Sandra Cisneros
Reading Warm-up A

Read the following passage. Pay special attention to the underlined words. Then, read it again, and complete the activities. Use a separate sheet of paper for your written answers.

The twister that carried Dorothy's house off to Oz was a tornado. A tornado is not the same as a <u>cyclone</u>. The word *cyclone* usually refers to a powerful windstorm that starts over the ocean somewhere in the tropics. These storms are also called hurricanes or typhoons, depending on their point of origin.

Tornadoes are twisting columns of air that extend from a thunderstorm to the ground. A tornado takes the form of a narrow funnel that skips across the earth and destroys everything in its path. The path of damage can be more than a mile wide and 50 miles long. The average tornado travels about 16 miles and stays in any one place for only about 30 seconds. With wind speeds in excess of 250 miles an hour, however, those 30 seconds are enough to reduce any tree or wooden house in the tornado's path to <u>kindling</u>.

Tornadoes come in all shapes and sizes. They are more likely to strike during the summer in the north and during the spring in the south. The largest known tornado outbreak <u>occurred</u> in 1974. During two terrible days in April, 148 tornados in eleven states injured more than 5,300 people. The <u>pulsing</u> lights of police cars and emergency vehicles flashed everywhere. Alabama, Kentucky, and Ohio were the states hardest hit.

If a tornado warning is sounded in your area, head for a storm cellar, basement, or inside room. Stay away from windows. Glass that has <u>shattered</u> and flying debris cause most tornado-related injuries.

Tornados can develop extremely rapidly. If the sky suddenly darkens, hail begins to fall, and you hear a loud roar, a twister may be on its way. Try to get to a safe place immediately. If you cannot, lie flat in the nearest ditch and cover your head. <u>Defiance</u> of the tornado's power is never a good idea. The tornado will win every time.

1. Underline the sentence that tells you what a <u>cyclone</u> is. Write a sentence for a radio announcement warning that a *cyclone* is on its way.

2. Underline the words that give a clue to the meaning of <u>kindling</u>. What is *kindling*?

3. Underline the words that tell what <u>occurred</u> in 1974. Give a synonym, or word with a similar meaning, for *occurred*.

4. Circle the word that hints at the meaning of <u>pulsing</u>. Write a sentence using *pulsing*.

5. Circle the word that tells what has <u>shattered</u>. Write a sentence about something else that might have *shattered*.

6. Underline the words that describe actions that are the opposite of <u>defiance</u> of the tornado's power. Explain why such *defiance* is never a good idea.

Name _____ Date _____

Poetry Collection: Ernest Lawrence Thayer, William Stafford, Sandra Cisneros
Reading Warm-up B

Read the following passage. Pay special attention to the underlined words. Then, read it again, and complete the activities. Use a separate sheet of paper for your written answers.

I could hardly sit still as my father parked our creaky old <u>sedan</u> next to the ball field. As soon as he stopped, I bolted out of the car and joined my teammates on the field.

This was the championship game, and excitement ran high among the Panthers. We were <u>confident</u> that we could win, but it was not going to be easy. The Eagles were an excellent team, and taking a <u>haughty</u> attitude toward our opponents was not going to help.

The Eagles were up first. Both teams played well, and the Panthers were ahead by one run at the top of the final inning. I was playing right field, and, with the stifling summer sun making me feel a little sleepy, I foolishly <u>indulged</u> my desire to close my eyes for a few seconds. Then, I heard a loud crack, and, as my eyes flew open, I saw the fly ball flying straight at me. The Eagles had two outs, so if I caught the ball before it hit the ground, the game would be over. I started thinking about how wonderful it would be to win the championship and, distracted by this vision of <u>grandeur</u>, I was not quite in position as the ball descended. With my arm outstretched, I dove toward the fence. The ball skimmed my glove, <u>rebounded</u> off the fence, and touched the ground. I quickly snatched it up, but it was too late—I had missed the catch!

Then, I heard the riotous cheering. Everyone thought I had caught the ball. I knew I would be hailed from this day forth as the hero who had won the championship for the Panthers . . . but it would all be based on a lie.

I looked at my teammates' smiling faces and felt a knot of indecision growing in my stomach. Then, I looked in the stands and saw my parents beaming at me with pride. At that moment, I knew exactly what I had to do.

Losing now might feel awful, but it would not feel half as bad as winning because of a lie.

1. Circle a word in the paragraph that means the same as <u>sedan</u>. Describe a *sedan* that you have seen.

2. Underline the words that tell what the Panthers were <u>confident</u> about. What reasons might they have for feeling *confident*?

3. Underline the phrase that explains why taking a <u>haughty</u> attitude would not be a good idea. In your own words, explain why taking a *haughty* attitude will not help the Panthers win.

4. Underline the words that tell what the narrator <u>indulged</u>. Explain when he might have more sensibly *indulged* himself.

5. Underline the words that tell what the vision of <u>grandeur</u> was. Tell about something you have seen that has *grandeur*.

6. Circle the word that tells what <u>rebounded</u>. What does *rebounded* mean?

© Pearson Education, Inc. All rights reserved.

Name _____ Date _____

Poetry Collection: Ernest Lawrence Thayer, William Stafford, Sandra Cisneros
Writing About the Big Question

How does communication change us?

Big Question Vocabulary

aware	communication	comprehension	discuss	empathy
exchange	illuminate	informed	interpretation	meaning
react	relationship	resolution	respond	understanding

A. *Use one or more words from the list above to complete each sentence.*

1. The chairperson announced, "We will not reach a _____ in this debate unless we all listen carefully to one another's viewpoints."

2. My _____ with Ken was damaged when I learned he was telling lies about me.

3. "It is my _____," Stacy said, "that the package will arrive at our office before 2 P.M."

4. "Let's _____ e-mail addresses," Matt urged, "so we can stay in touch."

5. That article helped a lot to _____ some obscure passages in the poem.

B. *Follow the directions in responding to each of the items below.*

1. List two different times when an **exchange** of ideas with someone else persuaded you to change your mind about someone or something.

   _____

   _____

2. Write two sentences to explain one of these experiences, and describe how it made you feel. Use at least two of the Big Question vocabulary words.

   _____

   _____

C. *Complete the sentence below. Then, write a short paragraph in which you connect the sentence to the Big Question.*

When a crowd communicates its support or disapproval, a person might **react** by

   _____

   _____

   _____

Name _____ Date _____

Poetry Collection: Ernest Lawrence Thayer, William Stafford, and Sandra Cisneros
Literary Analysis: Narrative Poetry

Narrative poetry is verse that tells a story and includes the same literary elements as narrative prose:

- a plot, or sequence of events
- specific settings
- characters who participate in the action

Also like narrative prose, such as a short story, a narrative poem conveys a **mood,** or **atmosphere**—an overall feeling created by the setting, plot, words, and images. For example, a narrative poem's mood can be gloomy, joyous, or mysterious. Poetry's emphasis on precise words and images makes mood a powerful element in a narrative poem.

DIRECTIONS: *As you read "Casey at the Bat," "Fifteen," and "Twister Hits Houston," answer the following questions.*

"Casey at the Bat"

1. What story does this poem tell?

    _____

2. Who are the two most important characters in the poem?

    _____

3. Briefly describe the poem's outcome.

    _____

4. How does Thayer use details of sound to contribute to the poem's setting?

    _____

    _____

"Fifteen"

5. Who is the speaker in this poem, and what occasion does he recall?

    _____

6. What is the principal conflict in "Fifteen"?

    _____

    _____

"Twister Hits Houston"

7. What details create suspense in this narrative poem?

    _____

    _____

8. How would you describe the atmosphere, or mood, at the end of the poem?

    _____

    _____

Poetry Collection: Ernest Lawrence Thayer, William Stafford, and Sandra Cisneros

Reading: Paraphrasing

Paraphrasing is restating in your own words what someone else has written or said. A paraphrase retains the essential meaning and ideas of the original but is simpler to read.

Paraphrasing is especially helpful when reading poetry because poems often contain **figurative language,** words and phrases that are used imaginatively rather than literally. To paraphrase lines in a narrative poem, **picture the action:**

- Based on details in the poem, form a mental image of the setting, the characters, and the characters' actions.
- To be sure that your mental picture is accurate, pay close attention to the way that the poet describes elements of the scene.
- Then, use your own words to describe your mental image of the scene and the action taking place in it.

DIRECTIONS: *On the lines provided, paraphrase the following passages from the narrative poems in this collection. Remember that a paraphrase is a restatement in your own words.*

1. And now the leather-covered sphere came hurtling through the air,
   And Casey stood a-watching it in haughty grandeur there.
   Close by the sturdy batsman the ball unheeded sped;
   "That ain't my style," said Casey. "Strike one," the umpire said. ("Casey at the Bat")

   _____

   _____

   _____

2. I admired all that pulsing gleam, the
   shiny flanks, the demure headlights,
   fringed where it lay; I led it gently
   to the road and stood with that
   companion, ready and friendly. I was fifteen. ("Fifteen")

   _____

   _____

   _____

3. Papa who was sitting on his front porch
   when the storm hit
   said the twister ripped
   the big black oak to splinter . . . ("Twister Hits Houston")

   _____

   _____

   _____

© Pearson Education, Inc. All rights reserved.

Name _____ Date _____

Poetry Collection: Ernest Lawrence Thayer, William Stafford, and Sandra Cisneros
Vocabulary Builder

Word List

defiance   demure   multitude   pallor   preceded   writhing

A. DIRECTIONS: *Match each word in Column A with the correct definition in Column B.*

Column A	Column B
___ 1. pallor	A. twisting
___ 2. writhing	B. modest
___ 3. demure	C. paleness

B. DIRECTIONS: *In each of the following items, think about the meaning of the italicized word and then answer the question.*

1. A *multitude* of townspeople attended the parade. Why might it have been hard to see the marchers?

   _____

2. Jean reacted with *defiance* when we asked her to deliver her report. Why might we have felt angry and hurt?

   _____

3. Nathaniel *preceded* his piano recital with a few informal comments about the composer. Which came first: his comments or his performance?

   _____

C. WORD STUDY: Use the context of each sentence and what you know about the Latin prefix *pre-* to rewrite the sentence so that it makes sense. Be careful not to change the word in italics.

1. Lucy was greatly interested in the comments by the authors in the *preface* at the end of the report.

   _____

   _____

2. At the parade, Mayor Vargas was scarcely visible because she *preceded* all the other marchers.

   _____

   _____

3. Thinking about yesterday's history test, Mark has a *premonition* that several questions would relate to the chapter review.

   _____

   _____

© Pearson Education, Inc. All rights reserved.

Name _____ Date _____

Poetry Collection: Ernest Lawrence Thayer, William Stafford, and Sandra Cisneros
Enrichment: Mathematics

Breaking Records

In "Casey at the Bat," the mighty Casey strikes out. We are led to believe, however, that Casey was normally a powerful hitter—perhaps capable of setting an all-time home run record.

In real life, Babe Ruth held the home run record in the major leagues for thirty-eight years. Before Hank Aaron began creeping up on Babe Ruth's record of 714 home runs, many baseball fans thought Ruth's record would never be broken. The following table shows the lifetime records of the top home run hitters in the major leagues. Players whose names are in boldface are still active in the major leagues, so their totals and ranks will have changed since this table was published.

All-time Home Run Leaders		
PLAYER	**HOME RUNS**	**RANK**
Hank Aaron	755	1
Babe Ruth	714	2
Barry Bonds	**703**	**3**
Willie Mays	660	4
Frank Robinson	586	5
Mark McGwire	583	6
Sammy Sosa	**574**	**7**
Harmon Killebrew	573	8

DIRECTIONS: *Use the statistics in the All-time Home Run Leaders table to answer the following questions.*

1. By how many home runs did the following players fall short of breaking Babe Ruth's record?
   A. Mays _____   B. Robinson _____   C. Killebrew _____

2. How many home runs behind Hank Aaron's mark did the following players finish their careers?
   A. Ruth _____   B. Mays _____   C. Robinson _____

3. What is the average number of home runs hit by the eight players listed in the table?

   _____

4. If a player averages forty-three home runs each season, how many years will he have to play to beat Hank Aaron's record? _____

5. Use the Internet to find out the latest home run totals for Barry Bonds and Sammy Sosa.
   A. Bonds _____   B. Sosa _____

Name _____ Date _____

Short Answer *Write your responses to the questions in this section on the lines provided.*

1. Use the following timeline to note the major events in "Casey at the Bat" by Ernest Lawrence Thayer. Record a key event in each box. Then, on the line below the timeline, tell which event creates the most suspenseful mood.

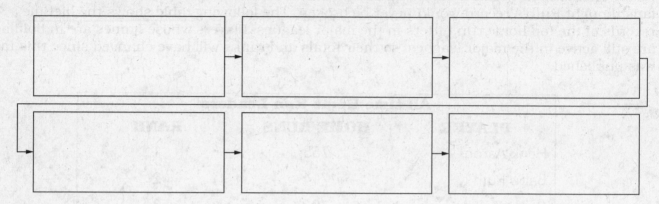

Most suspenseful event:

_____

2. In the fourth stanza of "Casey at the Bat" (lines 13–16), two events surprise the crowd. Picture the action as you reread the stanza. Then use your own words to paraphrase the action.

_____

_____

3. In line 32 of "Casey at the Bat," Casey says, "That ain't my style." Explain why he says this and what the comment reveals about his character.

_____

_____

_____

4. Before the third pitch to Casey, are the fans writhing? Why? Use the definition of the word *writhing* in your response.

_____

_____

5. Based on the second and third stanzas in "Fifteen" by William Stafford, what can the reader logically expect to happen in the fourth stanza? What happens instead?

_____

_____

© Pearson Education, Inc. All rights reserved.

6. The poem "Fifteen" describes a moment between childhood dreams and adult realities. Cite two lines from the poem that reflect a dream and a reality.

Childhood dream:

_____

_____

Adult reality:

_____

_____

7. At the end of "Fifteen," the owner of the motorcycle calls the speaker "a good man." What is the significance of this, in relation to the poem's title?

_____

_____

_____

8. In "Twister Hits Houston" by Sandra Cisneros, two characters tell their version of a story. Summarize each person's account.

Papa:

_____

_____

_____

Mama:

_____

_____

_____

9. In "Twister Hits Houston," how do Mama and Papa each seem to feel about their experience with the storm?

_____

_____

_____

10. Mama speaks the last three lines of "Twister Hits Houston." What new information does she give?

_____

_____

_____

© Pearson Education, Inc. All rights reserved.

Essay

Write an extended response to the question of your choice or to the question or questions your teacher assigns you.

11. Narrative poems, like short stories, tell a story. They include the elements of plot, setting, characters, and mood (or overall feeling). Choose one of the poems by Thayer, Stafford, and Cisneros in this collection, and write an essay in which you identify the elements of plot, setting, characters, and mood in that poem. In your view, which element is most strongly present? Explain, supporting your ideas with specific references to the text.

12. Most good stories include an element of suspense—the reader's feeling of curiosity, anxiety, or uncertainty about what will happen next. Revisit "Casey at the Bat" and "Fifteen." Then write an essay in which you compare and contrast the two poets' use of suspense in their works. Be sure to comment on how each poem's suspense relates to the mood, or atmosphere, at the end of each poem.

13. One glance at "Casey at the Bat" tells you that it is a poem, not a short story. And yet after reading the poem's first two lines, you know you have entered a storytelling world. Describe in an essay the ways in which the poem is like a short story and the ways in which it is different. Discuss at least three similarities and three differences, citing details from the poem to support your analysis. Then draw a conclusion about the story's form. If it were told in prose rather than poetry, what special qualities might it lose?

14. **Thinking About the Big Question: How does communication change us?** In "Twister Hits Houston," the characters describe a natural disaster over and over again. In a brief essay, tell why people might feel compelled to repeat disaster stories to anyone who will listen.

Oral Response

15. Go back to question 3, 6, or 7 or to the question your teacher assigns to you. Take a few minutes to expand your answer and prepare an oral response. Find additional details in the relevant poem that support your points. If necessary, make notes to guide your oral response.

Poetry Collection: Ernest Lawrence Thayer, William Stafford, and Sandra Cisneros
Selection Test A

Critical Reading *Identify the letter of the choice that best answers the question.*

____ 1. Which of the following most accurately describes Casey when he steps up to bat in Ernest Lawrence Thayer's poem?
A. angry
B. confident
C. nervous
D. scornful

____ 2. Which of the following details is most important to include in a paraphrase of "Casey at the Bat"?
A. Casey lets the first two pitches go by without swinging.
B. Casey doffs his hat to the crowd.
C. Casey pounds his bat on the plate.
D. Casey raises his hand when the crowd shouts "Kill the umpire!"

____ 3. In "Casey at the Bat," which of the following is the climax (the most exciting point in the narrative)?
A. Flynn hits a single.
B. Casey steps up to bat.
C. The umpire calls the first strike on Casey.
D. Casey swings at the third pitch.

____ 4. What is the best paraphrase of the following lines from "Casey at the Bat"?
   But Flynn let drive a "single," to the wonderment of all.
   And the much-despised Blakey "tore the cover off the ball."
A. Both Flynn and Blakey got hits.
B. Neither Flynn nor Blakey got on base.
C. Flynn got a single, but Blakey angrily destroyed the ball.
D. Flynn reached first base, but Blakey struck out.

____ 5. In "Fifteen," what does the motorcycle represent to the boy?
A. money
B. speed
C. danger
D. adventure

___ 6. In a paraphrase of the speaker's description of the motorcycle in "Fifteen," which of the following would you stress?

A. the speaker's lack of understanding

B. the speaker's admiration

C. the speaker's anxiety

D. the speaker's boredom

___ 7. Read the following lines from "Fifteen":

> Thinking, back farther in the grass I found
> the owner, just coming to, where he had flipped
> over the rail.

Which of the following best describes the function of these lines in the story the poem tells?

A. The lines present the chief conflict in the poem.

B. The lines reveal the speaker's identity.

C. The lines represent a turning point in the action.

D. The lines introduce the main character.

___ 8. Which of the following best describes William Stafford's theme, or overall message, in the poem "Fifteen"?

A. One should take proper safety precautions when riding a motorcycle.

B. Motorcycles are wonderful machines.

C. Adolescence can be a time of conflicts and difficult choices.

D. Riding in heavy traffic can be hazardous.

___ 9. In "Twister Hits Houston," what is Mama doing when the cyclone strikes?

A. cooking dinner

B. watching television

C. washing laundry

D. trying to change a lightbulb

___ 10. In "Twister Hits Houston," Sandra Cisneros most likely includes the details of the splintered oak tree, the green sedan, and the banging back door in order to accomplish which of the following?

A. enable the reader to picture the action

B. show that the speaker is an observant witness

C. hint that Papa exaggerates the story

D. show that Mama is courageous in a time of danger

____ 11. Read the final lines of "Twister Hits Houston":

> The light bulb is still sitting
> where I left it. Don't matter now.
> Got no electricity anyway.

Which of the following best describes the mood, or atmosphere, of these lines?

A. joyful   C. loving

B. confident   D. ironic

Vocabulary and Grammar

____ 12. Which of the following might you display if you believed you had seen a ghost?

A. anger   C. amusement

B. pallor   D. regret

____ 13. If tree branches were *writhing* in a high wind, which of the following would best describe them?

A. floating   C. falling

B. snapping   D. twisting

____ 14. In the following sentence, which words are the appositive phrase?

> The speaker, a boy of fifteen, finds the wrecked motorcycle south of the bridge and in back of the willows.

A. a boy of fifteen   C. south of the bridge

B. finds the wrecked motorcycle   D. in back of the willows

Essay

15. Because narrative poems, like short stories, tell a story, they include the elements of plot, setting, characters, and mood (or atmosphere). Choose one of the poems you have read in this collection. In an essay, identify and discuss the elements of plot, setting, characters, and mood in the poem you have chosen. Be sure to include specific references to the text.

16. One key element in storytelling is suspense—the reader's feeling of curiosity, uncertainty, or even anxiety about the outcome of events. Choose two of the poems in this collection, and write an essay in which you compare and contrast the ways in which the poets create suspense in the tales they tell. Be sure to comment on how the element of suspense relates to the mood, or atmosphere, at the end of each poem.

17. **Thinking About the Big Question: How does communication change us?** Sometimes people retell their story as a way to get control of a situation that has made them feel helpless. In an essay, tell what the characters in "Twister Hits Houston" say to regain control.

Poetry Collection: Ernest Lawrence Thayer, William Stafford, and Sandra Cisneros
Selection Test B

Critical Reading *Identify the letter of the choice that best completes the statement or answers the question.*

_____ 1. Which of the following is most likely the message of "Casey at the Bat"?
  A. Baseball players should not let pitches go by.
  B. Baseball fans should trust the umpire.
  C. People should not expect too much from their heroes.
  D. A ballgame is not worth getting excited about.

_____ 2. What distinguishes narrative poetry from other types of poetry is that narrative poetry
  A. expresses a theme or message.
  B. uses rhyme.
  C. tells a story.
  D. seeks to persuade readers.

_____ 3. Which of the following sums up the main conflict in "Casey at the Bat"?
  A. a disagreement between Casey and the umpire
  B. a game between Mudville and the opposing team
  C. a struggle between the umpire and the crowd
  D. a duel between Casey and the pitcher

_____ 4. What does the umpire do in "Casey at the Bat"?
  A. He calls the first two strikes on Casey.
  B. He calls all three strikes on Casey.
  C. He intimidates Casey into striking out.
  D. He favors the Mudville team's opponents.

_____ 5. Which of the following situations is most similar to the plot of "Casey at the Bat"?
  A. The tennis coach offers to play a match with you on Saturday and picks you up early.
  B. The world chess champion visits town and defeats twenty opponents at the same time.
  C. In the last seconds, the star quarterback's pass is intercepted and your school loses.
  D. Your soccer team wins by one goal in the last few moments of the game.

_____ 6. Which of the following best defines a paraphrase?
  A. a restatement in your own words of what someone else has written or said
  B. a very brief summary of any kind of lengthy text
  C. a direct quotation of a speaker's exact words
  D. a series of notes indicating questions for further research

_____ 7. In "Fifteen," what does the speaker find at the very beginning of the poem?
  A. a wrecked but running motorcycle
  B. a shortcut through the trees to the bridge
  C. an exhausted rider who has lost his way
  D. a man unconscious in the grass

____ 8. What does the boy in "Fifteen" consider doing?
  A. exploring the end of Seventeenth Street
  B. avoiding involvement in the mystery
  C. riding off on the motorcycle
  D. going for help

____ 9. Which of the following is the best description of the events in the poem "Fifteen"?
  A. a growing awareness of the physical dangers faced by adults
  B. a moment between childhood dreams and adult decisions
  C. nostalgia for a lost neighborhood in the 1950s
  D. the speaker's desire to escape his town

____ 10. Why is paraphrasing especially useful when you are reading poetry?
  A. Paraphrasing a poem helps you to analyze the rhyme scheme.
  B. Paraphrasing clarifies the important changes in the plot of a narrative poem.
  C. Paraphrasing helps you to identify the poem's mood, or atmosphere.
  D. Paraphrasing helps you interpret a poem's figurative language.

____ 11. In "Fifteen," which of the following best explains why the speaker repeats the phrase "I was fifteen" at the end of each stanza?
  A. The speaker wants to emphasize the maturity of his outlook at that age.
  B. He wants to stress that he was old enough to drive a motorcycle.
  C. He wants to underline the tension between his dreams and the reality of the situation.
  D. He wants to show that adolescence is always difficult and frustrating.

____ 12. In "Twister Hits Houston," where was the speaker when the cyclone hit?
  A. in the kitchen   C. in front of the television set
  B. on the front porch   D. not in the house

____ 13. Read the following lines from "Twister Hits Houston":
  [Papa] said the twister ripped
  the big black oak to splinter,
  tossed a green sedan into his garden,
  and banged the back door
  like a mad cat wanting in.

  If you use these details to picture the action, which of the following would best describe the twister?
  A. violent power
  B. unexpected occurrence
  C. shift in direction
  D. loud noise

____ 14. Which of the following best describes the mood at the end of "Twister Hits Houston"?
  A. intense relief   C. dry irony
  B. great happiness   D. wretched despair

_____ 15. In "Twister Hits Houston," Cisneros repeats several details in the poem in order to
A. emphasize the power of the cyclone.
B. stress that Mama and Papa told different versions of the story.
C. underline that the speaker did not witness the events.
D. suggest that the story of the cyclone was repeated many times.

Vocabulary and Grammar

_____ 16. Which of the following is the best synonym for *pallor*?
A. paleness   C. halo
B. shine   D. flush

_____ 17. Which of the following words is an antonym (a word that means the opposite) of *demure*?
A. modest   C. bold
B. generous   D. fearful

_____ 18. Which of the following best defines an appositive phrase?
A. a phrase that is connected by a pair of correlative conjunctions
B. a phrase placed near a noun or pronoun that it identifies, renames, or explains
C. a special type of subordinate clause
D. a phrase that modifies a verb, an adjective, or another adverb

_____ 19. Which of the following is the appositive phrase in the sentence "The author of the poem, a journalist named Ernest Lawrence Thayer, worked for many years as a sports reporter"?
A. The author of the poem
B. a journalist named Ernest Lawrence Thayer
C. for many years
D. as a sports reporter

Essay

20. The poems in this collection all exemplify narrative verse, or poetry that tells a story. Choose two of the poems, and write an essay comparing and contrasting the tales they tell. Are the stories meant purely for entertainment, in your view, or do they hint at a deeper message or lesson? Support your ideas with specific reference to the text of the selections.

21. No one reading "Casey at the Bat" would mistake it for a short story, yet the poem tells an exciting story. Describe in an essay the ways in which the poem is like a short story and the ways in which it is different. Discuss at least three similarities and three differences.

22. **Thinking About the Big Question: How does communication change us?** In "Twister Hits Houston," the characters describe a natural disaster over and over again. In a brief essay, tell why people might feel compelled to repeat disaster stories to anyone who will listen.

© Pearson Education, Inc. All rights reserved.

Vocabulary Warm-up Word Lists

Study these words from the poetry of Edgar Allan Poe, Edwin Muir, and Richard Wilbur. Then, apply your knowledge to the activities that follow.

Word List A

dank [DANGK] *adj.* unpleasantly chilly and damp or wet
   We were uncomfortable in the dank basement until we turned up the heat.

dazed [DAYZD] *adj.* unable to think clearly; confused
   I was dazed for a minute after bumping my head.

impenetrable [im PEN i truh buhl] *adj.* impossible to understand or hard to get through
   She could not make sense of the impenetrable essay.

iridescent [eer i DES uhnt] *adj.* showing many colors, which seem to change constantly
   The iridescent gem in her ring caught our attention.

pondered [PAHN derd] *v.* thought deeply and seriously about a subject
   He pondered the problem for a long time before stating his opinion.

undaunted [un DAWN tid] *adj.* not afraid or discouraged to continue something, even though it is dangerous or difficult
   Determined to reach the South Pole, the explorers were undaunted by the extreme cold.

Word List B

commotion [kuh MOH shuhn] *n.* noisy activity
   We rushed outside to see what the commotion was about.

hauled [HAWLD] *v.* pulled, often something heavy
   My father hauled the lawn mower out of the shed.

ominous [AHM uh nuhs] *adj.* creating the feeling that something bad will happen; threatening
   We looked for our umbrellas when the ominous clouds appeared.

pierce [PEERS] *v.* affect one's emotions deeply
   The stirring speech seemed to pierce me to my very soul.

servitude [SER vi tood] *n.* condition of having to serve someone else
   Wild dogs run free, but sled dogs are kept in servitude.

ungainly [un GAYN lee] *adj.* awkward; unattractive; clumsy
   Wearing high-heeled shoes always made Melissa feel ungainly.

© Pearson Education, Inc. All rights reserved.

Name _____ Date _____

Exercise A *Fill in each blank in the following paragraph with an appropriate word from Word List A. Use each word only once.*

My hobby is spelunking, which means I enjoy exploring caves. People expect caves to be [1] _____ and unpleasant, but most of them are really quite comfortable. The darkness in a cave can be [2] _____, so you should always bring along flashlights. Bring a map, too. Make sure you know how to read it, because it is easy to get lost. My best friend and I have been lost in caves on several occasions. We were a little [3] _____ the first time, but we soon got over our confusion. We [4] _____ our situation for a while and then came up with a plan. My friend remembered a beautiful, [5] _____ rock that glittered with color when we shone a flashlight at it. We used our flashlights to locate the rock and then found our way back to the cave entrance. [6] _____ by our frightening experience, we agreed to go spelunking again the very next weekend.

Exercise B *Decide whether each of the following statements is true or false. Explain your answers.*

1. It might be hard to sleep if there is a <u>commotion</u> outside.
   T / F _____

2. If you <u>hauled</u> an air conditioner up a flight of stairs, your arms might be sore.
   T / F _____

3. You would probably be pleased to hear an <u>ominous</u> piece of news.
   T / F _____

4. A silly limerick is likely to <u>pierce</u> your heart.
   T / F _____

5. Most prisoners would be grateful to have their period of <u>servitude</u> extended.
   T / F _____

6. Swans tend to be <u>ungainly</u> in water.
   T / F _____

Poetry Collection: Edgar Allan Poe, Edwin Muir, Richard Wilbur

Reading Warm-up A

Read the following passage. Pay special attention to the underlined words. Then, read it again, and complete the activities. Use a separate sheet of paper for your written answers.

My father and I did not agree on the subject of pets. I wanted a pet more than anything else in the world; he thought that keeping an animal in the house was a bad idea. Undaunted by his resistance, I did not give up. I finally persuaded him to get me a parakeet.

I have always loved reading and writing, so I named my new feathered friend Paragraph. Paragraph was a beautiful blue and yellow parakeet with feathers that appeared iridescent in the sunlight. My father and I agreed that I would take full responsibility for the care and feeding of our new family member. As my father put it, "Your pet, your problem."

Then, one day, Paragraph refused to come out of his cage. His feathers looked flat and dull, and he seemed to be dazed and confused. When I told my father that the bird was sick, he sat silently. Despite the impenetrable expression on his face, I knew exactly what he was thinking: your pet, your problem. I gazed out the window and pondered my next move. It was a dank and miserable afternoon, but I had to get Paragraph to the vet's office. It would be a long, hard ride by bike, but I had no choice.

Then, I saw my father reach into Paragraph's cage and gently remove the sick parakeet. He studied the bird for a long moment, carefully put him back inside, and covered the cage. He then took me in his arms and hugged me close.

"I will go warm up the car," he said.

1. Circle the word that tells who was underlined. Write a sentence explaining why the person might be *undaunted*.

2. Circle the word that tells what appeared iridescent. Write a sentence about something else that might be *iridescent*.

3. Circle the word that means almost the same as dazed. Why is the narrator concerned that Paragraph seems *dazed*?

4. Underline the words that tell what was impenetrable. Explain the meaning of *impenetrable* in the sentence.

5. Underline the words that tell what the narrator pondered. Why does the fact that the narrator *pondered* show you that the situation is difficult?

6. Circle the word that helps you to understand the meaning of dank. How would you dress on a *dank* day?

© Pearson Education, Inc. All rights reserved.

Poetry Collection: Edgar Allan Poe, Edwin Muir, Richard Wilbur
Reading Warm-up B

Read the following passage. Pay special attention to the underlined words. Then, read it again, and complete the activities. Use a separate sheet of paper for your written answers.

For thousands of years, people have had a special relationship with horses. The ancient Greeks and Romans raced horses and rode them into battle. During the Middle Ages, large, powerful horses were bred to carry knights in heavy suits of armor. Although horses were expected to work hard, they were generally well cared for in exchange for their years of loyal <u>servitude</u>.

Horses are well suited for working hard and running fast. They have long, muscular legs and keen sight and hearing. Newborn foals seem <u>ungainly</u> at first, but they are able to run about within hours of their birth. Horses have excellent memories and are easily trained; however, they startle easily and may try to flee at the first sign of a <u>commotion</u>.

Horses were unknown in the Americas until Spanish invaders brought them to Mexico in the early 1500s. Native Americans on the western plains soon began using them to hunt buffalo. During the American Revolution and the Civil War, horses <u>hauled</u> cannon and supply wagons. Horses also pulled streetcars through city streets and covered wagons across the prairies. Prior to the telegraph, stagecoaches and the Pony Express were the fastest means of coast-to-coast communication.

For those who raised and traded horses, the railroad ("iron horse") and automobile ("horseless carriage") were <u>ominous</u> developments that threatened to end the important role of horses in people's lives. Horse-drawn wagons that once delivered goods and services from place to place gradually gave way to motorized vehicles. The number of horses on farms declined sharply as tractors and other machinery replaced them.

Farmers around the world, though, still use horses to pull plows. Modern cowhands depend on horses to help them round up cattle. Many people today enjoy riding horses for pleasure. Stories about horses, such as the classic *Black Beauty*, can still <u>pierce</u> the hearts of people who have never even seen a real horse!

1. Underline the phrase that is a clue to the meaning of <u>servitude</u>. Tell about something or someone else who might have been in *servitude*.

2. Circle the words that tell what is <u>ungainly</u>. Give a synonym, or word with a similar meaning, for *ungainly*.

3. Underline the words that tell what horses may do at the first sign of a <u>commotion</u>. Describe what such a *commotion* could be.

4. Underline the word that has a meaning similar to <u>hauled</u>. Write a sentence about something else that would be *hauled*.

5. Circle the word that gives a clue to the meaning of <u>ominous</u>. Explain why the railroad and automobile were *ominous* developments.

6. Underline the words that tell what can <u>pierce</u> people's hearts. Why might such things *pierce* the heart?

Poetry Collection: Edgar Allan Poe, Edwin Muir, Richard Wilbur

Writing About the Big Question

How does communication change us?

Big Question Vocabulary

aware	communication	comprehension	discuss	empathy
exchange	illuminate	informed	interpretation	meaning
react	relationship	resolution	respond	understanding

A. *Use one or more words from the list above to complete each sentence.*

1. Reading an encyclopedia article usually improves your _____ of a topic.

2. During the debate, the candidates were each given a maximum of three minutes to _____ to the panel's questions.

3. The TV documentary made us keenly _____ of the worldwide problems of hunger and malnutrition.

4. I thought I understood that poem well, but Patrick presented a completely different _____.

5. When you _____ a problem or conflict with others, your _____ of ideas may often lead to a(n) _____.

B. *Follow the directions in responding to each of the items below.*

1. List two different times when another person's facial expression or body language has played an important part in your figuring out his or her real **meaning.**

   _____

   _____

2. Write two sentences to explain one of these experiences, and describe how it made you feel. Use at least two of the Big Question vocabulary words.

   _____

   _____

C. *Complete the sentence below. Then, write a short paragraph in which you connect the sentence to the Big Question.*

Having **empathy** for someone who is in a difficult situation might make a person realize that _____

_____

_____

_____

Poetry Collection: Edgar Allan Poe, Edwin Muir, and Richard Wilbur
Literary Analysis: Narrative Poetry

Narrative poetry is verse that tells a story and includes the same literary elements as narrative prose:

- a plot, or sequence of events
- specific settings
- characters who participate in the action

Also like narrative prose, such as a short story, a narrative poem conveys a **mood,** or **atmosphere**—an overall feeling created by the setting, plot, words, and images. For example, a narrative poem's mood can be gloomy, joyous, or mysterious. Poetry's emphasis on precise words and images makes mood a powerful element in a narrative poem.

DIRECTIONS: *As you read "The Raven," "The Horses," and "The Writer," answer the following questions.*

"The Raven"

1. Who is the speaker in the poem? What kind of person is this speaker?

   _____

2. Briefly describe the poem's setting.

   _____

3. What story does the poem tell?

   _____

"The Horses"

4. What events does the speaker in the poem recall?

   _____

   _____

5. Briefly describe the poem's setting.

   _____

6. On what emotional note does the poem end?

   _____

"The Writer"

7. What two stories are told by the poem's speaker?

   _____

   _____

8. How would you describe the atmosphere, or overall mood, of the poem?

   _____

Poetry Collection: Edgar Allan Poe, Edwin Muir, and Richard Wilbur

Reading: Paraphrasing

Paraphrasing is restating in your own words what someone else has written or said. A paraphrase retains the essential meaning and ideas of the original but is simpler to read.

Paraphrasing is especially helpful when reading poetry because poems often contain **figurative language,** words and phrases that are used imaginatively rather than literally. To paraphrase lines in a narrative poem, **picture the action:**

- Based on details in the poem, form a mental image of the setting, the characters, and the characters' actions.
- To be sure that your mental picture is accurate, pay close attention to the way that the poet describes elements of the scene.
- Then, use your own words to describe your mental image of the scene and the action taking place in it.

DIRECTIONS: *On the lines provided, paraphrase the following passages from the narrative poems in this collection. Remember that a paraphrase is a restatement in your own words.*

1. Eagerly I wished the morrow—vainly I had tried to borrow
   From my books surcease of sorrow—sorrow for the lost Lenore—
   For the rare and radiant maiden whom the angels name Lenore—
      Nameless here for evermore. ("The Raven")

   _____

   _____

   _____

2. Yet they waited,
   Stubborn and shy, as if they had been sent
   By an old command to find our whereabouts
   And that long-lost archaic companionship. ("The Horses")

   _____

   _____

   _____

3. I remember the dazed starling
   Which was trapped in that very room, two years ago;
   How we stole in, lifted a sash

   And retreated, not to affright it; ("The Writer")

   _____

   _____

   _____

© Pearson Education, Inc. All rights reserved.

Name _____   Date _____

Poetry Collection: Edgar Allan Poe, Edwin Muir, and Richard Wilbur
Vocabulary Builder

Word List

archaic   beguiling   impenetrable   iridescent   pondered   respite

A. DIRECTIONS: *Match each word in Column A with the correct definition in Column B.*

Column A	Column B
___ 1. beguiling	A. relief
___ 2. respite	B. charming
___ 3. archaic	C. old-fashioned

B. DIRECTIONS: *Revise each sentence so that the underlined vocabulary word is used logically. Be sure not to change the vocabulary word.*

1. The professor's lecture was so *impenetrable* that we all grasped his main ideas without difficulty.

_____

2. The *iridescent* fabric of the tablecloth was boring and unattractive.

_____

3. He *pondered* his dilemma, laughing and joking with friends at the party.

_____

C. WORD STUDY: Use the context of the sentences and what you know about the Latin prefix *im-* to answer to explain your answer to each question.

1. Can an *immutable* situation be changed? Why or why not?

_____

_____

2. If you speak in an *impersonal* tone, are people likely to feel that you care about them?

_____

_____

3. If someone acts with *impropriety*, is that person heaving politely?

_____

_____

© Pearson Education, Inc. All rights reserved.

Name _____ Date _____

Enrichment: Animals in Mythology and Folklore

Animals play a central role in all three poems in this collection. In the mythology and folklore of many cultures around the world, animals such as ravens and horses have been important characters. For example, in ancient Greek culture, the centaurs were half-human and half-equine, the horse Pegasus was able to fly through the air, and animals were the main characters in Aesop's *Fables*. In Native American mythology, Raven was associated with light and the creation of the world, while Coyote was renowned as a trickster figure.

DIRECTIONS: *Research how an animal of your choice has figured in the mythology and folklore of a particular culture. Then, compile a brief report of your findings. As you carry out your research, focus on such elements as the animal's appearance, the human characteristics associated with it, and the animal's symbolic meanings. Also, research the role the animal plays in important stories about nature, the origins of the world, and human behavior. Be prepared to present your report to the class as a whole.*

_____

_____

_____

_____

_____

_____

_____

_____

_____

_____

_____

_____

_____

_____

_____

_____

_____

_____

_____

_____

Poetry Collection: Edgar Allan Poe, Edwin Muir, and Richard Wilbur
Integrated Language Skills: Grammar

Appositive Phrases

An **appositive** is a noun or pronoun placed near another noun or pronoun to identify, rename, or explain it. Notice in the following example that the appositive is set off by commas, which indicates that it is not essential to the meaning of the sentence and can be removed.

> **Example:** The author of "The Raven," *Edgar Allan Poe*, was also a noted short-story writer.

In the following example, *Edgar Allan Poe* is not set off by commas because it is needed to complete the meaning of the sentence.

> **Example:** The American writer *Edgar Allan Poe* is often credited for the invention of the modern short story.

When an appositive has its own modifiers, it forms an **appositive phrase.** Appositive phrases are placed next to a noun or pronoun to add information and details.

> **Example:** We enjoyed reading Poe's "The Cask of Amontillado," *a thrilling tale of suspense.*

A. DIRECTIONS: *Underline the appositive phrase in each of the following sentences. Then, write the word or words that each appositive phrase renames.*

1. Hyperbole, a figure of speech involving deliberate exaggeration, appears in a wide variety of literary works.

   _____

2. For instance, Homer, the oral poet credited with composing the *Iliad* and the *Odyssey*, often uses hyperbole to describe the deeds of epic heroes.

   _____

3. Jonathan Swift employs the same device for fantastic effects in *Gulliver's Travels*, his pointed satire on human life and behavior.

   _____

B. Writing Application: *Write a brief paragraph in which you describe an appliance that you often use at home. Use at least three appositive phrases in your writing, and underline each appositive phrase you use.*

_____

_____

_____

_____

_____

_____

_____

© Pearson Education, Inc. All rights reserved.

Name _____ Date _____

Poetry Collection: Ernest Lawrence Thayer, William Stafford, Sandra Cisneros, Edgar Allan Poe, Edwin Muir, and Richard Wilbur
Support for Writing a Movie Scene

For your movie scene, use the following lines to make notes.

Details from "The Raven"

1. **Characters:** _____

_____

2. **Setting:** _____

_____

3. **Actions:** _____

_____

4. **Mood:** _____

Mood in Movie's Opening Scene: _____

_____

_____

_____

_____

Details Contributing to Mood: _____

_____

_____

_____

_____

Camera Angles, Lighting, and so on: _____

_____

_____

_____

_____

© Pearson Education, Inc. All rights reserved.

Poetry Collection: Ernest Lawrence Thayer, William Stafford, Sandra Cisneros, Edgar Allan Poe, Edwin Muir, and Richard Wilbur

Support for Extend Your Learning

Listening and Speaking

Use the following lines to make notes for your dialogue between the speaker and the motorcyclist in "Fifteen" or between the father and the daughter in "The Writer."

Details in Poem About Character, Setting, and Action:

_____

_____

_____

_____

_____

Main Concerns of Participants in Dialogue:

Main Concerns of Character A:

_____

_____

_____

_____

Main Concerns of Character B:

_____

_____

_____

_____

What we learn about their relationship:

_____

_____

_____

© Pearson Education, Inc. All rights reserved.

Poetry Collection: Edgar Allan Poe, Edwin Muir, Richard Wilbur
Open-Book Test

Short Answer *Write your responses to the questions in this section on the lines provided.*

1. In the second stanza of Edgar Allan Poe's "The Raven," the speaker says,

   And each separate dying ember wrought its ghost upon the floor.

   Restate this line in your own words.

   _____

2. What do you learn about the speaker's situation in the first and second stanzas of "The Raven"? Cite a detail from the poem to support your answer.

   _____

   _____

   _____

3. In the fourth stanza of "The Raven," the speaker opens the door only to find "Darkness there, and nothing more." What do you think this darkness represents?

   _____

   _____

4. In the seventh stanza of "The Raven," the bird enters the speaker's chamber. Use the chart to summarize how the speaker feels about the raven in each of the cited stanzas. Then answer the question that follows.

Stanza 10	Stanza 15	Stanza 17

   What is the speaker's state of mind at the poem's end?

   _____

5. In lines 17–18 of Edwin Muir's poem "The Horses," what does the speaker mean when he says "If on the stroke of noon a voice should speak, / We would not listen, . . ."?

   _____

   _____

   _____

6. What are the tractors compared to in the second stanza of "The Horses"? In your own words, what mental image does this comparison provide?

_____

_____

7. In "The Horses," which seem more archaic—the tractors or the horses? Base your explanation on the meaning of *archaic*.

_____

_____

_____

8. The main characters in Richard Wilbur's poem "The Writer" are the speaker's daughter and a trapped starling. How are these characters alike?

_____

_____

_____

9. In lines 16–30 of "The Writer," the speaker tells a story-within-a-story. What happens in the beginning, middle, and end of this story?

_____

_____

_____

10. What is the "It" in line 31 of "The Writer"? What do you think the speaker wishes for his daughter, "but harder" than before?

_____

_____

_____

Essay

Write an extended response to the question of your choice or to the question or questions your teacher assigns you.

11. The setting of a narrative poem can contribute to the work in many ways. It may play a key role in the story's plot. It might help establish a certain mood. Or it may relate to the poem's overall theme. Choose one of the poems by Poe, Muir, or Wilbur in this collection and, in an essay, discuss the role of the setting in the poem. Support your main ideas with specific references to the text.

12. Each of the poems by Poe, Muir, and Wilbur in this collection features an animal. In an essay, identify the animals in two of the poems and compare and contrast their roles. What does each animal do? What effect does it have on the speaker? What abstract idea might it symbolize or stand for? Support your claims with references to the text.

13. It could be said that Edwin Muir's poem "The Horses" contains two separate narratives: the speaker's grim account of the "seven days war" and his description of the more recent appearance of the horses. In an essay, compare and contrast these two stories. How is each story about an end and a beginning? What does each story have to say about human society? About technology? About the future?

14. **Thinking About the Big Question: How does communication change us?** In both "The Raven" and "The Horses," the speakers, in a state of desolation, expect a certain kind of communication—one from a bird and the other from a radio. In an essay, explain what kind of communication each speaker expects, whether it is forthcoming, and how this changes the speaker for the better or the worse.

Oral Response

15. Go back to question 3, 5, or 10 or to the question your teacher assigns to you. Take a few minutes to expand your answer and prepare an oral response. Find additional details in the relevant poem or poems that support your points. If necessary, make notes to guide your oral response.

Poetry Collection: Edgar Allan Poe, Edwin Muir, and Richard Wilbur

Selection Test A

Critical Reading *Identify the letter of the choice that best answers the question.*

____ 1. The primary subject of "The Raven" is which of the following?
A. a mysterious journey   C. a grieving man
B. a dead woman   D. a tormented dream

____ 2. Which of the following terms identifies the type of poem "The Raven" is?
A. narrative   C. lyric
B. epic   D. dramatic

____ 3. Which of the following is the term for a restatement in your own words of what someone else has written or said?
A. an elaboration   C. a paraphrase
B. a quotation   D. an allegory

____ 4. Which of the following best describes the atmosphere, or mood, at the end of "The Raven"?
A. angry   C. resigned
B. despairing   D. guilty

____ 5. In "The Raven," why does Poe repeat the line "Quoth the raven, 'Nevermore'"?
A. It is a logical reply to the words the speaker addresses to the raven.
B. It shows that the raven refuses to have anything to do with the speaker.
C. The word "Nevermore" expresses how unhappy the bird is.
D. It shows how smart the raven is because it can talk.

____ 6. In "The Horses," why does the speaker say that if the radios suddenly went on again, "We would not listen"?
A. The people have no time to listen to the radio.
B. The radios were all destroyed during the seven-day war.
C. The people do not want to return to the old way of life, which nearly destroyed the world.
D. The leaders of the community have warned people not to trust anyone but the horses.

____ 7. In the first section of "The Horses," on which of the following topics does the story focus?

A. the causes of the seven-day war

B. the destruction caused by the seven-day war

C. the weapons used in the seven-day war

D. the mysterious arrival of the horses

____ 8. Read the following lines from "The Horses":

> The tractors lie about our fields; at evening
> They look like dank sea-monsters, couched and waiting.
> We leave them where they are and let them rust.

The poet probably includes these details in order to do which of the following?

A. stress the defects of technology

B. show that the surviving humans have made wise choices

C. enable readers to picture the scene and the action

D. emphasize the survivors' need for food

____ 9. Which of the following best describes the atmosphere, or mood, in the final line of "The Horses"?

> Our life is changed; their coming our beginning.

A. melancholy

B. joyful

C. optimistic

D. critical

____ 10. In "The Writer," what is the speaker's daughter doing as the poem opens?

A. watching television

B. feeding her pet cat

C. sleeping in her bedroom

D. trying to write a story

____ 11. Read the following lines from "The Writer":

> Young as she is, the stuff
> Of her life is a great cargo, and some of it heavy:
> I wish her a lucky passage.

These lines compare the life of the speaker's daughter to which of the following?

A. a piece of clothing   C. a story

B. a sea journey   D. a bird

___ 12. In "The Writer," the story of the starling's successful efforts to free itself might best be interpreted as meaning which of the following?

  A. Practically everyone has the potential to become a successful writer.

  B. Everyone's life includes defeats as well as successes.

  C. The important thing in life is to keep on trying, even if you do not succeed all the time.

  D. People need to be cautious and avoid dangerous risks.

Vocabulary and Grammar

___ 13. Which of the following is the best synonym for *respite*?

  A. jealousy   C. relief

  B. regret   D. shame

___ 14. If a word or an expression is *archaic*, which of the following would best describe it?

  A. literal   C. trendy

  B. figurative   D. old-fashioned

___ 15. In the following sentence, which words are the appositive phrase?

  Edwin Muir, the poet and novelist, spent his early years on a farm in the Orkney Islands, north of the Scottish mainland.

  A. the poet and novelist   C. in the Orkney Islands

  B. on a farm   D. north of the Scottish mainland

Essay

16. Specific details of setting often contribute greatly to the plot, mood, theme, and total effect of a narrative poem. Choose one of the poems in this collection, and write an essay in which you discuss the role of setting in the poem. Consider especially how setting relates to two of the following elements: plot, mood, theme, or the poem's total effect. Support your main ideas with specific references to the text of the poem you have chosen.

17. **Thinking About the Big Question: How does communication change us?** In the poems "The Raven" and "The Horses," the speakers expect a certain kind of communication. In "The Raven," the bird is expected to speak. In "The Horses," communication is expected from the radio. In an essay, choose a poem and explain what the speaker in the poem expects to hear. Then tell how the expectation of communication changes the speaker for better or the worse.

Poetry Collection: Edgar Allan Poe, Edwin Muir, and Richard Wilbur
Selection Test B

Critical Reading *Identify the letter of the choice that best completes the statement or answers the question.*

____ 1. Which of the following terms designates poems that tell a story and include characters, settings, and a specific atmosphere, or overall mood?
   A. lyric
   B. narrative
   C. dramatic
   D. symbolic

____ 2. In the first stanza of "The Raven," what inference might you make about the speaker based on the "many a quaint and curious volume of forgotten lore" that he is reading?
   A. He has a restless imagination.
   B. He is extremely practical.
   C. He keeps up with the latest news.
   D. He has a quirky sense of humor.

____ 3. In "The Raven," what does the bust of the goddess Pallas above the speaker's door represent?
   A. life
   B. beauty
   C. wisdom
   D. love

____ 4. In "The Raven," the darkness that the narrator looks into after he opens the chamber door represents which of the following?
   A. the blackness of the night
   B. the darkness of the grave
   C. the evil of the narrator's soul
   D. the blackness of the raven

____ 5. Read the following lines from "The Raven":
   Deep into that darkness peering, long I stood there wondering, fearing,
   Doubting, dreaming dreams no mortal ever dared to dream before;

   From these lines, you can infer that the speaker is which of the following?
   A. distracted
   B. courageous
   C. weak
   D. terrified

____ 6. Because poetry often contains figurative language, it is often helpful to do which of the following when you are reading a poem?
   A. express the essential ideas and meaning of the text in a paraphrase
   B. write your own set of footnotes for a passage
   C. research the author's life and times
   D. convert a narrative passage into dramatic form

_____ 7. What is the most frightening effect of war on the world as it is described in "The Horses"?
   A. the arrival of wild animals   C. death, destruction, and silence
   B. being without radio announcements   D. being without computers

_____ 8. A flashback in a narrative describes events that occurred before the time of the main story. In "The Horses," which of the following is the subject of a flashback?
   A. the arrival of the horses
   B. the seven-day war
   C. the rusting of the tractors
   D. the hope of the speaker

_____ 9. What does the speaker in "The Horses" mean when he says that if they "speak again" on the radio, "we will not listen"?
   A. He is giving up radio, television, and other aspects of technology forever.
   B. He no longer wants to listen to people who represent the old, destroyed world.
   C. He does not want to know what is going to happen next.
   D. He does not believe that the seven-day war has really ended.

_____ 10. Read these lines from "The Horses":
   We heard a distant tapping on the road,
   A deepening drumming; it stopped, went on again
   And at the corner changed to hollow thunder.

   Edwin Muir probably included these details in order to
   A. stress the ferocity of the horses.
   B. hint at the guilt of the humans in the poem.
   C. enable the reader to picture the action.
   D. create imaginative sound effects.

_____ 11. At the end of "The Horses," what is the speaker's tone, or attitude toward his subject?
   A. angry   C. hopeful
   B. despairing   D. restrained

_____ 12. In the first four stanzas of "The Writer," how does the speaker describe the process of writing?
   A. Writing is an amusing diversion for people in their spare time.
   B. Writing offers a welcome distraction from anxieties and care.
   C. Writing requires sustained thought and concentration.
   D. Writing is like a ship that travels smoothly over the ocean.

_____ 13. In "The Writer," whom does the speaker directly address at the end of the poem when he says, "I wish / What I wished you before, but harder"?
   A. his wife   C. the reader
   B. his daughter   D. his son

_____ 14. In "The Writer," the speaker most likely recalls the story of the trapped starling because
   A. he is moved by the plight of injured wild animals.
   B. his daughter wrote a poem about the event.
   C. the incident suggests a parallel in his mind to his daughter's struggle to write.
   D. the efforts of the starling were doomed to failure.

© Pearson Education, Inc. All rights reserved.

____ 15. What can you infer from the following lines from "The Writer" about the speaker's underlying message?

> It is always a matter, my darling,
> Of life or death, as I had forgotten.

A. Writing can become a life-or-death struggle.
B. In writing, as elsewhere in life, it is vital to keep on trying.
C. The more you struggle at writing, the less you can accomplish.
D. Some people are not cut out to be writers.

Vocabulary and Grammar

____ 16. Which of the following is the best synonym for *beguiling* in this line from "The Raven"?

> But the raven still beguiling all my sad soul into smiling,

A. negotiating
B. releasing
C. charming
D. reflecting

____ 17. Which of the following is the best antonym for *archaic*?

A. antique
B. innovative
C. inflexible
D. temporary

____ 18. An appositive must always be which of the following parts of speech?

A. a conjunction
B. a verb
C. a noun or pronoun
D. an adjective or adverb

____ 19. In the following sentence, which words are the appositive phrase?

> Sandra Cisneros, who was born in Chicago and lived for some of her childhood in Mexico City, began to write her first novel, *The House on Mango Street,* while still a college student.

A. who was born in Chicago
B. and lived for some of her childhood
C. *The House on Mango Street*
D. while still a college student

Essay

20. Why do you think Edgar Allan Poe chose to tell the tale of "The Raven" in the form of a narrative poem rather than as a short story? Both literary forms have the same elements—plot, characters, setting, and atmosphere (or mood). In an essay, discuss what effect the form of a narrative poem has upon Poe's story.

21. Edwin Muir's poem "The Horses" might be said to contain two stories: the speaker's grim account of the seven-day war and his description of the more recent, mysterious appearance of the horses. In an essay, discuss how these stories compare and contrast with each other. Be sure to comment on the deeper message or theme they may suggest about human life and behavior.

22. **Thinking About the Big Question: How does communication change us?** In both "The Raven" and "The Horses," the speakers, in a state of desolation, expect a certain kind of communication—one from a bird, and the other from a radio. In an essay, explain what kind of communication each speaker expects; whether it is forthcoming; and how this changes the speaker for the better or the worse.

Vocabulary Warm-up Word Lists

Study these words from the poetry of Emily Dickinson, Robert Frost, and T. S. Eliot. Then, apply your knowledge to the activities that follow.

Word List A

defy [dee FY] *v.* refuse to obey someone or something
   Thirteen colonies dared to <u>defy</u> England and declare independence.

despair [di SPAIR] *n.* someone or something that makes others lose hope or feel frustrated
   Our dog barks constantly and is the <u>despair</u> of the neighborhood.

equally [EE kwuhl ee] *adv.* to the same degree; in the same amount
   She is <u>equally</u> interested in sports and music.

hence [HENS] *adv.* away from this place or time
   The knight left this castle and went <u>hence</u> to defend his honor.

outwardly [OWT werd lee] *adv.* in appearance or behavior; on the surface
   She looked <u>outwardly</u> happy even though she was actually upset.

stifled [STY feld] *v.* smothered; stopped from happening, growing, or being expressed
   To be polite, I <u>stifled</u> a yawn.

Word List B

fiend [FEEND] *n.* evil spirit or person
   In the movie, a <u>fiend</u> was on the loose and was shooting poison arrows.

heroism [HEER oh iz uhm] *n.* very great courage; very courageous actions
   Many brave soldiers will be honored with medals for their <u>heroism</u>.

respectable [ri SPEK tuh buhl] *adj.* proper in behavior or appearance
   He is a <u>respectable</u> business owner and would not cheat a customer.

rifled [RY fuhld] *v.* searched through a place to steal things from it
   She knows someone <u>rifled</u> her purse because her wallet is missing.

statures [STACH erz] *n.* peoples' physical height; also, their reputations or achievements
   The <u>statures</u> of several national leaders were hurt by the scandal.

undergrowth [UN der grohth] *n.* bushes and small trees that grow around bigger trees
   Clear the woods of <u>undergrowth</u> to avoid a fire in the dry season.

© Pearson Education, Inc. All rights reserved.

Name _____ Date _____

Poetry Collection: Emily Dickinson, Robert Frost, T. S. Eliot
Vocabulary Warm-up Exercises

Exercise A *Fill in each blank in the following paragraph with an appropriate word from Word List A. Use each word only once.*

In 1920, U.S. women won the right to vote. Finally, the rules that had

[1] _____ their ability to express political views were changed. Women

had fought hard and often had to [2] _____ the law to achieve this

victory. Marches and picketing made them the [3] _____ of officials who

were frustrated by their demands. At first, many people did not want women to be

treated [4] _____ and have the same rights as men. However,

over time, more and more people realized that even though women might appear

[5] _____ weaker than men, they had the inward intelligence to make

voting decisions. By gaining the right to vote, women sent a message to the future:

"From this time [6] _____, women will be treated as true citizens!"

Exercise B *Answer the questions with complete explanations.*

Example: Where would you be likely to find <u>undergrowth</u>?
You would find <u>undergrowth</u>, or bushes and other plants that grow around trees, in a forest.

1. Would you likely want a <u>fiend</u> as a friend? Explain.

   _____

2. When the police search a house, would they be said to have <u>rifled</u> through it? Explain.

   _____

3. If a team that is considered excellent is defeated by a supposedly weaker team, what happens to the <u>statures</u> of both? Explain.

   _____

4. Would most people be eager to perform an act of <u>heroism</u>? Explain.

   _____

5. What would be <u>respectable</u> clothing to wear to a formal event, such as a wedding? Explain.

   _____

Poetry Collection: Emily Dickinson, Robert Frost, T. S. Eliot
Reading Warm-up A

Read the following passage. Pay special attention to the underlined words. Then, read it again, and complete the activities. Use a separate sheet of paper for your written answers.

Louis Armstrong is remembered as an extraordinary jazz trumpeter with a wide, sparkling grin. However, his early years were far from bright and promising. It was a chance encounter with a music teacher that changed everything.

Armstrong was born on August 4, 1901, in New Orleans, Louisiana. He grew up in a poor neighborhood that he described as "The Battlefield." It was filled with tough characters who were the <u>despair</u> of those who lived there. Young Louis did not cause as much unhappiness and irritation to others as the Battlefield toughs. However, by the time he was age twelve, he was in trouble. Some New Year's Eve mischief resulted in his arrest.

The court saw Armstrong as a poor adolescent with little supervision. It believed he would continue to <u>defy</u> the law and break the rules. Armstrong was sent to live in a "waif's home" for African American boys.

<u>Outwardly</u>, he seemed like other kids. However, that outside appearance was hiding an amazing ability inside. Early on, he showed some of that skill by singing on the streets for change and trying to learn the cornet. At the home, the music director, Peter Davis, recognized that Armstrong had tremendous talent to develop.

Armstrong was instructed <u>equally</u> in vocal and instrumental music. Giving the same degree of attention to both musical skills helped develop both talents in him.

Looking back on his experience in the boys' home, Armstrong called it "the greatest thing that ever happened to me." There, the love of music and the skill to produce it that had been <u>stifled</u> inside of him were set free. "From this time <u>hence</u>," young Louis must have thought, "I will be known as a musician." By the time of his death in 1971, his achievements were legendary. Through his original compositions and his inspired playing, Armstrong helped invent the American music called jazz.

1. Circle who or what was the <u>despair</u> of the neighborhood. Underline the phrase that is a clue to the meaning of *despair*.

2. Circle the phrase that is a clue to the meaning of <u>defy</u>. Imagine if everyone tried to *defy* the rules, and tell what would happen.

3. Underline the sentence that helps explain the meaning of <u>outwardly</u>. Give a word or phrase that is a synonym, or word with a similar meaning, for *outwardly*.

4. Circle the words that are a clue to the meaning of <u>equally</u>. Describe two activities that you enjoy *equally*, and explain why.

5. Underline what was stifled in Louis Armstrong. Circle the phrase that is an opposite action to <u>stifled</u>. Use your own words to explain the meaning of *stifled*.

6. Circle the phrase that is a clue to the meaning of <u>hence</u>. To what part of Armstrong's life does *hence* refer?

Poetry Collection: Emily Dickinson, Robert Frost, T. S. Eliot
Reading Warm-up B

Read the following passage. Pay special attention to the underlined words. Then, read it again, and complete the activities. Use a separate sheet of paper for your written answers.

London is a very old city. However, it did not have a city-wide police force until 1829. The first police commissioners were Colonel Sir Charles Rowan and Sir Richard Mayne. Both men were committed to protecting <u>respectable</u> citizens who followed the rules and contributed to society. They helped organize London's Metropolitan Police Service—more commonly known as "Scotland Yard." The name comes from the original location of the police headquarters off an area called Great Scotland Yard.

It was Sir Rowan who figured out how best to prevent crime and catch criminals. He was a former British soldier who was admired for his <u>heroism</u> and courage. Sir Rowan had fought against the French Army. He recalled small patrols of soldiers scouting to gather information. Police officers on foot, he thought, could also be effective in watching out for criminals. He organized his police into patrols who walked a certain area, or "beat."

At first, London residents were uncertain about the new police. The commissioners understood that for the police to be effective, people had to admire them and hold them in high regard. Individual officers strived to be polite and helpful to law-abiding citizens. Over time, the <u>statures</u> of both the patrols and Scotland Yard increased.

However, as with any large city, there was plenty of lawlessness, even with a police force. Criminals hid in the shadows of buildings and behind bushes and other <u>undergrowth</u>, ready to attack unsuspecting victims.

Scotland Yard still works to solve crimes big and small. It might be searching for the <u>fiend</u> who committed a cold-blooded murder. Or, it might be finding pickpockets who have <u>rifled</u> and searched through tourists' pockets and purses and stolen their vacation money. However big or small the case, Scotland Yard is on the job.

1. Underline the phrase that describes <u>respectable</u> citizens. Tell how the meaning of *respectable* is connected to the idea of getting respect from others.

2. Circle a word that is a clue to the meaning of <u>heroism</u>. Why do most people admire someone who shows *heroism*?

3. Circle a phrase that is a clue to the meaning of <u>statures</u>. Underline what made a difference in raising the *statures* of the police and Scotland Yard.

4. Circle the word that is a clue to the meaning of <u>undergrowth</u>. Where might you find *undergrowth* in a city, and why?

5. Circle the phrase that is a clue to the meaning of <u>fiend</u>. What qualities make a person a *fiend*?

6. Underline the phrase that is a clue to the meaning of <u>rifled</u>. What might a desk that had been *rifled* look like? Explain your answer.

© Pearson Education, Inc. All rights reserved.

Poetry Collection: Emily Dickinson, Robert Frost, T. S. Eliot
Writing About the Big Question

How does communication change us?

Big Question Vocabulary

aware	communication	comprehension	discuss	empathy
exchange	illuminate	informed	interpretation	meaning
react	relationship	resolution	respond	understanding

A. *Use one or more words from the list above to complete each sentence.*

1. Although the Martinez family spent a year away in Spain, we stayed in regular _____ with them by e-mail.

2. In order to _____ ideas effectively, you need to listen carefully to the other group members.

3. The twin sisters' _____ is so close that one can usually tell what the other is thinking, even without speaking.

4. In an oral presentation, graphic aids like charts can help you _____ your _____ for the audience.

B. *Follow the directions in responding to each of the items below.*

1. List two different times when good **communication** with another person helped you solve a problem or overcome a challenge.

   _____

   _____

2. Write two sentences to explain one of these experiences, and describe how it made you feel. Use at least two of the Big Question vocabulary words.

   _____

   _____

C. *Complete the sentence below. Then, write a short paragraph in which you connect the sentence to the Big Question.*

   Other people can make someone **aware** of his or her potential by _____

   _____

   _____

   _____

   _____

   _____

Poetry Collection: Robert Frost, Emily Dickinson, and T. S. Eliot
Literary Analysis: Rhyme and Meter

Rhyme is the repetition of sounds at the ends of words. There are several types of rhyme:

- **Exact rhyme:** the repetition of words that end with the same vowel and consonant sounds, as in *end* and *mend*
- **Slant rhyme:** the repetition of words that end with similar sounds but do not rhyme perfectly, as in *end* and *stand*
- **End rhyme:** the rhyming sounds of words at the ends of lines
- **Internal rhyme:** the rhyming of words within a line

A **rhyme scheme** is a regular pattern of end rhymes in a poem or stanza. A rhyme scheme is described by assigning one letter of the alphabet to each rhyming sound. For example, in "Uphill" by Christina Rossetti, the rhyme scheme is *abab*:

Does the road wind uphill all the <u>way</u>?	*a*
Yes, to the very <u>end</u>.	*b*
Will the day's journey take the whole long <u>day</u>?	*a*
From morn to night, my <u>friend</u>.	*b*

Meter is the rhythmical pattern in a line of poetry. Meter results from the arrangement of stressed (´) and unstressed (ˇ) syllables. When you read aloud a line with a regular meter, you can hear the steady, rhythmic pulse of the stressed syllables:

"and maggie discovered a shell that sang"

"Let not Ambition mock their useful toil"

Not all poems include rhyme, a rhyme scheme, or a regular meter. However, poets often use one or more of these techniques to create musical effects and achieve a sense of unity.

DIRECTIONS: *Read this stanza from "Dream Variations," a poem by Langston Hughes. Identify the rhyme scheme and think about how it emphasizes the speaker's meaning. Also think about Hughes's use of meter in these lines. Then, answer the questions on the lines provided.*

> To fling my arms wide
> In some place of the sun,
> To whirl and to dance
> Till the white day is done.
> 5 Then rest at cool evening
> Beneath a tall tree
> While night comes on gently,
>   Dark like me—
> That is my dream!

1. What is the rhyme scheme of this stanza?

   _____

2. How does the rhyme scheme help to set off the last line in the stanza?

   _____

3. Is the meter in these lines regular or irregular? Explain your answer.

   _____

© Pearson Education, Inc. All rights reserved.

Name _____ Date _____

Poetry Collection: Robert Frost, Emily Dickinson, and T. S. Eliot
Reading: Paraphrasing

Paraphrasing is restating in your own words what someone else has written or said. A paraphrase should retain the essential meaning and ideas of the original but should be simpler to read. One way to simplify the text that you are paraphrasing is to **break down long sentences.** Divide long sentences into parts and paraphrase those parts.

- If a sentence contains multiple subjects or verbs, see if it can be separated into smaller sentences with a single subject and a single verb.
- If a sentence contains colons, semicolons, or dashes, create separate sentences by treating those punctuation marks as periods.
- If a sentence contains long phrases or long passages in parentheses, turn each phrase or parenthetical passage into a separate sentence.

Poets often write sentences that span several lines to give their poems fluidity. By breaking down long sentences and paraphrasing them, you can enjoy a poem's fluid quality without missing its meaning.

DIRECTIONS: *On the lines provided, paraphrase the following passages from the poems in this collection. Remember that a paraphrase is a restatement in your own words. In your paraphrases, use short sentences with simple structures.*

1. Then took the other, as just as fair,
   And having perhaps the better claim,
   Because it was grassy and wanted wear;
   Though as for that, the passing there
   Had worn them really about the same. ("The Road Not Taken")

   _____

   _____

   _____

2. The Heroism we recite
   Would be a normal thing
   Did not ourselves the Cubits warp
   For fear to be a King—("We never know how high we are")

   _____

   _____

   _____

3. And when the Foreign Office find a Treaty's gone astray,
   Or the Admiralty lose some plans and drawings by the way,
   There may be a scrap of paper in the hall or on the stair—
   But it's useless to investigate—*Macavity's not there!* ("Macavity: The Mystery Cat")

   _____

   _____

   _____

© Pearson Education, Inc. All rights reserved.

Poetry Collection: Robert Frost, Emily Dickinson, and T. S. Eliot
Vocabulary Builder

Word List

bafflement   depravity   disclosed   diverged
levitation   rifled   warp

A. DIRECTIONS: *Match each word in Column A with the correct definition in Column B.*

Column A	Column B
___ 1. diverged	A. twist
___ 2. warp	B. corruption
___ 3. bafflement	C. branched out
___ 4. depravity	D. puzzlement

B. DIRECTIONS: *In each of the following items, think about the meaning of the italicized word and then answer the question.*

1. While traveling in India, you observe an entertainer practicing *levitation*. What would likely be your reaction? Explain.

   _____

2. The burglars *rifled* through their victim's belongings. Would the burglars have searched thoroughly or rapidly?

   _____

3. If someone *disclosed* a secret, would he or she keep it or not? Explain.

   _____

C. WORD STUDY: Use the context of the sentences and what you know about the Latin suffix *-ment* to explain your answer to each question.

1. If you experience *astonishment*, are you surprised or not?

   _____

   _____

2. Is an *amendment* to a document an addition or a subtraction?

   _____

   _____

3. Does a *postponement* mean that something will be done now or later?

   _____

   _____

© Pearson Education, Inc. All rights reserved.

Poetry Collection: Robert Frost, Emily Dickinson, and T. S. Eliot
Enrichment: Workplace Skills

Setting and Achieving Short-term Goals

In "We never know how high we are," Emily Dickinson stresses the value of dreams and goals as well as the human potential to fulfill them. What dream or goal have you nurtured from an early age? Think about that goal, and consider what short-term goals you might need to achieve it. Short-term goals are small but important steps that pave the way toward your greater goal. For instance, you might get a part-time job in order to save money for college. You could reach your long-term goal of entering the military by keeping in shape and maintaining good grades throughout high school. Whatever your dream or goal, setting and achieving short-term goals can help you realize it.

A. DIRECTIONS: *Answer these questions to help you identify your long-term and short-term goals.*

1. What is your dream or long-term goal?

   _____

2. How far in the future is your goal or dream?

   _____

3. What skills might you need to learn or further develop to help you reach your goal?

   _____

   _____

4. List two or three actions that you could take to help you reach your dream or goal.

   _____

   _____

5. Will your short-term goals take place over a period of weeks? Months? Years?

   _____

B. DIRECTIONS: *Choose one of the paths toward your dream. Write a paragraph in which you define your long-term dream or goal. Then, identify the short-term goals that will lead you to achieve your long-term goal. Explain how the short-term goals relate to one another.*

_____

_____

_____

_____

_____

_____

_____

_____

_____

© Pearson Education, Inc. All rights reserved.

Name _____ Date _____

Short Answer *Write your responses to the questions in this section on the lines provided.*

1. Paraphrase the first four lines of Emily Dickinson's poem "We never know how high we are."

   _____

   _____

   _____

2. According to the speaker in "We never know how high we are," do we *warp* ourselves to become great? Use the meaning of *warp* in your response.

   _____

   _____

   _____

3. In "The Road Not Taken" by Robert Frost, what do the diverging roads mean to you?

   _____

   _____

4. What rhyme scheme does Frost use in stanzas one and two in "The Road Not Taken"? Is there a second rhyme scheme in this poem?

   _____

   _____

5. In "The Road Not Taken," does the speaker have a difficult time choosing one road over the other? Can you tell, based on the last two lines, whether this is the right choice? Explain.

   _____

   _____

   _____

6. In "The Road Not Taken," the speaker says that in the future, he will "be telling this with a sigh." Why might the speaker sigh when he recalls the choice he made?

   _____

   _____

   _____

7. In "The Road Not Taken," the poet uses a regular meter. How does this steady rhythm reflect the action in the poem?

_____

_____

_____

8. What type of rhyme does T. S. Eliot use at the ends of lines 39–40 of "Macavity: The Mystery Cat"? Define this type of rhyme, and tell what the rhyming words are.

_____

_____

_____

9. Why is Macavity considered the "bafflement of Scotland Yard"? Use the definition of the word *bafflement* in your response.

_____

_____

_____

10. The name *Macavity* sounds like and perhaps suggests the word *cavity*. If this is intentional by the poet, what underlying meaning might he be trying to express?

_____

_____

_____

Essay

Write an extended response to the question of your choice or to the question or questions your teacher assigns you.

11. "We never know how high we are" and "The Road Not Taken" offer two different approaches to life. In an essay, discuss one of these poems and tell how the speaker views life's choices and challenges. Be sure to support your ideas with specific references to the poem. Then paraphrase the poem's overall message.

12. What kind of a person is the speaker in "The Road Not Taken"? Would you like having this person as a mentor, or guide, in life? Why or why not? Write an essay answering these questions. First, describe the traveler's character, using information from the poem. Then, explain which of the character's qualities would make him a useful—or not useful—guide.

13. In many poems, meter and rhyme work together to create musical effects. In turn, these musical effects can help to achieve a sense of unity in the poem. In an essay, compare and contrast the uses of meter and rhyme in any two of the poems in this collection by Emily Dickinson, Robert Frost, and T. S. Eliot. Support your ideas with specific references to the texts.

14. **Thinking About the Big Question: How does communication change us?**
Imagine that you are eighty years old and you want to send a poetic message to your youthful self. Which poem would you send: "We never know how high we are" or "The Road Not Taken"? What would you want your younger self to learn from this poem? Use specific references to the poem to support what you say in your essay.

Oral Response

15. Go back to question 3, 5, or 6 or to the question your teacher assigns to you. Take a few minutes to expand your answer and prepare an oral response. Find additional details in the poem or poems by Dickinson, Frost, and Eliot that support your points. If necessary, make notes to guide your oral response.

© Pearson Education, Inc. All rights reserved.

Poetry Collection: Robert Frost, Emily Dickinson, and T. S. Eliot

Selection Test A

Critical Reading *Identify the letter of the choice that best answers the question.*

_____ 1. What must the speaker in "The Road Not Taken" decide?
  A. which friend to invite on a journey
  B. which road to travel
  C. which road to cover with gravel
  D. which vehicle to drive down the road

_____ 2. In "The Road Not Taken," what ultimately draws the traveler to the road he takes despite the fact that the differences between the two roads are slight?
  A. The road is grassy and seems to have been traveled by fewer people.
  B. The road seems longer, so it will provide the traveler with more exercise.
  C. The road is paved and seems to lead to people and communities.
  D. The road is bumpy and full of potholes, so the traveler thinks other people will avoid it.

_____ 3. A metaphor is a direct comparison of two unlike things without the use of a comparative word such as *like* or *as*. In "The Road Not Taken," the two roads are metaphors for which of the following?
  A. stages of life
  B. life and death
  C. ways of life
  D. commitment and compassion

_____ 4. Which of the following is a helpful technique to use when you want to paraphrase a text?
  A. Skim the text rapidly.
  B. Break down long sentences.
  C. Read only the first few lines.
  D. Use a dictionary.

_____ 5. Which of the following defines *internal rhyme*?
  A. exact rhyme at the ends of lines
  B. words with similar sounds that do not rhyme perfectly
  C. the rhyming of words within a line
  D. the use of a single rhyme throughout a poem

© Pearson Education, Inc. All rights reserved.

____ 6. What does the speaker in "We never know how high we are" believe about dreaming?

    A. It is a waste of time.

    B. It leads to false hopes.

    C. It enables us to achieve greatness.

    D. It should be discouraged.

____ 7. Which of the following best defines the term *meter*?

    A. the length of the lines in a poem

    B. the number of lines in a poem

    C. the number of stanzas in a poem

    D. the rhythmical pattern in a line of poetry

____ 8. What is the rhyme scheme in these lines from "We never know how high we are"?

    The Heroism we recite

    Would be a normal thing

    Did not ourselves the Cubits warp

    For fear to be a King—

    A. *abab*

    B. *abba*

    C. *aaab*

    D. *abcb*

____ 9. In "We never know how high we are," Emily Dickinson focuses on which of the following conflicts?

    A. good vs. evil

    B. life vs. death

    C. love vs. hatred

    D. confidence vs. fear

____ 10. According to the speaker in "Macavity: The Mystery Cat," what do people say about other cats who are guilty of wicked deeds?

    A. They will replace Macavity when he leaves town.

    B. They try to find Macavity and beat him at his own game.

    C. They can outsmart Macavity in many different ways.

    D. They are nothing more than agents for Macavity, who controls their operations.

____ 11. What makes Macavity "the Napoleon of Crime"?

    A. his short and plump appearance

    B. the fact that he would like to be an emperor

    C. the fact that he is a leader in the criminal world

    D. his ability to get away with his crimes

© Pearson Education, Inc. All rights reserved.

_____ **12.** The atmosphere, or overall mood, in "Macavity: The Mystery Cat" might best be described as which of the following?
    A. affectionate
    B. detached
    C. humorous
    D. ominous

Vocabulary and Grammar

_____ **13.** Which of the following is the best synonym for *warp*?
    A. bark   **C.** trace
    B. distort   **D.** plunder

_____ **14.** Which of the following most nearly means the opposite of *depravity*?
    A. shame   **C.** integrity
    B. guilt   **D.** ambiguity

_____ **15.** Which of the following always appears in an infinitive?
    A. *for*   **C.** *-ing*
    B. *to*   **D.** have

Essay

16. In "Macavity: The Mystery Cat," how does T. S. Eliot create humor by contrasting serious details and events with amusing and ridiculous details and events? In an essay, discuss Eliot's use of contrast for entertainment in the poem.

17. "The Road Not Taken" and "We never know how high we are" present two contrasting approaches to life. In an essay, discuss the different ways in which the speakers in these poems view human nature and behavior. Be sure to support your ideas with specific references to the poems.

18. **Thinking About the Big Question: How does communication change us?** Imagine that you are eighty years old and you want to send a poetic message to your youthful self. Which poem would you send to warn your younger self that choices in life can have significant effects? Would you send "We never know how high we are" or "The Road Not Taken"? Use specific references to the poem in an essay to explain your choice.

© Pearson Education, Inc. All rights reserved.

Name _____   Date _____

Selection Test B

Critical Reading *Identify the letter of the choice that best completes the statement or answers the question.*

____ 1. Which of the following items best defines the term *slant rhyme*?
   A. words that end with the same consonant and vowel sounds at the ends of lines
   B. the rhyming of words within a line
   C. verse that does not employ any kind of rhyme
   D. repetition of words that end with similar sounds but do not rhyme perfectly

____ 2. Which of the following is the best paraphrase of the line, "Two roads diverged in a yellow wood"?
   A. Two roads met in the forest.
   B. In the autumn forest, there was a fork in the path.
   C. Two roads lay side by side in the woods.
   D. The roads in the woods were confusing.

____ 3. The lines "Two roads diverged in a wood, and I— / I took the one less traveled by, / And that has made all the difference" contain figurative language that compares choosing one road over another to
   A. running in a marathon.   C. planting flowers and trees.
   B. making peace with an enemy.   D. making an important life decision.

____ 4. When the speaker in "The Road Not Taken" predicts that he will someday tell about his decision "with a sigh," what does he mean?
   A. He will feel sad because the road he has chosen will probably not lead to success.
   B. He will be depressed at the thought of having to return to the woods.
   C. He will feel some regret, wondering if his life would have been different if he had chosen the other road.
   D. He will feel disappointment because he knows that when he returns, the road will probably no longer be there.

____ 5. What is the rhyme scheme in this stanza from "The Road Not Taken"?
   > And both that morning equally lay
   > In leaves no step had trodden black.
   > Oh, I kept the first for another day!
   > Yet knowing how way leads on to way,
   > I doubted if I should ever come back.

   A. *abbab*   C. *ababa*
   B. *abaab*   D. *abbba*

____ 6. Which of the following best describes the overall mood in "The Road Not Taken"?
   A. reflective   C. skeptical
   B. argumentative   D. angry

____ **7.** Which of the following best defines a *paraphrase*?
   A. an extensive research report
   B. a direct quotation from a text
   C. a restatement of a text in your own words
   D. a list of sources used for research

____ **8.** In "We never know how high we are," Emily Dickinson deals with which of the following?
   A. the limitations that our own ignorance imposes on us
   B. the results of prejudice
   C. the way in which fear restricts our potential for success
   D. the dangers of materialism and greed

____ **9.** Which of the following statements is true about Emily Dickinson's use of rhyme in "We never know how high we are"?
   A. She uses internal rhyme but no end rhyme.
   B. She uses slant rhyme but no exact rhyme.
   C. She uses exact rhyme at the end of some lines.
   D. She does not use any kind of rhyme.

____ **10.** In "We never know how high we are," what do the skies symbolize?
   A. self-confidence   C. limitless possibility
   B. success   D. wishful thinking

____ **11.** On the whole, the tone, or attitude, of the speaker in "We never know how high we are" might best be described as
   A. pessimistic.   C. cheerful.
   B. angry.   D. encouraging.

____ **12.** Which of the following is the best definition of the term *meter*?
   A. a type of figurative language
   B. the stanzaic form of a poem
   C. the rhythmical pattern in a line of poetry
   D. a symbolic reading of poetry

____ **13.** In "Macavity: The Mystery Cat," which of the following lines features a humorous contrast between the formal diction of the speaker and the actual behavior of Macavity?
   A. "Macavity's a Mystery Cat: he's called the Hidden Paw—"
   B. "Macavity's a ginger cat, he's very tall and thin;"
   C. "His coat is dusty from neglect, his whiskers are uncombed."
   D. "He's outwardly respectable. (They say he cheats at cards.)"

____ **14.** In "Macavity: The Mystery Cat," which of the following lines is humorous because it combines serious details with ridiculous, amusing details?
   A. "And when the Foreign Office find a Treaty's gone astray, / Or the Admiralty lose some plans and drawings by the way, / There may be a scrap of paper in the hall or on the stair—"
   B. "You'll be sure to find him resting, or a-licking of his thumbs, / Or engaged in doing complicated long division sums."
   C. "Macavity, Macavity, there's no one like Macavity,"
   D. "He always has an alibi, and one or two to spare;"

© Pearson Education, Inc. All rights reserved.

Vocabulary and Grammar

____ 15. Which of the following is the best synonym for *diverged*?
A. grouped
B. branched out
C. anticipated
D. reflected

____ 16. Which of the following is the best antonym for *bafflement*?
A. obstruction
B. confusion
C. comprehension
D. reduction

____ 17. Infinitive phrases can function as which of the following?
A. nouns or pronouns
B. adjectives
C. verbs or adverbs
D. nouns, adjectives, or adverbs

____ 18. Which of the following is the infinitive phrase in the sentence, "Born in the United States, T. S. Eliot settled in England as a young man to work as a teacher."
A. Born in the United States
B. settled in England
C. as a young man
D. to work as a teacher

Essay

19. In a short essay, describe the character of Macavity the Mystery Cat. What details does T. S. Eliot use to show Macavity's personality and appearance? How do people feel about Macavity?

20. In many poems, meter and rhyme function to create musical effects, a specific atmosphere or mood, and unity of composition. In an open-book essay, compare and contrast the uses of meter and rhyme in two of the poems in this collection. Be sure to support your main ideas with specific references to the texts.

21. The speaker in Robert Frost's poem "The Road Not Taken" says that one day he will sigh when he tells the story of choosing one road over the other. In an essay, describe the significance of the two roads in the woods, and discuss why the speaker might sigh as he thinks about the road he chose and the road he did not choose. As you write your essay, keep the following questions in mind: What did the speaker give up when he chose one road over another? What might he be wondering about the road he did not take?

22. **Thinking About the Big Question: How does communication change us?** Imagine that you are eighty years old and you want to send a poetic message to your youthful self. Which poem would you send: "We never know how high we are" or "The Road Not Taken"? What would you want your younger self to learn from this poem? Use specific references to the poem to support what you say in your essay.

Vocabulary Warm-up Word Lists

Study these words from the poetry of Robert Frost, E. E. Cummings, and William Shakespeare. Then, apply your knowledge to the activities that follow.

Word List A

ballad [BAL uhd] *n.* long song or poem that tells a story
   "John Henry" is a <u>ballad</u> about a worker with amazing strength.

desire [di SYR] *n.* strong wish or longing
   Carly has the <u>desire</u> to do well and works hard to get good grades.

eventful [ee VENT fuhl] *adj.* full of interesting or important happenings
   It was an <u>eventful</u> holiday, with lots of visitors and activities.

favor [FAY ver] *v.* prefer something or someone to other things or people
   Most of my friends choose chocolate ice cream, but I <u>favor</u> vanilla.

stranded [STRAND id] *adj.* stuck in a place
   It was feared that the <u>stranded</u> spaceship might never return to Earth.

whatever [whuht EV er] *pron.* anything that
   We are leaving soon and must get rid of <u>whatever</u> we cannot carry.

Word List B

befriended [bee FREND ed] *v.* made friends with, especially with someone who needs help
   On the plane, our family <u>befriended</u> a child who was flying alone.

childishness [CHYLD ish nes] *n.* immature behavior not appropriate for one's age
   A teenager who throws temper tantrums shows <u>childishness</u>.

mewling [MYOO ling] *adj.* crying weakly
   We found three abandoned kittens in a box, all <u>mewling</u> for food.

oblivion [uh BLIV ee uhn] *n.* state of forgetting or of unconsciousness
   A vacation on a tropical island is an ideal trip to <u>oblivion</u>.

saws [SAWZ] *n.* sayings; proverbs
   "Beggars can't be choosers" is one of my brother's favorite <u>saws</u>.

unwillingly [un WILL ing lee] *adv.* doing in a way that shows you do not want to
   He answered <u>unwillingly</u> and would not share everything he knew.

© Pearson Education, Inc. All rights reserved.

Poetry Collection: Robert Frost, E. E. Cummings, William Shakespeare
Vocabulary Warm-up Exercises

Exercise A *Fill in each blank in the following paragraph with an appropriate word from Word List A. Use each word only once.*

"Casey at the Bat" is a favorite [1] _____ for those who love a baseball

story. This poetic telling of an exciting and [2] _____ game must appeal to

any player who has ever been in Casey's place. Surely, many have a strong wish and

[3] _____ to hit a grand-slam home run and be the hero of a game. Most

fans probably [4] _____ this heart-stopping moment in a game over an easy

victory. Suspense, drama, and the opportunity for baseball glory—all of these things and

[5] _____ else is needed in a great sports story are in place as Casey goes to

bat. First it is strike one, and then strike two. Like a [6] _____ sailor on an

island, Casey is stuck at home plate, unable to get to a base and help his team score. Then,

alas, it is strike three and Casey is out!

Exercise B *Decide whether each of the following statements is true or false. Explain your answers.*

1. Someone <u>mewling</u> might be weak and sick.
   T / F _____

2. <u>Childishness</u> is a way for older people to feel young.
   T / F _____

3. A friend who greets you <u>unwillingly</u> is upset about something.
   T / F _____

4. <u>Saws</u> are phrases that people generally have never heard before.
   T / F _____

5. One enemy of mine <u>befriended</u> by another enemy of mine is double trouble for me.
   T / F _____

6. <u>Oblivion</u> is not a good state to be in when you are driving.
   T / F _____

Poetry Collection: Robert Frost, E. E. Cummings, William Shakespeare
Reading Warm-up A

Read the following passage. Pay special attention to the underlined words. Then, read it again, and complete the activities. Use a separate sheet of paper for your written answers.

The element of fire requires four components. Fire needs oxygen to burn. It needs fuel—something to burn—and fire is not choosy. From gas to oil to wood to paper, <u>whatever</u> is available will be consumed. There also must be heat energy. Heat raises a fuel source to the temperature where it will go up in flames. Finally, fire needs a rapid chain reaction that starts the burning process and keeps it going.

Firefighters learn that to stop a fire, they must remove one of these components. That is why water is commonly used to cool a fire. The <u>desire</u> to reduce a fire's fuel source is the strong hope behind the development of "flame-retardant" materials that do not burn easily.

However, even with modern knowledge, a major fire is sure to be <u>eventful</u>, filled with dramatic moments and nonstop activity. History is filled with tragic examples of cities going up in flames.

Among the first recorded fires is the burning of Rome in A.D. 64. Most fires are fed by oxygen in the air, and accounts show that wind fanned the flames. The fire is thought to have started among the wooden shops and goods in a merchant area of the city. In the narrow streets, flames spread quickly, trapping people. These <u>stranded</u> victims were unable to get away, and many died.

A famous myth of this fire is that "the Emperor Nero fiddled while Rome burned." He was accused of being outside the city, playing music while watching the fire. Nero was known as an entertainer. However, it is unlikely that he would sing a <u>ballad</u> of Rome's destruction or any musical story at such a time. Nero's actions afterward included opening his royal gardens and surviving public buildings to the homeless. He also directed the rebuilding of Rome. The decision to <u>favor</u> marble and stone over wood created a more fireproof city.

1. Circle the four things that are represented by the word <u>whatever</u> in the passage. Give a phrase defining the pronoun **whatever**.

2. Circle the words that give the meaning of <u>desire</u> in the passage. Describe a **desire** that you have connected with your future.

3. Underline the phrase that explains <u>eventful</u>. Give an antonym, or word with opposite meaning, for **eventful**.

4. Underline the words and phrases that give clues to the meaning of <u>stranded</u>. If you were in a **stranded** car, what might be the problem and what would be a safe thing to do?

5. Circle the words that are a clue to the meaning of <u>ballad</u>. Is a **ballad** a kind of song you like? Why or why not?

6. Circle the phrase that is a clue to the meaning of <u>favor</u>. Why would Romans **favor** marble and stone over wood after the great fire?

© Pearson Education, Inc. All rights reserved.

Poetry Collection: Robert Frost, E. E. Cummings, William Shakespeare
Reading Warm-up B

Read the following passage. Pay special attention to the underlined words. Then, read it again, and complete the activities. Use a separate sheet of paper for your written answers.

Many sea creatures lead complicated lives. We may think of fish as residing in comfortable <u>oblivion</u> in watery homes, unaware of more than their immediate surroundings. However, the salmon is a good example of the complexity of life in the ocean.

Salmon live in the sea but make a difficult journey upstream to fresh water to spawn, or reproduce. A female lays thousands of eggs in a stream nest, which are fertilized by a male. After the eggs hatch, the young salmon go through the different growth stages. Eventually, they return to the ocean to mature into adult salmon. Then, as if they had outgrown <u>childishness</u> and accepted adult responsibilities, they travel back upstream to spawn. There, they usually die. Yet the salmon do not appear to take this journey <u>unwillingly</u>. Instead, they swim with great strength, fighting strong currents, until they arrive at their freshwater home.

Relationships among sea dwellers can also be complicated. An interesting example involves the shark. Weak and injured creatures, violently thrashing or quietly <u>mewling</u>, attract the shark. Yet, along with the shark come slender pilot fish, <u>befriended</u> by this fearsome predator. The shark, of course, is not a friend to humans. However, it helps the pilot fish by letting it eat its leftovers without attacking this "freeloading" fish. The relationship between the two is a surprising example of one of the old <u>saws</u> that many people know: "Live and let live."

1. Circle a word that is a clue to the meaning of <u>oblivion</u>. Then, give a word that means the opposite of *oblivion*.

2. Underline the phrase that shows what it means to outgrow <u>childishness</u>. Then, explain whether or not fish can really act with *childishness*.

3. Underline the phrase that shows that the fish do not travel <u>unwillingly</u>. Then, explain how a person who was taking a trip *unwillingly* might act.

4. Circle the word that is a clue to the meaning of <u>mewling</u>. Give another word that means the same as *mewling*.

5. Underline the name of the creature that is <u>befriended</u>. Explain which part of the word *befriended* suggests its meaning.

6. Underline the example of one of the <u>saws</u> that many people know. Then, give one of the *saws* you know, explaining what it has in common with other *saws*.

Poetry Collection: Robert Frost, E. E. Cummings, William Shakespeare

Writing About the Big Question

THE BIG ?

How does communication change us?

Big Question Vocabulary

aware	communication	comprehension	discuss	empathy
exchange	illuminate	informed	interpretation	meaning
react	relationship	resolution	respond	understanding

A. *Use one or more words from the list above to complete each sentence.*

1. Because he was so shy, Mark found _____ with strangers difficult.

2. Many schools have started conflict management programs that help students find a(n) _____ to their disputes.

3. Building your vocabulary helps improve your _____ of a reading passage.

4. The goal of a panel discussion is usually for the panelists to _____ ideas.

5. _____ with less fortunate people is one of Sue's most attractive character traits.

B. *Follow the directions in responding to each of the items below.*

1. Assume that you are about to make a documentary film or video. List two different topics that you might choose in order to make your audience better **informed.**

   _____

   _____

2. Write two sentences to explain your reasons for choosing one of the topics. Use at least two of the Big Question vocabulary words.

   _____

   _____

C. *Complete the sentence below. Then, write a short paragraph in which you connect the sentence to the Big Question.*

Communication between two people can seem like action in a play when _____

   _____

   _____

   _____

   _____

Poetry Collection: Robert Frost, E. E. Cummings, and William Shakespeare
Literary Analysis: Rhyme and Meter

Rhyme is the repetition of sounds at the ends of words. There are several types of rhyme:

- **Exact rhyme:** the repetition of words that end with the same vowel and consonant sounds, as in *end* and *mend*
- **Slant rhyme:** the repetition of words that end with similar sounds but do not rhyme perfectly, as in *end* and *stand*
- **End rhyme:** the rhyming sounds of words at the ends of lines
- **Internal rhyme:** the rhyming of words within a line

A **rhyme scheme** is a regular pattern of end rhymes in a poem or stanza. A rhyme scheme is described by assigning one letter of the alphabet to each rhyming sound. For example, in "Uphill" by Christina Rossetti, the rhyme scheme is *abab*:

Does the road wind uphill all the <u>way</u>?	*a*
Yes, to the very <u>end</u>.	*b*
Will the day's journey take the whole long <u>day</u>?	*a*
From morn to night, my <u>friend</u>.	*b*

Meter is the rhythmical pattern in a line of poetry. Meter results from the arrangement of stressed (´) and unstressed (˘) syllables. When you read aloud a line with a regular meter, you can hear the steady, rhythmic pulse of the stressed syllables:

"and maggie discovered a shell that sang"

"Let not Ambition mock their useful toil"

Not all poems include rhyme, a rhyme scheme, or a regular meter. However, poets often use one or more of these techniques to create musical effects and achieve a sense of unity.

DIRECTIONS: *Read this stanza from "The Day-Breakers," a poem by Arna Bontemps. Identify the rhyme scheme and think about how it emphasizes the speaker's meaning. Also, think about the poet's use of meter in these lines. Then, answer the questions on the lines provided.*

The Day-Breakers
    We are not come to wage a strife
with swords upon this hill:
it is not wise to waste the life
against a stubborn will.

5   Yet would we die as some have done:
beating a way for the rising sun.

1. What is the rhyme scheme of this poem?

_____

2. How does the rhyme scheme help to set off the last two lines?

_____

3. Is the meter in these lines regular or irregular? Explain your answer.

_____

_____

Poetry Collection: Robert Frost, E. E. Cummings, and William Shakespeare
Reading: Paraphrasing

Paraphrasing is restating in your own words what someone else has written or said. A paraphrase should retain the essential meaning and ideas of the original but should be simpler to read. One way to simplify the text that you are paraphrasing is to **break down long sentences.** Divide long sentences into parts and paraphrase those parts.

- If a sentence contains multiple subjects or verbs, see if it can be separated into smaller sentences with a single subject and a single verb.
- If a sentence contains colons, semicolons, or dashes, create separate sentences by treating those punctuation marks as periods.
- If a sentence contains long phrases or long passages in parentheses, turn each phrase or parenthetical passage into a separate sentence.

Poets often write sentences that span several lines to give their poems fluidity. By breaking down long sentences and paraphrasing them, you can enjoy a poem's fluid quality without missing its meaning.

DIRECTIONS: *On the lines provided, paraphrase the following passages from the poems in this collection. Remember that a paraphrase is a restatement in your own words. In your paraphrases, use short sentences with simple structures.*

1. But if it had to perish twice,
   I think I know enough of hate
   To say that for destruction ice
   Is also great
   And would suffice. ("Fire and Ice")

   _____

   _____

   _____

2. molly befriended a stranded star
   whose rays five languid fingers were ("maggie and milly and molly and may")

   _____

   _____

3. All the world's a stage,
   And all the men and women merely players:
   They have their exits and their entrances;
   And one man in his time plays many parts,
   His acts being seven ages. ("The Seven Ages of Man")

   _____

   _____

   _____

Poetry Collection: Robert Frost, E. E. Cummings, and William Shakespeare
Vocabulary Builder

Word List

languid   oblivion   stranded   suffice   treble   woeful

A. DIRECTIONS: *Match each word in Column A with the correct definition in Column B.*

Column A	Column B
___ 1. suffice	A. high-pitched voice
___ 2. languid	B. weak
___ 3. woeful	C. be enough
___ 4. treble	D. sorrowful

B. DIRECTIONS: *Revise each sentence so that the underlined vocabulary word is used logically. Be sure not to change the vocabulary word.*

1. The amount of lemonade in that pitcher will <u>suffice</u>, so we will need to make more.

   _____

2. Their behavior was extremely <u>languid</u>, and we could not believe the amount of energy they displayed.

   _____

3. We were <u>stranded</u> in the middle of nowhere, so we felt extremely happy.

   _____

4. He dreamed of losing himself in <u>oblivion</u>, where he could happily mingle with the friends whose company he most enjoyed.

   _____

C. WORD STUDY: Use the context of the sentences and what you know about the Latin suffix *-ion* to explain your answer to each question.

1. If a restaurant serves dishes from many different countries, could its menu be described as a *fusion*?

   _____

   _____

2. If someone at a trial pleads guilty, does the plea amount to an *admission* of guilt?

   _____

   _____

3. If a person suffers from *delusions* of grandeur, does he or she have a mental or emotional disorder?

   _____

   _____

© Pearson Education, Inc. All rights reserved.

Poetry Collection: Robert Frost, E. E. Cummings, and William Shakespeare
Enrichment: Music

In William Shakespeare's "The Seven Ages of Man," the speaker argues that each person "plays many parts" throughout life and that these roles can be divided into seven ages, or phases. The speaker then describes his perspective on each of the seven ages. How does your perspective differ from his? How would you describe each of the seven ages presented in the poem? What words or images do you associate with infancy, childhood, and so on? How would you translate and present those images through music?

A. DIRECTIONS: *Complete the following chart by writing down the first words or images that you associate with each of the seven ages, as outlined in Shakespeare's poem.*

1. the infant:
2. the schoolchild:
3. the lover:
4. the soldier:
5. the justice:
6. the old person:
7. the second childhood/death:

B. DIRECTIONS: *Use the information you gathered in the chart to help you research and identify music to represent your interpretation of each of the seven ages. Try to collect a variety of music from different centuries and composers. List the selections and artists in the following chart and briefly explain why you chose the music. Then, if possible, check out from a library one or two recordings of your selections to share with the rest of the class.*

Title of Music	Musician/Composer	Explanation
1. _____	_____	_____
2. _____	_____	_____
3. _____	_____	_____
4. _____	_____	_____
5. _____	_____	_____
6. _____	_____	_____
7. _____	_____	_____

© Pearson Education, Inc. All rights reserved.

Name _____   Date _____

Integrated Language Skills: Grammar

Infinitives and Infinitive Phrases

An **infinitive** is a verb form preceded by the word *to* that acts as a noun, an adjective, or an adverb. An **infinitive phrase** is an infinitive with its modifiers or complements. Like infinitives, infinitive phrases can function as nouns, adjectives, or adverbs. Unlike a **prepositional phrase** that begins with *to* and ends with a noun or pronoun, an infinitive phrase always ends with a verb.

Infinitive:	The schoolboy liked *to complain.* (acts as a noun, functioning as the direct object of the sentence)
Infinitive Phrase:	During the storm, I was afraid *to go outdoors.* (acts as an adverb by modifying *afraid*)
Prepositional Phrase:	The girls traveled *to the beach.*

A. DIRECTIONS: *On the line provided, write the infinitive phrase in each sentence. Be sure to write the entire infinitive phrase: the infinite with all of its modifiers or complements. Then, identify whether the infinitive phrase functions as a noun, an adjective, or an adverb.*

1. On the beach, the girls found plenty of shells to collect.

   _____

2. May wanted to keep the smooth round stone.

   _____

3. Maggie pointed out that iridescent shells are sometimes hard to find.

   _____

4. Molly was afraid to admit her fear of the little crab.

   _____

5. The beach was an ideal place to enjoy the warm, sunny afternoon.

   _____

B. Writing Application: *Write a brief paragraph describing one of your favorite hobbies. Use at least three infinitive phrases in your writing, and underline each infinitive phrase you use.*

_____

_____

_____

_____

_____

_____

_____

© Pearson Education, Inc. All rights reserved.

Name _____ Date _____

Poetry Collection: Robert Frost, Emily Dickinson, T. S. Eliot, E. E. Cummings, and William Shakespeare

Support for Writing a Poem

Make prewriting notes for your poem by thinking about the issues below.

Rhyme Scheme:

_____

_____

_____

Topic/Event/Experience/Emotion:

_____

_____

_____

Images/Details/Phrases/Words:

_____

_____

_____

_____

_____

_____

_____

Main Idea/Theme:

_____

_____

_____

_____

_____

© Pearson Education, Inc. All rights reserved.

Name _____ Date _____

Poetry Collection: Robert Frost, Emily Dickinson, T. S. Eliot, E. E. Cummings, and William Shakespeare

Support for Extend Your Learning

Listening and Speaking

Use the following chart to make notes to prepare for your panel discussion on possible interpretations of each poem.

Title of Poem: _____

Possible Interpretations of Poem's Theme or Main Idea (Check the one you favor.)
1. _____   _____   Support in Text: _____   _____   _____   _____   _____   _____   2. _____   _____   Support in Text: _____   _____   _____   _____   _____   Panel's Position Statement: _____   _____

© Pearson Education, Inc. All rights reserved.

Name _____ Date _____

Poetry Collection: Robert Frost, E. E. Cummings, William Shakespeare
Open-Book Test

Short Answer *Write your responses to the questions in this section on the lines provided.*

1. In the poem "Fire and Ice," how does Robert Frost use human emotions to present fire and ice as opposites? What do these emotions have in common?

   _____

   _____

2. What is the most frequent rhyming sound in the first four lines of "Fire and Ice"? What is the most frequent rhyming sound in the last five lines of "Fire and Ice"?

   _____

   _____

3. Meter is the rhythm pattern in a line of poetry. Which line of "Fire and Ice" does not have a regular meter?

   _____

   _____

4. In E. E. Cummings's poem "maggie and milly and molly and may," Molly is "chased by a horrible thing." What do you think the "horrible thing" is? Quote a line from the poem to support your answer.

   _____

   _____

   _____

5. Give an example of slant rhyme and the line numbers where it occurs in "maggie and milly and molly and may."

   _____

   _____

6. Paraphrase the second stanza of the poem "maggie and milly and molly and may."

   _____

   _____

   _____

7. In "The Seven Ages of Man" by William Shakespeare, what do the players' exits and entrances refer to in line 3?

   _____

   _____

8. In "The Seven Ages of Man," the speaker describes seven stages in a person's life. Look for words such as *At first, And then, Last,* to help you find each stage. Use your own words to write the seven ages in order along the timeline. Then answer the question that follows.

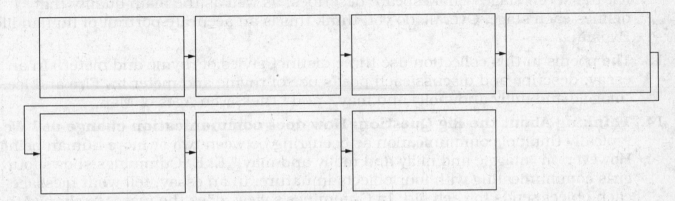

What stage might you add to the timeline?

_____

9. How many stressed and unstressed syllables are there in each line of lines 2–4 of "The Seven Stages of Man"? Is the meter in these lines regular or irregular?

_____

_____

10. In your opinion, does the speaker of "The Seven Ages of Man" see the human condition as woeful? Why? Base your response on the definition of *woeful.*

_____

_____

_____

Essay

Write an extended response to the question of your choice or to the question or questions your teacher assigns you.

11. In both "Fire and Ice" and "maggie and milly and molly and may," the poets Frost and Cummings show how human feelings are reflected in nature. In an essay, explain how each poem does this. What specific objects or elements from nature does each poet include? What does each object show or tell about human nature? What overall message about human nature does each poem express? Support your ideas with references to the poems.

12. William Shakespeare describes the various stages of human life in "The Seven Ages of Man." The poet does not mean each stage literally; for example, he is not saying that every person becomes a soldier and a judge. Instead, he uses the stages to suggest that every person exhibits certain qualities at each stage of life. In an essay, list the seven stages Shakespeare describes, as well as the main quality that defines each stage. Overall, do you think this is an accurate portrait of human life? Explain.

13. The poems in this collection use three distinct styles of rhyme and meter. In an essay, describe and discuss each poet's use of rhyme and meter in "Fire and Ice," "maggie and milly and molly and may," and "The Seven Ages of Man."

14. **Thinking About the Big Question: How does communication change us?** We typically think of communication as occurring between two or more human beings. However, in "maggie and milly and molly and may," E. E. Cummings shows four girls communicating with four objects in nature. In an essay, tell what message each object sends to each girl. In Cummings's view, does the message change the girl? If so, how? If not, what exactly does it do?

Oral Response

15. Go back to question 1, 3, or 10 or to the question your teacher assigns to you. Take a few minutes to expand your answer and prepare an oral response. Find additional details in the poem or poems that support your points. If necessary, make notes to guide your oral response.

Name _____ Date _____

Poetry Collection: Robert Frost, E. E. Cummings, and William Shakespeare
Selection Test A

Critical Reading *Identify the letter of the choice that best answers the question.*

_____ 1. Which of the following is Robert Frost's basic subject in the poem "Fire and Ice"?
  A. the destructive potential of human emotions
  B. the power of love
  C. the change of seasons
  D. the cruelty of war

_____ 2. Which of the following best defines a *paraphrase*?
  A. a highly condensed summary
  B. a restatement of a text in your own words
  C. an analysis of the structure of a text
  D. a quotation of a speaker's exact words

_____ 3. What is the rhyme scheme in the following lines from "Fire and Ice"?
  I think I know enough of hate
  To say that for destruction ice
  Is also great
  And would suffice.
  A. *abba*
  B. *aabb*
  C. *abcb*
  D. *abab*

_____ 4. In "Fire and Ice," which of the following best describes the speaker's tone, or attitude toward the subject?
  A. sympathetic
  B. amused
  C. ironic
  D. cheerful

_____ 5. Which of the following defines the term *meter*?
  A. the number of syllables in a line of verse
  B. the number of lines in a poem
  C. the number of lines in a stanza
  D. the rhythmical pattern in a line of poetry

Unit 4 Resources: Poetry
© Pearson Education, Inc. All rights reserved.
199

____ **6.** Which of the following serves as the setting in "maggie and milly and molly and may"?
    A. a train journey
    B. the beach
    C. a shopping mall
    D. a zoo

____ **7.** Read the following lines from "maggie and milly and molly and may":
    milly befriended a stranded star
    whose rays five languid fingers were
    Which of the following do these lines illustrate?
    A. internal rhyme
    B. exact rhyme
    C. slant rhyme
    D. onomatopoeia

____ **8.** As in the following lines, what kind of feeling is conveyed by the use of parenthetical expressions in "maggie and molly and milly and may"?
    For whatever we lose (like a you or a me)
    It's always ourselves we find in the sea
    A. playful
    B. gruesome
    C. cruel
    D. foolish

____ **9.** Which of the following is most relevant to the poet's overall message in "maggie and milly and molly and may"?
    A. the pleasure of recreation and discovery
    B. the deadening effect of routine
    C. the dangers of the sea
    D. the foolishness of the four girls

____ **10.** What is the basic subject of "The Seven Ages of Man" by William Shakespeare?
    A. the failure of human beings to live life to the fullest
    B. the inability of human beings to predict the time of their own death
    C. the conflicts that make human life stressful
    D. the different phases of human life and their distinguishing characteristics

© Pearson Education, Inc. All rights reserved.

____ 11. In "The Seven Ages of Man," the sixth stage, which "shifts / Into the lean and slippered pantaloon, / With spectacles on nose and pouch on side," describes which of the following?

A. a corrupt judge

B. an overdressed aristocrat

C. a thin, foolish old man

D. a playwright

____ 12. Which of the following best describes the overall atmosphere, or mood, in "The Seven Ages of Man"?

A. passionately enthusiastic

B. amusedly detached

C. pessimistic and gloomy

D. upbeat and optimistic

Vocabulary and Grammar

____ 13. Which of the following is the best synonym for *treble*?

A. triple

B. trembling

C. tentative

D. high-pitched

____ 14. Which of the following means most nearly the opposite of *languid*?

A. energetic

B. lazy

C. drowsy

D. slow

____ 15. Which of the following is always the last word in an infinitive phrase?

A. the word *to*

B. an adverb

C. a verb

D. a preposition

Essay

16. In "Fire and Ice" and "maggie and milly and molly and may," Robert Frost and E. E. Cummings present two very different portraits of human nature. Write an essay in which you contrast the poets' themes, or overall messages, in these works. In your essay, be sure to comment on how the poets' use of rhyme and meter contribute to a distinctive overall atmosphere, or mood, in each poem.

17. How do you feel about the view of life presented in Shakespeare's "The Seven Ages of Man"? Do you think it is an accurate portrayal, or is it too cynical? Write an essay explaining your point of view. Be sure to support your position with quotations from the poem. You may keep your book open as you write your essay.

18. **Thinking About the Big Question: How does communication change us?** In "maggie and milly and molly and may," E. E. Cummings writes about four girls who each get a message from an object in nature. In an essay, list each object along with the girl who finds the object. Then tell what each object communicates, or says, to each girl.

Poetry Collection: Robert Frost, E. E. Cummings, and William Shakespeare

Selection Test B

Critical Reading *Identify the letter of the choice that best completes the statement or answers the question.*

_____ 1. What emotions does the speaker in "Fire and Ice" associate with fire and ice?
   A. love and compassion
   B. desire and hatred
   C. excitement and happiness
   D. indifference and uneasiness

_____ 2. In his discussion about fire and ice, what does Robert Frost want readers to realize about human nature?
   A. Humans are capable of destroying themselves with hatred and desire.
   B. Humans are capable of starting fires and causing other disasters.
   C. The world will definitely be destroyed by fire and ice.
   D. People need to prepare for natural disasters.

_____ 3. Which of the following is an example of slant rhyme?
   A. *clanging* and *bells*   C. *prove* and *glove*
   B. *buzz* and *pop*   D. *fire* and *desire*

_____ 4. Which of the following defines the term *meter*?
   A. the emotional intensity of a poem
   B. the atmosphere, or mood, of a poem
   C. the rhythmical pattern in a line of poetry
   D. the stanza form of a poem

_____ 5. Why do poets often write sentences that span several lines?
   A. to make paraphrasing easier
   B. to give their poems fluidity
   C. for the sake of the rhyme scheme
   D. to establish parallelism

_____ 6. What kind of feeling does Cummings convey with the rhyme and rhythm in "maggie and milly and molly and may"?
   A. calm   C. haunting
   B. dramatic   D. playful

_____ 7. In "maggie and milly and molly and may," when "molly was chased by a horrible thing," the thing she saw was probably a
   A. starfish.   C. crab.
   B. seagull.   D. storm.

_____ 8. In Cummings's poem, one girl comes home with a stone "as small as a world and as large as alone." The poet intends to suggest that the girl
   A. left the beach before the others to bring home a trivial thing.
   B. ignored the real beauty of the ocean in favor of shore objects.
   C. reflected on the whole world and on her feelings while viewing the stone.
   D. tried to preserve things while the other girls did not.

_____ 9. Which of the following best interprets the meaning of "maggie and milly and molly and may"?
   A. A day at the beach is only a waste of time.
   B. The seashore is a place of rediscovery.
   C. Friends do not always enjoy the same pursuits.
   D. It is easy to make new friends at the beach.

_____ 10. When Shakespeare says that "All the world's a stage" and continues that idea in the next four lines, what figure of speech is he using?
   A. extended simile
   B. extended symbolism
   C. extended metaphor
   D. extended personification

_____ 11. In "The Seven Ages of Man," which of the following words best conveys the speaker's description of the infant "mewling and puking in the nurse's arms"?
   A. helpless
   B. cute
   C. disgusting
   D. comical

_____ 12. In "The Seven Ages of Man," calling the soldier "jealous in honor, sudden and quick in quarrel" is another way of saying that he is
   A. brave.
   B. honorable.
   C. modest.
   D. impulsive.

_____ 13. The reader can infer that the speaker in "The Seven Ages of Man" finds people
   A. interesting and amusing.
   B. bothersome and irritating.
   C. weak and foolish.
   D. sincere and good-hearted.

_____ 14. Read the following lines from "The Seven Ages of Man":
   And then the whining schoolboy, with his satchel,
   And shining morning face, creeping like snail
   Unwillingly to school.

   Which of the following is the best paraphrase of these lines?
   A. The schoolboy complains because his satchel is so heavy.
   B. Reluctant to go to school, the complaining boy moves as slowly as he can.
   C. The boy cannot wait to get to school in the morning.
   D. The schoolboy should have washed his face before he set out for school.

Vocabulary and Grammar

____ **15.** If a quantity of something *suffices*, it is which of the following?

A. excessive

B. enough

C. scanty

D. expensive

____ **16.** Which of the following means most nearly the opposite of *woeful*?

A. lamentable

B. melancholy

C. enigmatic

D. cheerful

____ **17.** Which of the following items is an example of an infinitive?

A. is writing

B. has written

C. will write

D. to write

____ **18.** Which of the following is the infinitive phrase in this sentence?

Robert Frost is known for his appearance at the inauguration of President John F. Kennedy, where he had been invited to recite two of his poems.

A. for his appearance

B. at the inauguration

C. of President John F. Kennedy

D. to recite two of his poems

Essay

19. In the poem "Fire and Ice," what is the poet's purpose in describing the destruction of the world by fire and ice? What human failings does Robert Frost emphasize? What attitude does he express toward the world? Discuss these questions in an essay.

20. William Shakespeare describes the various ages of human life in "The Seven Ages of Man." In an essay, write a summary, describing each of those seven ages. Then, draw a conclusion about what message Shakespeare conveys about life in this poem. You may keep your book open as you write this essay.

21. The three poems in this collection exhibit a variety of styles. In "Fire and Ice," for example, Robert Frost uses brief lines, rhyme, and a varying rhythm. In "maggie and milly and molly and may," E. E. Cummings mixes end rhyme with slant rhyme in longer lines. In "The Seven Ages of Man," Shakespeare uses a form known as blank verse, which consists of unrhymed lines of iambic pentameter, or five-stress lines in a rising rhythm. Write an essay in which you discuss these poets' use of rhyme, rhythm, and meter. In your discussion, relate these elements to other important elements of each poem, such as atmosphere, tone, and theme.

22. **Thinking About the Big Question: How does communication change us?** We typically think of communication as occurring between two or more human beings. However, in "maggie and milly and molly and may," E. E. Cummings shows four girls communicating with four objects in nature. In an essay, tell what message each object sends to each girl. In Cummings's view, does the message change the girl? If so, how? If not, what exactly does it do?

Vocabulary Warm-up Word Lists

Study these words from the poetry of Alice Walker, Bashō, Chiyojo, Walt Whitman, and William Shakespeare. Then, apply your knowledge to the activities that follow.

Word List A

grievances [GREEV uhn sez] *n.* complaints about people or situations that are unfair
  The employees had <u>grievances</u> about working weekends without pay.

heavily [HEV i lee] *adv.* very much or in large amounts
  The success of an outdoor party depends <u>heavily</u> on the weather.

husky [HUS kee] *adj.* sounding deep and low or hoarse and scratchy
  Her voice turned <u>husky</u> because of her cold.

madly [MAD lee] *adv.* in a wild, uncontrolled way
  I was in such a rush, I ran around <u>madly</u> gathering my things.

robust [roh BUST] *adj.* strong and healthy
  Good diet and plenty of exercise can help anyone feel more <u>robust</u>.

vanished [VAN isht] *adj.* of something that has disappeared, especially in a sudden way
  The Coast Guard has boats out looking for the <u>vanished</u> ship.

Word List B

fragrant [FRAY gruhnt] *adj.* having a pleasant smell
  Her perfume was <u>fragrant</u> and had the scent of roses.

intermission [in ter MISH uhn] *n.* break in an activity
  The contest will stop for an <u>intermission</u> so all players can rest.

melodious [muh LOH dee uhs] *adj.* having a pleasant tune or sound
  Listening to a quiet, <u>melodious</u> song is a great way to relax.

precious [PRESH uhs] *adj.* valuable; not to be taken for granted
  Voting is a <u>precious</u> right for many people throughout the world.

starched [STARCHT] *adj.* made stiff and neat using a powder called laundry starch
  The <u>starched</u> collar was uncomfortable and rubbed against her neck.

summon [SUH muhn] *v.* call forth or gather together
  The president will <u>summon</u> his top advisers to meet on the crisis.

Poetry by Alice Walker, Bashō, Chiyojo, Walt Whitman, William Shakespeare
Vocabulary Warm-up Exercises

Exercise A *Fill in each blank in the following paragraph with an appropriate word from Word List A. Use each word only once.*

The painting had disappeared from the museum and now the [1] _____
art had created a mystery. The ticket seller recalled a nervous woman with a deep,
[2] _____ voice who asked twice what time the museum closed for the day.
The coat-check attendant remembered a [3] _____ man in a thick jacket
who would have the strength and energy to grab the painting and run. The parking assistant was certain it was a couple that came dashing [4] _____ from the
museum, shouting wildly for their car. The police were looking for a team of thieves, for
the painting was [5] _____ protected and stealing it would take a great
deal of planning. The police suspected that it was an "inside job" and that unhappy
employees with [6] _____ were involved. Who do you think did it?

Exercise B *Revise each sentence so the underlined vocabulary word is used in a logical way. Be sure to keep the vocabulary word in your revision.*

1. There is nothing I enjoy more than listening to a <u>fragrant</u> garden.
   _____

2. A <u>precious</u> memory is something to forget as quickly as possible.
   _____

3. He always looks so sloppy in his <u>starched</u> shirts.
   _____

4. <u>Summon</u> your friends when you want to be alone.
   _____

5. During the <u>intermission</u> of the game, we watched our team score.
   _____

6. Her <u>melodious</u> voice was loud and harsh.
   _____

Poetry by Alice Walker, Bashō, Chiyojo, Walt Whitman, William Shakespeare
Reading Warm-up A

Read the following passage. Pay special attention to the underlined words. Then, read it again, and complete the activities. Use a separate sheet of paper for your written answers.

The value of friendship is hard to measure. We depend <u>heavily</u> on our best chums for large amounts of understanding and acceptance. True pals work through petty differences or even serious <u>grievances</u> and complaints of unfairness. Friendships can also lead to collaborations that produce memorable results. The business world offers some profitable examples.

Bill Hewlett and Dave Packard were college classmates in California, graduating in 1934. However, it was in the setting of a camping and fishing trip that a strong, <u>robust</u> friendship between them grew. Both were engineers and their many conversations included lots of talk of ideas. Fours years later, they started working together out of a garage and, in 1939, they formed a company. They decided on whose name would be first with a coin tossed in the air. It might seem as if they began a little <u>madly</u>, with a wild and crazy start, but today Hewlett-Packard is among the largest technology companies in the world.

Another friendship produced one of the most popular board games ever. In December 1979, two friends in Montreal, Canada, were sitting around a kitchen table. They wanted to play a game but were missing some pieces. So, they came up with their own game. That's how Chris Haney and Scott Abbott created Trivial Pursuit. However, it was not an instant success. They went to toy fairs and talked to people about the game until their voices were <u>husky</u> and tired. Yet, like true friends, they stood by their product and each other. Eventually, they found a company to manufacture it. Today, Trivial Pursuit is sold in nineteen different languages and thirty-three countries.

Some friends make money together and some just make good times. Lasting friendships are the greatest; <u>vanished</u> friendships that disappear without a trace are surely the saddest. Whatever your friendships, make the most of them!

1. Circle the words that are a clue to the meaning of <u>heavily</u>. Underline what the passage indicates we depend *heavily* on friends to give us.

2. Underline the phrase that is a clue to the meaning of <u>grievances</u>. Explain how someone can work out *grievances* with friends.

3. Circle a word that is a clue to the meaning of <u>robust</u>. Would most people want their best friendships to be *robust*? Include the meaning of *robust* in your answer.

4. Circle the phrase that gives a clue to the meaning of <u>madly</u>. Give a word that is the opposite of *madly*.

5. Circle the word and underline the phrase that explains why someone might get a <u>husky</u> voice. Give a word that means the same as *husky* does in this passage.

6. Underline a phrase that is a clue to the meaning of <u>vanished</u>. Explain what the passage means by the phrase "*vanished* friendship."

Name _____ Date _____

Poetry by Alice Walker, Bashō, Chiyojo, Walt Whitman, William Shakespeare
Reading Warm-up B

Read the following passage. Pay special attention to the underlined words. Then, read it again, and complete the activities. Use a separate sheet of paper for your written answers.

In 1856, the great educator Booker T. Washington was born into slavery on a small tobacco farm in Virginia. Even as a child, there was no <u>intermission</u> from work and no break from effort for Washington. Throughout his life, though, Washington was able to <u>summon</u> amazing strength, endurance, and determination. Gathering these resources to meet each challenge, he became an extraordinary achiever.

As a boy, Washington worked inside the home of his enslaver, James Burroughs. Young Booker's daily task was to operate a lever that moved a huge ceiling fan above the dining room. The fan would keep flies away from the food on the <u>starched</u> and ironed tablecloth. The family cook was Washington's mother, Jane. He probably grew up with fond memories of the <u>fragrant</u> smells of his mother's cooking.

Washington viewed an education as <u>precious</u> and valuable. After slavery came to an end, he made every effort to get schooling. When he was sixteen, he walked more than 200 miles to enroll in the Hampton Institute, a school for African Americans. Later, he became a teacher there.

For Washington, the most <u>melodious</u> and pleasant tune was the tinkling of school bells. In 1881, he got the opportunity to lead a brand-new school for black students in Alabama. At the Tuskegee Institute, he taught students his philosophy of independence and self-reliance through hard work. Students learned trades such as masonry, shoemaking, printing, and carpentry along with reading, writing, and math. The school's success made Washington one of the most important educators of his time.

1. Underline the phrase that gives a clue to the meaning of <u>intermission</u>. What *intermission* from work do many people today enjoy?

2. Underline what Booker T. Washington was able to <u>summon</u>. Circle the word that is a clue to the meaning of *summon*.

3. Circle the word that is a clue to the meaning of <u>starched</u>. Describe what a *starched* tablecloth would look like.

4. Circle a word clue for the meaning of <u>fragrant</u>. If Washington's mother had been a bad cook and burned all the food, would you still use *fragrant* in this sentence? Explain.

5. Circle a word that is a clue to the meaning of <u>precious</u>. Give a word that is the opposite of *precious*.

6. Underline the words that are a clue to the meaning of <u>melodious</u>. Describe a sound that you would call *melodious*.

Name _____ Date _____

Writing About the Big Question

How does communication change us?

Big Question Vocabulary

aware	communication	comprehension	discuss	empathy
exchange	illuminate	informed	interpretation	meaning
react	relationship	resolution	respond	understanding

A. *Use one or more words from the list above to complete each sentence.*

1. Good _____ often helps deepen a(n) _____
   between two people.

2. Kyra was _____ that she would have to improve her reading
   _____ skills if she were to score well on that test.

3. We workers attended the meeting to _____ our grievances, but the
   management seemed to _____ with hostility.

4. The professor's _____ of that story helped _____
   the _____ for us.

B. *Follow the directions in responding to each of the items below.*

1. List two poems from this unit that have changed your perception of a person, place,
   event, or situation.

   _____

   _____

2. Write two sentences to explain how the poem changed your perception, and
   describe how this experience made you feel. Use at least two of the Big Question
   vocabulary words.

   _____

   _____

C. *Complete the sentence below. Then, write a short paragraph in which you connect the
sentence to the Big Question.*

A powerful poem makes us **aware** of _____

_____

_____

_____

© Pearson Education, Inc. All rights reserved.

Name _____ Date _____

Poetry by Alice Walker, Bashō, Chiyojo, Walt Whitman, William Shakespeare
Literary Analysis: Lyric Poetry

Lyric poetry is poetry with a musical quality that expresses the thoughts and feelings of a single speaker. Unlike a narrative poem, a lyric does not try to tell a complete story. Instead, it describes an emotion or a mood, often by using vivid imagery, or language that appeals to the senses. A lyric poem is relatively short and usually achieves a single, unified effect.

There are a variety of lyric forms that can create different effects:

- A **sonnet** is a fourteen-line poem that is written in iambic pentameter and that rhymes. Two common sonnet types are the Italian, or Petrarchan, and the English, or Shakespearean. The English, or Shakespearean, sonnet consists of three quatrains, or four-line stanzas, and a final rhyming couplet.
- A **haiku** is an unrhymed Japanese verse form arranged into three lines of five, seven, and five syllables. A haiku often uses a striking image from nature to convey a strong emotion.
- A **free verse** poem does not follow a regular pattern. Free verse employs sound and rhythmic devices, such as alliteration and repetition, and may even use rhyme—but not in a regular pattern, as in metered poetry.

DIRECTIONS: *Analyze each poem. On the chart, write the type of lyric in the first column. Then, in the remaining columns, briefly describe the speaker of the poem, identify the speaker's emotion, and quote an example of a striking image or sound device.*

Author	Type of Lyric	Speaker	Emotion	Image/Sound Device
Walker				
Bashō				
Chiyojo				
Whitman				
Shakespeare				

Name _____ Date _____

Poetry by Alice Walker, Bashō, Chiyojo, Walt Whitman, William Shakespeare
Vocabulary Builder

Word List

intermission   stout   wail   woes

A. DIRECTIONS: *Revise each sentence so that the underlined vocabulary word is used logically. Be sure not to change the vocabulary word.*

1. Because she is <u>stout</u> of heart, she faces her future with great fear.

   _____

2. The film was 3 hours long with no <u>intermission</u>; we were grateful for the break.

   _____

3. He was cheerful as he recounted to us his many <u>woes</u> of the past year.

   _____

4. So many misfortunes in a single day caused her to <u>wail</u> with happiness.

   _____

B. DIRECTIONS: *On the line, write the letter of the choice that is the best synonym, or word with a similar meaning, for each numbered word.*

___ 1. wail
    A. strike
    B. publish
    C. grieve
    D. crawl

___ 2. woes
    A. signals
    B. factories
    C. songs
    D. sorrows

___ 3. intermission
    A. analysis
    B. break
    C. communication
    D. alliance

___ 4. stout
    A. plentiful
    B. sturdy
    C. weary
    D. energetic

© Pearson Education, Inc. All rights reserved.

Poetry by Alice Walker, Bashō, Chiyojo, Walt Whitman, William Shakespeare
Support for Writing to Compare

Use a chart like the one shown to make prewriting notes for an essay comparing the relationship between lyric form and meaning in two poems from the selections.

Title of Poem 1: _____

Lyric Form: _____

Characteristics of Form: _____
_____
_____

**Relationship of Poem's
Form to Its Meaning:** _____
_____
_____
_____

Title of Poem 2: _____

Lyric Form: _____

Characteristics of Form: _____
_____
_____

**Relationship of Poem's
Form to Its Meaning:** _____
_____
_____
_____

Comparing Literary Works: Alice Walker, Bashō, Chiyojo, Walt Whitman, William Shakespeare

Open-Book Test

Short Answer *Write your responses to the questions in this section on the lines provided.*

1. At the end of "Women," poet Alice Walker points out that the women's efforts toward education for their children were quite remarkable. Why does she find these efforts so remarkable? Cite lines from the poem to support your answer.

   _____

   _____

2. What woes did the women in Alice Walker's poem experience? Base your response on the definition of the word *woes*.

   _____

   _____

   _____

3. In what way are Three Haiku by Bashō and Chiyojo similar in their use of imagery?

   _____

   _____

4. In "I Hear America Singing," one of poet Walt Whitman's purposes is to rejoice over the different types of people in America. Cite a line from the poem that supports this idea.

   _____

   _____

5. What lyric form of verse does Whitman use in "I Hear America Singing"? How does this form reflect the main idea of the poem?

   _____

   _____

6. In Sonnet 30 by William Shakespeare, what change in feeling does the speaker have in the last two lines? What causes this change?

   _____

   _____

7. How are the lyric forms of "Women" and "I Hear America Singing" similar? What main feeling does each poem convey?

   _____

   _____

8. How are the women in "Women" like the speaker in Chiyojo's haiku "Bearing no flowers, . . ."? How might Walker's women and Chiyojo's speaker be seen as different?

_____

_____

_____

9. Which poem—"Women," "I Hear America Singing," or "Sonnet 30"—uses a regular rhyme scheme? How do the rhyming sounds help bring the feeling of the poem to life?

_____

_____

_____

10. Use the chart to list a single image from "Women," Three Haiku, "I Hear America Singing," and "Sonnet 30" that has stayed in your mind. Then, answer the questions that follow the chart.

"Women"	Three Haiku	"I Hear America Singing"	"Sonnet 30"

Of these images, which is the most powerful?

_____

What feeling does it convey?

_____

Essay

Write an extended response to the question of your choice or to the question or questions your teacher assigns you.

11. A lyric poem usually describes a feeling or a mood, which helps communicate the thoughts of a single speaker. From among "Women," Three Haiku, "I Hear America Singing," and Sonnet 30, choose two poems in this collection. Then, write an essay in which you describe both the mood and the speaker of each poem. Do you enjoy stepping into the mind and thoughts of this speaker? Why? Which poem is more powerful? In what ways? Use references to the poems to support your ideas.

12. In "Women," Alice Walker describes the struggle of her mother's generation to secure an education for their children. Write an essay in which you describe how two of the poems in this collection offer a lesson to future generations. First, briefly identify the theme, or overall message, of each poem. Then explain how the poet uses the elements of speaker, imagery, and mood to make this message memorable. In your view, which message is the most important for future generations? Why?

13. The form of a lyric poem contributes to its overall meaning. For example, the brief form of the haiku encourages a poet to use one or two images to convey a single feeling, whereas the sonnet requires the poet to develop ideas logically and sequentially, often leading to a change in mood. In an essay, compare and contrast the way form adds meaning and enhances mood in two of the poems in this group. Support your ideas with specific references to the text.

14. **Thinking About the Big Question: How does communication change us?** Which poem in this collection caused you to think differently about something you took for granted before? Explain in a brief essay, supporting your ideas with specific references to the text.

Oral Response

15. Go back to question 4, 8, or 10 or to the question your teacher assigns to you. Take a few minutes to expand your answer and prepare an oral response. Find additional details in the relevant poem or poems that support your points. If necessary, make notes to guide your oral response.

Poetry by Alice Walker, Bashō Chiyojo, Walt Whitman, William Shakespeare
Selection Test A

Critical Reading *Identify the letter of the choice that best answers the question.*

____ 1. In "Women," Alice Walker mentions that the women of her mama's generation had "fists as well as/ Hands." What quality in the women does this detail emphasize?
  A. refinement
  B. tall stature
  C. determination
  D. compassion

____ 2. What did the women in Alice Walker's poem succeed in discovering for their children?
  A. good jobs
  B. equality of opportunity
  C. an education
  D. better housing

____ 3. "Women" by Alice Walker is an example of which type of poetry?
  A. narrative
  B. dramatic
  C. epic
  D. lyric

____ 4. In which country did haiku develop as a form of poetry?
  A. Greece
  B. Japan
  C. India
  D. Mexico

____ 5. In the haiku by Bashō, which of the following does the speaker focus on?
  A. the calm beauty of the evening
  B. the destructive power of nature
  C. the decline of religious belief
  D. the pleasures of writing poetry

____ 6. In "I Hear America Singing," what impresses the speaker the most about America and Americans?
  A. the businesses
  B. the variety
  C. the hugeness
  D. the technology

_____ 7. "I Hear America Singing" illustrates what type of lyric poem?

    A. sonnet

    B. haiku

    C. free verse

    D. ode

_____ 8. Tone is the writer's attitude toward his or her subject, characters, or audience. Which of the following best describes the speaker's tone in "I Hear America Singing"?

    A. frightened

    B. enthusiastic

    C. resigned

    D. regretful

_____ 9. In Shakespeare's Sonnet 30, why is the speaker sad as the poem begins?

    A. He has been forced to leave home.

    B. He finds it hard to adjust to a life of poverty.

    C. His efforts to marry the woman he loves have failed.

    D. He remembers past disappointments and sorrows.

_____ 10. The theme of a literary work is its main idea or underlying message. Which of the following best states the theme of Sonnet 30?

    A. the inevitability of death

    B. the power of friendship

    C. the risks of life

    D. the importance of faith

_____ 11. The speakers in "Women," "I Hear America Singing," and Sonnet 30 all have in common which of the following?

    A. the use of free verse

    B. the ability to be inspired by other people

    C. the reluctance to become distracted from their work

    D. admiration for the beauty of nature

_____ 12. In this group, which lyric is inspired most vividly by the beauty of nature?

    A. the haiku by Bashō

    B. "Women"

    C. "I Hear America Singing"

    D. Sonnet 30

© Pearson Education, Inc. All rights reserved.

Vocabulary

____ **13.** Which of the following is the best synonym, or word with a similar meaning, for *stout* as Alice Walker uses it in these lines from "Women"?

> My mama's generation
> Husky of voice—Stout of
> Step

    A. lazy
    B. hurried
    C. sturdy
    D. irregular

____ **14.** Which word is most nearly opposite to *wail*?
    A. lament
    B. rejoice
    C. postpone
    D. hurry

Essay

15. Lyric poems usually describe an emotion or a mood, and they feature the thoughts and feelings of a single speaker. Choose two of the poems in this collection. Then, write an essay discussing why they may be classified as lyric poems. In your essay, describe the mood and speaker in each poem. Consider also especially vivid imagery or effective sound devices. Then, explain why the mood and speaker help show that the poem is a lyric.

16. In lyric poems, vivid imagery often expresses the mood of the work, making the speaker's emotion clearer and more powerful. Choose two of the poems in this group. In an essay, compare and contrast the use of imagery in these works. Consider whether the images are happy or sad, whether they are full of energy or calm, and whether they are strong or gentle. Then, explain how the poet's sensory language shows the speaker's emotion or adds to the overall mood.

17. **Thinking About the Big Question: How does communication change us?** The poets in this collection, Alice Walker, Bashō, Chiyojo, Walt Whitman, and William Shakespeare, each communicate ideas. The ideas may help you think differently about something we take for granted or something we do not usually notice. Which poem in this collection causes you to think about something in a different way? How did you think about your choice before reading the poem? How have your ideas changed after reading the poem? Explain in a brief essay. Support your ideas with specific references to the text.

© Pearson Education, Inc. All rights reserved.

Poetry by Alice Walker, Bashō, Chiyojo, Walt Whitman, William Shakespeare
Selection Test B

Critical Reading *Identify the letter of the choice that best completes the statement or answers the question.*

_____ 1. Which of the following statements about lyric poetry is *not* accurate?
   A. A sonnet is a type of lyric poem.
   B. A lyric poem attempts to tell a complete story.
   C. Lyric poems typically have a musical quality.
   D. Lyric poems often use vivid imagery and describe an emotion or a mood.

_____ 2. To what is Alice Walker referring when she writes that the women led armies "Across mined/ Fields/ Booby-trapped/ Ditches"?
   A. World War II military weapons and technology
   B. assistance given to the military to restore order
   C. the danger of pursuing education in the segregated South
   D. the difficulties involved in getting a library card in the segregated South

_____ 3. At the end of "Women," what point does the poet make to show how remarkable the women's efforts toward education were?
   A. The women valued education deeply without having had any themselves.
   B. There were more difficulties and obstacles than the women could have imagined.
   C. Books and desks were hard to come by in the segregated South.
   D. The women had so little chance of success.

_____ 4. Which word best describes the speaker's mood in Bashō's haiku about temple bells and fragrant blossoms?
   A. content
   B. excited
   C. restless
   D. melancholy

_____ 5. When the speaker in Chiyojo's first haiku asks the dragonfly catcher, "How far have you gone today/ In your wandering?", which of the following is the poet expressing?
   A. anger at the dragonfly catcher's disappearance
   B. concern for the dragonfly catcher's safety
   C. a desire to join the dragonfly catcher's wanderings
   D. resentment of the dragonfly catcher's freedom

_____ 6. Haiku often contain which of the following?
   A. explicit mention of the speaker's identity
   B. references to mythology
   C. a striking image from nature
   D. the theme of romantic love

_____ 7. Choose the phrase that best describes the workers mentioned in "I Hear America Singing."
A. people doing odd jobs just to get by
B. people working hard and being satisfied by their work
C. people working themselves to exhaustion
D. people putting in their time at work just to get paid

_____ 8. In "I Hear America Singing," what is the meaning of the line "Each singing what belongs to him or her and to none else"?
A. The song each worker sings, like the task he or she performs, fully expresses his or her own being.
B. No two workers ever sing the same song.
C. Each worker makes up his or her own words to whatever song comes to mind.
D. The workers are singing about the tools and equipment that belong to them.

_____ 9. What is one theme, or underlying message or insight about life, that Whitman conveys in "I Hear America Singing"?
A. Americans are hard workers and good singers.
B. America is the sum of different contributions from many people.
C. Every American has a job unlike anyone else's.
D. The spirit of America lives in popular music and the people's songs.

_____ 10. In Sonnet 30 by William Shakespeare, what is the cause of the speaker's unhappiness?
A. the pain of love
B. his financial losses
C. his memories of past sorrows
D. the absence of a dear friend

_____ 11. The last lines of Shakespeare's Sonnet 30 ("But if the while I think on thee, dear friend, / All losses are restored and sorrows end.") are an example of which of the following?
A. refrain
B. couplet
C. quatrain
D. hexameter

_____ 12. Which of the following words best describes the mood of the speaker at the end of Sonnet 30?
A. regretful
B. sentimental
C. serene
D. guilty

_____ 13. Which of the following do the speakers in "Women" and "I Hear America Singing" seem to have in common?
A. enthusiasm and admiration
B. melancholy and regret
C. reverence for nature
D. a skeptical attitude toward their subject

© Pearson Education, Inc. All rights reserved.

____ 14. Both sonnets and haiku are examples of which type of poetry?
  A. dramatic
  B. free verse
  C. epic
  D. lyric

____ 15. The speakers in Alice Walker's "Women" and William Shakespeare's Sonnet 30 would probably agree with which of the following statements?
  A. Idealism is less important in life than realism.
  B. Our connections with others can help us surmount hardships and obstacles in life.
  C. Recollections of the natural world's beauty can inspire us in a time of trouble.
  D. Disappointments are an inevitable part of life.

Vocabulary

____ 16. When Walt Whitman writes in "I Hear America Singing" that he hears the ploughboy's song "at noon intermission," what does he mean by *intermission*?
  A. entertainment   C. recess
  B. lunchtime   D. vacation

____ 17. In "Women," Alice Walker describes the women of her mama's generation as "Stout of / Step." What is the best synonym for *stout* in this phrase?
  A. fleet   C. sturdy
  B. ponderous   D. faltering

____ 18. The speaker in Shakespeare's Sonnet 30 refers to his "old woes." What does he mean by *woes*?
  A. sighs   C. sorrows
  B. friends   D. loves

Essay

19. In "Women," Alice Walker describes the struggle of her mother's generation to gain an education for their children. Write an essay in which you describe the lesson that two of these poems can give to future generations. In your essay, briefly identify the theme, or overall message, of each poem. Support your discussion with details about the speaker, imagery, and mood of each poem. Then, explain which theme represents the most important lesson for future generations.

20. The form of a lyric poem contributes to the poem's overall meaning. For instance, the brief form of haiku requires a poet to use one or two images with maximum impact. By contrast, the sonnet form encourages a poet to develop ideas logically, using elaboration and contrast. To give unity to free verse, poets often use devices such as related images. Write an essay in which you compare and contrast the way form adds meaning in two of the poems in this group. Support your ideas with references to each poem's form and overall meaning.

21. **Thinking About the Big Question: How does communication change us?** Which poem in this collection caused you to think differently about something you took for granted before? Explain in a brief essay, supporting your ideas with specific references to the text.

Writing Workshop
Response to Literature

Prewriting: Narrowing Your Topic

Use the questions in the following chart to help you focus your response.

Question	Your Response:
What is your purpose?	
What types of details will you need?	
What examples from the literary work will support your ideas?	

Drafting: Providing Supporting Details

Use the following chart to record the evidence for every claim you make in your essay.

What claims do you make?	Quotations	Examples	Paraphrases
First:			
Second:			
Third:			
Fourth:			

© Pearson Education, Inc. All rights reserved.

Writing Workshop
Response to Literature: Integrating Grammar Skills

Revising Common Usage Problems

Words with similar meanings are often confused. Be careful to use the following words correctly in your writing.

- *Among*, a preposition, usually implies three or more.
- *Between*, also a preposition, is usually used only between two things.

Second prize was shared *among* five winners.
First prize was *between* Sondra and Paul.

- *Like*, a preposition, means "similar to" or "such as."
- *As, as if*, and *as though* are subordinating conjunctions that introduce clauses.

A champion *like* Sondra practices for hours every day.
Sondra performed her routine in under ten minutes, just *as* she planned.
Paul performs *as if* (or *as though*) he has already won first prize.

Identifying Correct Usage

A. DIRECTIONS: *Complete each sentence by circling the correct choice in parentheses.*

1. Carly was (between, among) the best sprinters in Orlando.
2. Sarah runs just (like, as) her sister Kate did.
3. The winner will probably be (between, among) Carly and Sarah.
4. I will probably be last (between, among) the runners.
5. You look (like, as if) you ran for hours.

Fixing Common Usage Problems

B. DIRECTIONS: *On the lines provided, rewrite these sentences with correct usage. If a sentence is correct as presented, write* correct.

1. We watched a tennis match among Sol and Roberto.

_____

2. Sol played like he needed a good nap.

_____

3. Roberto was like a tiger.

_____

4. He moved up to the net, just like he practiced.

_____

5. Between the three of them, who do you think will take home the trophy?

_____

© Pearson Education, Inc. All rights reserved.

Name _____ Date _____

Unit 4 Vocabulary Workshop—1
Connotation and Denotation

Sometimes it is tricky to use the exact word that connotes your exact meaning. Using a word with a negative connotation when you mean something positive can be disastrous!

DIRECTIONS: *The following conversation has gone bad because of words with unintended connotations. Circle those words and then replace them with words that have positive connotations. You can use a thesaurus to help you.*

© Pearson Education, Inc. All rights reserved.

Name _____ Date _____

Unit 4 Vocabulary Workshop—2
Connotation and Denotation

Sometimes it is difficult to tell whether a person means something in a positive or a negative way. That is why it is important to choose words carefully!

DIRECTIONS: *Are you getting a compliment, an insult, or something in between? Write your imagined response to each of the following sentences. The first has been done for you. Note how the connotation of one word in each sentence can change your response.*

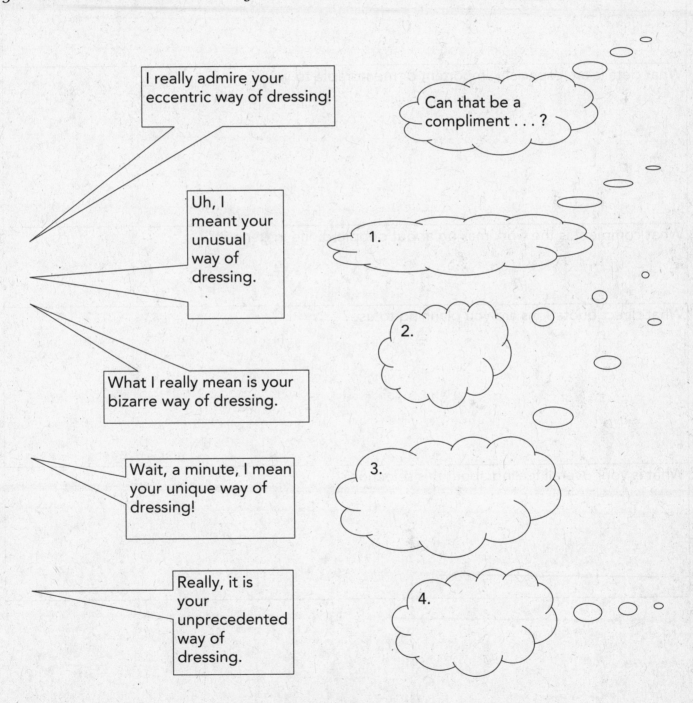

I really admire your eccentric way of dressing!

Can that be a compliment . . . ?

Uh, I meant your unusual way of dressing.

1.

2.

What I really mean is your bizarre way of dressing.

3.

Wait, a minute, I mean your unique way of dressing!

Really, it is your unprecedented way of dressing.

4.

© Pearson Education, Inc. All rights reserved.

Communications Workshop
Oral Interpretation of Literature

After choosing a selection, fill out the following chart. Use your notes to plan and organize your interpretation to the class.

Title of poem, story, or play: _____

What is the main idea of this selection?
What details are especially important or memorable to you?
What comment is the work making about people or life in general?
What direct quotations are you planning to use?
What is your overall feeling about this selection?

Unit 4: Poetry
Benchmark Test 8

Literary Analysis: Lyric Forms *Read the selection. Then, answer the questions that follow.*

1. Which of the following poetic forms has 14 lines?
   A. sonnet
   B. haiku
   C. free verse
   D. tanka

2. Which of the following describes the rhyme pattern of a free verse poem?
   A. unrhymed
   B. couplet
   C. iambic pentameter
   D. Irregular

Read the poem. Then, answer the question that follows.

> First autumn morning:
> the mirror I stare into
> shows my father's face.
>
> —Kijo Murakami

3. What is the form of this poem?
   A. sonnet
   B. free verse
   C. limerick
   D. haiku

Literary Analysis: Narrative Poetry

4. Which of the following characteristics is included in a narrative poem?
   A. a monologue and a setting
   B. plot and mood
   C. characters and stage directions
   D. a universal theme and an epic hero

5. In what way is narrative poetry like narrative prose?
   A. It concerns itself with the same topics.
   B. It has characters.
   C. It uses figurative language.
   D. It has the same literary elements.

© Pearson Education, Inc. All rights reserved.

6. What is a synonym for *mood* in a poem or other literary work?
   A. metaphors
   B. thoughtfulness
   C. atmosphere
   D. language

7. Which of these words might describe the mood of a narrative poem?
   A. difficult
   B. wonderful
   C. astonished
   D. lengthy

Literary Analysis: Rhyme

8. What kind of rhyme is being used in the following example?

   When Polly was in a bad mood,

   she found it very hard to be good.

   A. exact
   B. slant
   C. end
   D. internal

9. What kind of rhyme is being used in the following example?

   It is important to be polite,

   Even when you think you are right.

   A. exact
   B. slant
   C. end
   D. internal

10. What is meter as used in poetry?
    A. pattern of internal and external rhymes
    B. pattern of regular and irregular rhythms
    C. arrangement of exact and slant rhymes
    D. arrangement of stressed and unstressed syllables

© Pearson Education, Inc. All rights reserved.

Name _____ Date _____

Reading Skill: Paraphrasing *Read the poem. Then, answer the questions that follow.*

1 Let me not to the marriage of true minds
2 Admit impediments. Love is not love
3 Which alters when it alteration finds,
4 Or bends with the remover to remove.
5 O, no! It is an ever -fixed mark
6 That looks on tempests and is never shaken;
7 It is the star to every wandering bark,
8 Whose worth's unknown, although his height be taken.
9 Love's not Time's fool, though rosy lips and cheeks
10 Within his bending sickle's compass come;
11 Love alters not with his brief hours and weeks,
12 But bears it to even to the edge of doom.
13 If this be error, and upon me proved,
14 I never writ, nor no man ever loved.

—*Sonnet 116* by William Shakespeare

11. Which of the following is the best paraphrase of lines 2 and 3?
A. Love does not change when circumstances change.
B. Love does not last.
C. Marriage should be considered seriously.
D. Marriage does not alter people.

12. How does picturing the image in lines 5 and 6 help the reader?
A. The reader decides whether he or she agrees with the writer.
B. The reader works through the argument logically.
C. The reader pictures his or her own life.
D. The reader can understand the metaphor.

Read the poem. Then, answer the questions that follow.

1 Whose woods these are I think I know.
2 His house is in the village though;
3 He will not see me stopping here
4 To watch his woods fill up with snow.

5 My little horse must think it queer
6 To stop without a farmhouse near
7 Between the woods and frozen lake
8 The darkest evening of the year.

—from "Stopping by Woods on a Snowy
Evening" by Robert Frost

© Pearson Education, Inc. All rights reserved.

Name _____ Date _____

13. Which is the best paraphrase of the first line?
    A. I believe I know who owns these woods.   C. I don't care who owns these woods.
    B. I don't know who owns these woods.   D. I know who owns these woods.

14. Which of the following techniques can help the reader paraphrase a passage?
    A. predicting what will happen next   C. breaking down long sentences
    B. identifying synonyms and antonyms   D. using a dictionary

15. Which of the following sentences most clearly paraphrases the second stanza?
    A. My little horse must think it queer to stop without a farmhouse near between the woods and frozen lake the darkest evening of the year.
    B. My little horse must think it queer to stop without a farmhouse near. It's between the woods and frozen lake on the darkest evening of the year.
    C. My little horse must think it queer to stop. There's no farmhouse near. We're between the woods and frozen lake. It's the darkest evening of the year.
    D. My little horse must think it queer to stop at a farmhouse. We're between the woods and frozen lake on the darkest evening of the year.

Reading Informational Material: Paraphrase Main Idea

16. Which of the following Web sites would you use to paraphrase information about Robert Frost?
    A. www.poetry.com   C. www.robertfrost/mypoetry/aol.com
    B. www.frost/harvard.edu   D. www.ampoets/bob435.org

17. Which of the following sources would be the best to consult if you want to paraphrase a main idea on a topic?
    A. a student Web site   C. a chat room
    B. a professor's Web site   D. an online encyclopedia

18. Why is it important to paraphrase difficult informational text?
    A. Paraphrasing is not important.
    B. Paraphrasing is only important when reading a short story
    C. Paraphrasing difficult text is important because it helps promote understanding.
    D. Paraphrasing difficult text is important because it helps promote fluency.

Vocabulary: Prefixes and Suffixes

19. The words *predict, prevent,* and *precede* share the prefix *pre-*. What does *pre-* most likely mean?
    A. not   C. know ahead of time
    B. before   D. with

20. The prefix *im-* can mean both "in/into and not." What is the meaning of the word formed by adding *im-* to *-merse*?
    A. below the surface   C. very large
    B. not merciful   D. above the surface

21. In the following sentence, what does the word *impenetrable* mean?

The castle walls were four feet thick and heavily guarded: the confident king believed his fortress to be impenetrable.

A. not conquerable   C. not accessible

B. not flammable   D. not destructible

22. In the following sentence, what is the meaning of the word *bafflement*?

The toll collector had not witnessed such bafflement since the time a car had driven through his booth in reverse.

A. clarity   C. defiance

B. confusion   D. bravery

23. The words *confusion*, *elation*, and *indecision* share the suffix *-ion*. What does *-ion* most likely mean?

A. full of   C. quality

B. without   D. condition

24. In the following sentence, what does the word *oblivion* mean?

Ted accidentally dropped his watch overboard and watched helplessly as it disappeared into oblivion.

A. the unknown   C. the sea

B. the depths   D. obscurity

Grammar

25. Which is a reason a writer would add an appositive phrase to a sentence?

A. to qualify a verb

B. to add information to a noun or pronoun

C. to add an adjective phrase to a noun

D. to replace a noun or pronoun

26. Which of the following sentences contains an appositive phrase that is used correctly?

A. Although it was night, we decided to go for a walk.

B. Mr. Smith, our science teacher, also coached baseball.

C. We decided to go for a long, calming walk.

D. Gerry was a very hard worker and a good student.

27. Identify the infinitive in the following sentence:

I wanted to go to that movie.

A. wanted   C. to that

B. to go   D. movie

© Pearson Education, Inc. All rights reserved.

Name _____ Date _____

28. In which sentence does the infinitive phrase act as a noun?
   A. Jean likes to speak her mind.
   B. I hate to go to the supermarket.
   C. To play the piano requires a lot of practice.
   D. I love to swim in the ocean.

29. Why is the word *between* in the following sentence used incorrectly?

   We could never choose between the many vacation destinations.

   A. The word *between* should be used with only two elements.
   B. The word *between* should be replaced with *from.*
   C. The word *between* should be used as a preposition.
   D. The word *between* should never have a direct object.

30. Why is the word *like* used incorrectly in the following sentence?

   It looks like we are in for a long, boring lecture.

   A. The word *like* should be used only as a verb, meaning "enjoy."
   B. The word *like* should never be used as a preposition.
   C. The word *like* should be used only a preposition.
   D. The word *like* is a conjunction that introduces a clause.

Spelling: Affixes

31. What is the correct spelling of the word *pronounce* when the suffix *-able* is added?
   A. pronounseable   C. pronouncable
   B. pronounceable   D. pronounceble

32. Which of the following words is spelled incorrectly?
   A. consumtion   C. reunify
   B. maintenance   D. unbearable

33. Which of the following words has both a prefix and a suffix?
   A. antebellum   C. laziness
   B. counteracting   D. picnicked

ESSAY

34. Describe your bedroom at its messiest. Include exact details and organize them in a way that makes sense, for example from top to bottom or from left to right.

35. Poetry is a written form that includes not only description but also emotion. What words might a poet use to express an emotion about the first day of summer?

36. Imagine that you go around a corner and see something absolutely amazing. What is it? Write a poem that uses exact end rhyme to describe what you see.

Vocabulary in Context 4—Part 1

Identify the answer choice that best completes the statement.

1. She was very lively and had a _____ personality.
   A. heartily
   B. vivacious
   C. ordinary
   D. precise

2. I measured the powdered drink, incorrectly, and it was too _____ to drink.
   A. watery
   B. pestilence
   C. bitterly
   D. infectious

3. I know she was arrested, but I do not know what her _____ was supposed to be.
   A. peril
   B. defect
   C. vengeance
   D. offense

4. The next time you have a cough and cold, I may have a better _____ for you.
   A. remedy
   B. fate
   C. prevent
   D. contagion

5. The wedding cake was so beautifully decorated that the bride declared, "It is _____!"
   A. envious
   B. lamentable
   C. perfection
   D. satisfaction

6. She takes good care of her sick mother and sister and has a real _____ to them.
   A. devotion
   B. predicament
   C. disobedient
   D. demonstrative

7. The circus wagon was brightly painted, but the decorations were overdone and _____.
   A. garish
   B. merrily
   C. unsavory
   D. unruly

© Pearson Education, Inc. All rights reserved.

8. An employer wants to know if the company can depend on you and if you are_____ .
   A. patience
   B. boundless
   C. aptitude
   D. reliable

9. After the bank robbery, the police questioned everyone and used that information to make other_____ .
   A. resolution
   B. inquiries
   C. authority
   D. transcription

10. When you graduate from high school, what course do you_____ to follow next?
    A. achieve
    B. intend
    C. depart
    D. inevitable

11. When I was a wrestler last year, he was always my main_____ .
    A. adversary
    B. alliance
    C. assiduous
    D. allotment

12. I intend to buy a sports car and have come to see what is_____ .
    A. disposition
    B. enthralled
    C. convenient
    D. available

13. We did not know where to eat in the city, but this restaurant was_____ to us by a friend.
    A. unaccustomed
    B. assurance
    C. recommended
    D. banished

14. The townsfolk had just finished cleaning up after the great storm when another_____ befell them.
    A. intrusion
    B. calamity
    C. interpretation
    D. rebellious

Unit 4 Resources: Poetry
© Pearson Education, Inc. All rights reserved.
234

15. The lion roared loudly and scratched the dirt_____ .
    A. violently
    B. abruptly
    C. cowardly
    D. obviously

16. The day that my car broke down, I inherited ten thousand dollars; I guess it was_____ !
    A. characteristic
    B. ventured
    C. fate
    D. conclusion

17. The florist arranged the flowers in a huge metal_____ .
    A. ornament
    B. urn
    C. tombstone
    D. sheath

18. It looks as if it will be an early winter, from all_____ .
    A. discrimination
    B. hoaxes
    C. indications
    D. misgivings

19. Will you permit me to treat you to a_____ this afternoon?
    A. banqueting
    B. luncheon`
    C. marketplace
    D. ruse

20. When a deer ran in front of our car, we quickly_____ to avoid hitting it.
    A. protruded
    B. asserted
    C. lessened
    D. swerved

Name _____ Date _____

Diagnostic Tests and Vocabulary in Context
Use and Interpretation

The Diagnostic Tests and Vocabulary in Context were developed to assist teachers in making the most appropriate assignment of *Prentice Hall Literature* program selections to students. The purpose of these assessments is to indicate the degree of difficulty that students are likely to have in reading/comprehending the selections presented in the *following* unit of instruction. Tests are provided at six separate times in each in each grade level—a *Diagnostic Test* (to be used prior to beginning the year's instruction) and a *Vocabulary in Context,* the final segment of the Benchmark Test appearing at the end of each of the first five units of instruction. Note that the tests are intended for use not as summative assessments for the prior unit, but as guidance for assigning literature selections in the upcoming unit of instruction.

The structure of all Diagnostic Tests and Vocabulary in Context in this series is the same. All test items are four-option, multiple-choice items. The format is established to assess a student's ability to construct sufficient meaning from the context sentence to choose the only provided word that fits both the semantics (meaning) and syntax (structure) of the context sentence. All words in the context sentences are chosen to be "below-level" words that students reading at this grade level should know. All answer choices fit *either* the meaning or structure of the context sentence, but only the correct choice fits *both* semantics and syntax. All answer choices—both correct answers and incorrect options—are key words chosen from specifically taught words that will occur in the subsequent unit of program instruction. This careful restriction of the assessed words permits a sound diagnosis of students' current reading achievement and prediction of the most appropriate level of readings to assign in the upcoming unit of instruction.

The assessment of vocabulary in context skill has consistently been shown in reading research studies to correlate very highly with "reading comprehension." This is not surprising as the format essentially assesses comprehension, albeit in sentence-length "chunks." Decades of research demonstrate that vocabulary assessment provides a strong, reliable prediction of comprehension achievement— the purpose of these tests. Further, because this format demands very little testing time, these diagnoses can be made efficiently, permitting teachers to move forward with critical instructional tasks rather than devoting excessive time to assessment.

It is important to stress that while the Diagnostic and Vocabulary in Context were carefully developed and will yield sound assignment decisions, they were designed to *reinforce*, not supplant, teacher judgment as to the most appropriate instructional placement for individual students. Teacher judgment should always prevail in making placement—or indeed other important instructional—decisions concerning students.

© Pearson Education, Inc. All rights reserved.

Diagnostic Tests and Vocabulary in Context
Branching Suggestions

These tests are designed to provide maximum flexibility for teachers. Your *Unit Resources* books contain the 40-question **Diagnostic Test** and 20-question **Vocabulary in Context** tests. At *PHLitOnline,* you can access the Diagnostic Test and complete 40-question Vocabulary in Context tests. Procedures for administering the tests are described below. Choose the procedure based on the time you wish to devote to the activity and your comfort with the assignment decisions relative to the individual students. Remember that your judgment of a student's reading level should always take precedence over the results of a single written test.

Feel free to use different procedures at different times of the year. For example, for early units, you may wish to be more confident in the assignments you make—thus, using the "two-stage" process below. Later, you may choose the quicker diagnosis, confirming the results with your observations of the students' performance built up throughout the year.

The **Diagnostic Test** is composed of a single 40-item assessment. Based on the results of this assessment, make the following assignment of students to the reading selections in Unit 1:

Diagnostic Test Score	Selection to Use
If the student's score is 0–25	more accessible
If the student's score is 26–40	more challenging

Outlined below are the three basic options for administering **Vocabulary in Context** and basing selection assignments on the results of these assessments.

1. For a one-stage, quicker diagnosis using the *20-item* test in the *Unit Resources:*

Vocabulary in Context Test Score	Selection to Use
If the student's score is 0–13	more accessible
If the student's score is 14–20	more challenging

2. If you wish to confirm your assignment decisions with a *two-stage* diagnosis:

Stage 1: Administer the 20-item test in the *Unit Resources*	
Vocabulary in Context Test Score	Selection to Use
If the student's score is 0–9	more accessible
If the student's score is 10–15	(Go to Stage 2.)
If the student's score is 16–20	more challenging

Stage 2: Administer items 21–40 from *PHLitOnline*	
Vocabulary in Context Test Score	Selection to Use
If the student's score is 0–12	more accessible
If the student's score is 13–20	more challenging

3. If you base your assignment decisions on the full 40-item **Vocabulary in Context** from *PHLitOnline:*

Vocabulary in Context Test Score	Selection to Use
If the student's score is 0–25	more accessible
If the student's score is 26–40	more challenging

© Pearson Education, Inc. All rights reserved.

Name _____ Date _____

Grade 9—Benchmark Test 7
Interpretation Guide

For remediation of specific skills, you may assign students the relevant Reading Kit Practice and Assess pages indicated in the far-right column of this chart. You will find rubrics for evaluating writing samples in the last section of your Professional Development Guidebook.

Skill Objective	Test Items	Number Correct	Reading Kit
Literary Analysis			
Figurative language	1, 2, 3, 4		pp. 152, 153
Sound Devices	5, 6, 7, 8		pp. 154, 155
Imagery	9, 10		pp. 156, 157
Reading Skill			
Read Fluently	11, 12, 13, 14, 15		pp. 158, 159
Follow Technical Directions	16, 17, 18		pp. 160, 161
Vocabulary			
Roots and Prefixes *-fer-, -vert-, ana-, mono-*	19, 20, 21, 22, 23, 24		pp. 162, 163
Grammar			
Prepositions and Objects of Prepositions	25, 26, 27		pp. 164, 165
Prepositional Phrases	28, 29, 30		pp. 166, 167
Vary Sentences With Phrases	31, 32, 33		pp. 168, 169
Writing			
Description of a Scene	34	Use rubric	pp. 170, 171
Editorial	35	Use rubric	pp. 172, 173
Descriptive Essay	36	Use rubric	pp. 174, 175

Name _____ Date _____

Grade 9—Benchmark Test 8
Interpretation Guide

For remediation of specific skills, you may assign students the relevant Reading Kit Practice and Assess pages indicated in the far-right column of this chart. You will find rubrics for evaluating writing samples in the last section of your Professional Development Guidebook.

Skill Objective	Test Items	Number Correct	Reading Kit
Literary Analysis			
Lyric Poetry	1, 2, 3		pp. 180, 181
Narrative Poetry	4, 5, 6, 7		pp. 176, 177
Rhyme	13, 14, 15		pp. 178, 179
Reading Skill			
Paraphrase	8, 9, 10, 11, 12		pp. 182, 183
Paraphrase Main Idea	16, 17, 18		pp. 184, 185
Vocabulary			
Prefixes and Suffixes *pre-, im-, -ion, -ment*	19, 20, 21, 22, 23, 24		pp. 186, 187
Grammar			
Appositive Phrases	25, 26		pp. 188, 189
Infinitives and Infinitive phrases	27, 28		pp. 190, 191
Common Usage problems	29, 30		pp. 192, 193
Spelling			
Words With Affixes	31, 32, 33		pp. 194, 195
Writing			
Description	34	Use rubric	pp. 196, 197
Poem	35	Use rubric	pp. 198, 199
Poem with Rhyme	36	Use rubric	pp. 200, 201

© Pearson Education, Inc. All rights reserved.

ANSWERS

Big Question Vocabulary—1, p. 1

Sample Answer

Hi Peter. This is Micah. I am calling because there is something that I want to **discuss** with you. I really value our **relationship** and I know that you always have **empathy** for me when I am upset. The other day, you did not even stop to say hello when you passed by me. My **interpretation** of this is that you are angry. If you are, please tell me why so we can reach a **resolution**.

Big Question Vocabulary—2, p. 2

Sample Answers

1. This story was **communicated** to me by radio.
2. I was **informed** of a hurricane in New Orleans that caused death and destruction.
3. I do not **understand** why the people were not evacuated sooner.
4. My **comprehension** would be improved by reading a more detailed account in the newspaper.
5. I can **respond** to this story by providing donations to a local charity that is helping hurricane victims.

Big Question Vocabulary—3, p. 3

Sample Answers

Douglas: What is the **meaning** of this strike? Please **illuminate** me.

Striker: The newspaper staff has not had a raise in seven years. We need more money.

Douglas: I wasn't **aware** of that! I am glad to have this **exchange** with you.

Striker: Will you **react** to your new knowledge by signing my petition?

The Poetry of Pat Mora

Vocabulary Warm-up Exercises, p. 8

A.
1. sighs
2. pale
3. thorns
4. scratches
5. tangles
6. retreat

B. Sample Answers
1. The farmer chasing the rabbit might make the rabbit *scurry* out of the farmer's vegetable garden.
2. Weather that is likely to accompany *lightning* might be cold temperatures, wind, and rain.
3. *Gusts* of wind would blow the laundry on a clothesline around; they might also get the laundry dirty if they raised dust and dirt in the area.
4. A desert is more likely to be a *tumbleweed* area because tumbleweeds must dry out before they break from their roots.

5. No, small children cannot pick up *boulders* because the large rocks are too heavy for them.
6. Anna *tosses* her hair because she is flirting with Billy, and she wants him to notice how pretty her hair is.

Reading Warm-up A, p. 9

Sample Answers

1. (with dismay); Mike *sighs* to show that he feels put-upon when his mother asks him to clean his room.
2. Marsha's hair; *Tangles* are snarls.
3. (dark); *Pale* means "of a whitish or grayish color."
4. at the back door; Michelle *scratches* her name in the dirt with a stick.
5. grab at their clothes; People working in rose gardens protect themselves from *thorns* by wearing leather gloves.
6. (to the safety of the cellar); I like to *retreat* sometimes to a secluded area of the beach near my home.

Reading Warm-up B, p. 10

Sample Answers

1. gets up close; A mouse might *scurry* away if a cat were chasing it.
2. (jagged bolts); The *lightning* struck about a mile from the water tower.
3. forming into whirlwinds; *Gusts* of wind might cause waves in the water on a lake.
4. (debris); No, I am not likely to find *tumbleweed* debris in a big city because tumbleweeds grow wild in the desert.
5. as if they were pebbles; The difference between *boulders* and pebbles is in their size: Boulders are very large, and pebbles are very small.
6. (through the air); Phyllis *tosses* the ball to James.

Pat Mora

Listening and Viewing, p. 11

Sample Answers

Segment 1. Mora believes it is important to use one's native language because it is special and should be honored. Mora uses both English and Spanish because she is of Mexican American heritage and likes to share her two cultures with her readers.

Segment 2. The poem describes the wildness of a dust storm in the desert. It is written in the shape of a tornado—the lines of the poem placed chaotically on the page. Students may suggest that the poem's shape draws the reader into the storm and symbolizes the chaos a tornado causes.

Segment 3. She listens intently to the sounds in the poem, rethinks ideas, and tries to transform her first draft into the best poem possible. Students may suggest that revising a first draft improves the final product by helping them to express ideas more clearly and—in a poem—more creatively.

Segment 4. If you view writing as exploring, you will play with words and not tense up because you know that you do not have to keep what you initially write. Students may feel that exploring lets them be creative and does not box them in.

Learning About Poetry, p. 12

1. A; 2. C; 3. A; 4. B; 5. C

The Poetry of Pat Mora

Model Selection: Poetry, p. 13

Sample Answers

1. A. personification
   B. sight, hearing, and touch
2. A. spews/spooks; women/windows/when; skirt/starts/spin
   B. gusts/thunder; spooks/to; skirt/its/spin
3. A. "house smelled like/rose powder"; "formal/as your father"
   B. The father is called a judge because he is strict. He insists that Spanish be spoken and that the children use proper manners. He is "without a courtroom" because he is an ordinary husband and father.

Open-Book Test, p. 14

Short Answer

1. It is a narrative poem, because narrative poems tell stories in verse.
   Difficulty: *Average* **Objective:** *Literary Analysis*
2. The poet is using onomatopoeia, or the use of a word whose sound imitates its meaning.
   Difficulty: *Average* **Objective:** *Literary Analysis*
3. The line contains the onomatopoeia *babbling brook*, a metaphor comparing the brook to a child, and the personification of the brook as a child.
   Difficulty: *Challenging* **Objective:** *Literary Analysis*
4. a stanza
   Difficulty: *Easy* **Objective:** *Literary Analysis*
5. They sing lullabies to calm their children during a howling desert storm.
   Difficulty: *Average* **Objective:** *Interpretation*
6. Mora repeats the initial consonant /s/ in the words *sound, spins, sleep, sand, stinging, skin,* and *stars.*
   Difficulty: *Average* **Objective:** *Literary Analysis*
7. Possible answer: "Uncoiling" suggests a spinning release of energy, like that of a desert dust storm.
   Difficulty: *Challenging* **Objective:** *Interpretation*
8. Her mother found public speaking undoable as a child. The poet concludes that her mother finally "spoke up" through the voices of her children.
   Difficulty: *Easy* **Objective:** *Interpretation*
9. The next generation, taught to speak up, does speak up, which is a courageous and spirited act.
   Difficulty: *Average* **Objective:** *Vocabulary*

10. Sample answer: "Uncoiling": She sighs clouds; "A Voice": Your breath moves . . . like the wind moves through the trees.
    These sounds are similar because both are soft and gentle.
    Difficulty: *Average* **Objective:** *Literary Analysis*

Essay

11. In "Uncoiling," Mora compares the desert storm to a powerful woman. The desert tosses her long hair, sighs and closes her eyes, throws back her head, howls and roars, and spins herself to sleep with sand stinging her ankles.
    Difficulty: *Easy* **Objective:** *Essay*
12. Students may respond that both the poet's mother in "A Voice" and the desert storm "woman" in "Uncoiling" find and use their voices, but that the storm's "voice" is a natural, spontaneous phenomenon, while the poet's mother's voice is a belief or value that is ultimately expressed through her children.
    Difficulty: *Average* **Objective:** *Essay*
13. Students who choose "Uncoiling" may say that the "journey" of that poem is focused mainly on the "scenery" of the desert storm, but that it is a rapid and intense journey that leads to the storm's own exhaustion. Students who choose "A Voice" may say that the poem's journey meanders through the past, finally arriving at a moment of homage and gratitude to the poet's mother.
    Difficulty: *Challenging* **Objective:** *Essay*
14. Students may respond that English changed the poet's mother in both positive and negative ways: On one hand, it allowed her to live in America with greater ease and gave her a sense of power in conflicts; but on the other hand, she was uncomfortable using it at home with her father and in public with strangers. Students may also respond that ultimately, the English language became a positive source of expression and independence for later generations.
    Difficulty: *Average* **Objective:** *Essay*

Oral Response

15. Oral responses should be clear, well organized, and well supported by appropriate examples from the selections.
    Difficulty: *Average* **Objective:** *Oral Interpretation*

Selection Test A, p. 17

Learning About Poetry

1. **ANS:** C   **DIF:** Easy   **OBJ:** Literary Analysis
2. **ANS:** B   **DIF:** Easy   **OBJ:** Literary Analysis
3. **ANS:** D   **DIF:** Easy   **OBJ:** Literary Analysis
4. **ANS:** C   **DIF:** Easy   **OBJ:** Literary Analysis
5. **ANS:** C   **DIF:** Easy   **OBJ:** Literary Analysis

Critical Reading

6. ANS: B   DIF: Easy   OBJ: Literary Analysis
7. ANS: A   DIF: Easy   OBJ: Literary Analysis
8. ANS: B   DIF: Easy   OBJ: Comprehension
9. ANS: D   DIF: Easy   OBJ: Literary Analysis
10. ANS: B   DIF: Easy   OBJ: Interpretation
11. ANS: C   DIF: Easy   OBJ: Comprehension
12. ANS: B   DIF: Easy   OBJ: Literary Analysis
13. ANS: A   DIF: Easy   OBJ: Interpretation
14. ANS: C   DIF: Easy   OBJ: Interpretation
15. ANS: C   DIF: Easy   OBJ: Literary Analysis

Essay

16. Students should include discussion and evaluation of two images. Evaluate students' essays for clarity, coherence, and specific references to the text.

    Difficulty: *Easy*

    Objective: *Essay*

17. Students should point out that Mora's theme in "Uncoiling" is the power of nature and the relative powerlessness of humans before the awesome storm. In "A Voice," the speaker celebrates the achievements and example of Mom, whose determination to "do the undoable" has served as an inspiring example for her four children. Any reasonable theme statement should be accepted if students support it adequately with evidence from the poem.

    Difficulty: *Easy*

    Objective: *Essay*

18. Students may respond that English changed the poet's mother in both good and bad ways. On one hand, it allowed her to live in America with greater ease and gave her a sense of power in conflicts. On the other hand, speaking English made the mother uncomfortable when she used it at home with her father and in public with strangers. Students may also say that ultimately, the English language became a positive source of expression and independence for the mother's four children.

    Difficulty: *Average*

    Objective: *Essay*

Selection Test B, p. 20

Learning About Poetry

1. ANS: D   DIF: Average   OBJ: Literary Analysis
2. ANS: C   DIF: Average   OBJ: Literary Analysis
3. ANS: C   DIF: Average   OBJ: Literary Analysis
4. ANS: B   DIF: Challenging   OBJ: Literary Analysis
5. ANS: A   DIF: Average   OBJ: Literary Analysis
6. ANS: B   DIF: Average   OBJ: Literary Analysis
7. ANS: B   DIF: Challenging   OBJ: Literary Analysis

Critical Reading

8. ANS: C   DIF: Average   OBJ: Comprehension
9. ANS: A   DIF: Average   OBJ: Literary Analysis
10. ANS: C   DIF: Average   OBJ: Interpretation
11. ANS: D   DIF: Challenging   OBJ: Comprehension
12. ANS: D   DIF: Average   OBJ: Interpretation
13. ANS: B   DIF: Challenging   OBJ: Interpretation
14. ANS: A   DIF: Average   OBJ: Comprehension
15. ANS: B   DIF: Average   OBJ: Literary Analysis
16. ANS: C   DIF: Average   OBJ: Interpretation
17. ANS: D   DIF: Average   OBJ: Literary Analysis
18. ANS: A   DIF: Average   OBJ: Interpretation
19. ANS: A   DIF: Average   OBJ: Interpretation

Essay

20. Students' essays should discuss several images and identify the senses to which the images appeal. Students should also evaluate, in general, the effectiveness of Mora's use of imagery in the poem they have chosen.

    Difficulty: *Average*

    Objective: *Essay*

21. Students should identify some of the sound effects Mora uses in the poems. For instance, students might cite the lurching, powerful rhythm in "Uncoiling." In the same poem, the phrase "howling/leaves off trees" illustrates assonance. In "A Voice," alliteration is exemplified in "You liked winning with words." Evaluate students' essays for clarity and coherence.

    Difficulty: *Average*

    Objective: *Essay*

22. You may choose to allow your students to use their books for this essay. Students should discuss specific examples of the three types of figurative language. They should also evaluate the effectiveness of each example. For instance, students should recognize that personification is a core element of "Uncoiling," in which the storm is compared to a frenzied, fearsome woman. Both poems contain many similes and metaphors. Evaluate students' essays for clarity, coherence, and the appropriate use of examples from the selections.

    Difficulty: *Challenging*

    Objective: *Essay*

23. Students may respond that English changed the poet's mother in both positive and negative ways: On one hand, it allowed her to live in America with greater ease and gave her a sense of power in conflicts; but on the other hand, she was uncomfortable using it at home with her father and in public with strangers. Students may also respond that ultimately, the English language

became a positive source of expression and independence for later generations.

Difficulty: *Average*
Objective: *Essay*

Poetry Collection: Langston Hughes, William Wordsworth, Gabriela Mistral, Jean de Sponde

Vocabulary Warm-up Exercises, p. 24

A.
1. soundlessly
2. sparkling
3. sprightly
4. fast
5. battered
6. deferred

B. Sample Answers
1. T; An *academic* scholarship has to do with education, so it is more likely to go to a good student.
2. F; *Inward* thoughts are the private thoughts in a person's mind, and a person is not likely to share them freely with strangers.
3. T; An *immovable* object is impossible to move, so it might stay permanently in one place.
4. T; A *theory* is an idea about something, but if it is not proven, it might not be true. Believing something that might not be true could be risky.
5. F; Someone enjoying *solitude* is alone, so the person would not be at a party with other people.
6. T; The *margin* of a lake is its edge, and the edge of a lake is sometimes a beach.

Reading Warm-up A, p. 25

Sample Answers
1. (avoided); The problem of writing a poem is *deferred* by Molly, who puts off or delays writing it.
2. (firm and secure); miles of granite extending to the earth's core
3. (silence); *Loudly* is an antonym for *soundlessly*.
4. like generously sprinkled diamonds; *Shining* is a synonym for *sparkling*.
5. (lively); attitude of the ballet dancers her mother loved
6. (knocked down); The *battered* tree is on the ground, probably with limbs broken and bark fallen off.

Reading Warm-up B, p. 26

Sample Answers
1. (thinkers); Academic thinkers are interested in studying the reasons behind things, while practical researchers look for ways to do things.
2. (edge); Standing on the *margin* of the land above a river would mean standing on the edge of a cliff, looking far down on the water below.
3. being alone; separated from the rest of the world; Nature is a good place to find *solitude* because it is generally quiet and not filled with people.

4. (idea); A *theory* is not the same as a fact because it is an idea someone has about the facts.
5. (inner); *Inward* resolve is the commitment that a person has inside. Outward success involves things outside the person such as a good experiment or praise from other people.
6. (determined); *Unchanging* is a synonym for *immovable*.

Writing About the Big Question, p. 27

A.
1. communication, comprehension
2. empathy, understanding
3. meaning
4. discuss
5. aware

B. Sample Answers
1. I did not know the person's native language; I had an entirely different viewpoint.
2. I became **aware** that my classmate Ron had a totally different opinion about the election of class officers. Afterward, I was able to **discuss** our disagreements calmly.

C. Sample Answer

When the speaker of a poem asks the audience to respond to a question, the reader is encouraged to think about his or her own past experiences. This often helps the reader connect with the poem. Asking yourself how you would respond to the speaker's question creates a link. This helps you understand the poem's theme or overall message.

Literary Analysis: Figurative Language, p. 28

Sample Answers
1. simile—The "smell" [of a dream deferred] is compared to the stink of rotten meat using the word *like*.
2. metaphor—The speaker compares life to a broken-winged bird without using *like* or any other comparative word.
3. personification—The daffodils are spoken of as if they are human; they have "sprightly heads" and are dancing.
4. metaphor—Memory is directly compared to an "inward eye" without using *like* or any other comparative word.
5. personification—The wind is spoken of as if it were human, as a wanderer and as loving.
6. paradox—The lines express an apparent contradiction.

Reading: Read Fluently, p. 29

1. Major pauses at the end of lines 2 and 4; minor pause at the end of line 3; no pause at all at the end of line 1
2. Minor pauses after *life, idea,* and *you;* major pauses after *all* and *dear*
3. No pause at all after *they* and *thought*

Vocabulary Builder, p. 30

A. 1. A; 2. B 3. B; 4. A
B. Sample Answers
1. No, because people at a lively party would probably not be thoughtful.

Unit 4 Resources: Poetry

2. You would not be happy because you would have to wait some time to be paid for work you had already completed.

3. No, it would not, since a *paradoxical* statement would involve an apparent contradiction.

4. No, it will not heal quickly, since *fester* means "to cause the formation of pus in," as with a sore.

C. 1. B; 2. D; 3. A; 4. C

Enrichment: Nature in Art, p. 31

A. Sample Answers

1. Students might list the comparison of the daffodils to the stars; the descriptions of their movements in the breeze, which is like dancing; and the descriptions of their position by the lake. Students might also list the descriptions of the lake and its waves.

2. Students are likely to say that Wordsworth expresses his fascination with nature. He seems to derive much comfort and joy from his observations of the natural world. Students might say that his descriptions of nature are inviting and create a new appreciation for nature in them.

B. Students should choose three works of art that express a variety of attitudes toward and perspectives on nature. Students who complete the assignment successfully should be able to describe each work in considerable detail and should interpret the attitudes toward nature and emotions that the work suggests. Students can work from pictures of works of art in art books, prints, photographs, or actual pieces of fine art.

Open-Book Test, p. 32

Short Answer

1. A dream deferred is a dream that is postponed, or put off until another time, because it is not yet possible.
Difficulty: *Average*   **Objective:** *Vocabulary*

2. Sample answer: "Does it dry up / like a raisin in the sun?" A dream that is not followed or pursued may lose its power and shape, just as a grape does when it becomes a raisin.
Difficulty: *Average*   **Objective:** *Literary Analysis*

3. Sample answer: "Hold fast to dreams" is an encouraging or hopeful piece of advice, but the images of the "broken-winged bird" and "barren field / Frozen with snow" create a hopeless mood.
Difficulty: *Challenging*   **Objective:** *Interpretation*

4. Sample answer: Life is a broken-winged bird. Life cannot move forward and cannot reach its full potential.
Difficulty: *Challenging*   **Objective:** *Literary Analysis*

5. One sentence
Difficulty: *Average*   **Objective:** *Reading*

6. Sample answer: He is lonely; he sees the daffodils and feels joyful; he is pensive in solitude; he remembers the daffodils and feels pleasure.
Joyful, because the sight and the memory of the daffodils bring the speaker joy.
Difficulty: *Average*   **Objective:** *Interpretation*

7. Sample answers: The sea rocks her waves as a human parent might rock a child. The wind wanders through fields as a nighttime wanderer might.
Difficulty: *Easy*   **Objective:** *Literary Analysis*

8. Sample response: Gabriela Mistral might mean that the sea is like a goddess and/or that the sea is beautiful or awesome.
Difficulty: *Average*   **Objective:** *Interpretation*

9. The lines are paradoxical because one would have to be standing *on* the world in order to move the world—which is impossible, except in a metaphorical sense relating to the superhuman feelings associated with love.
Difficulty: *Challenging*   **Objective:** *Literary Analysis*

10. Sample answer: A lever is like love because it makes a person feel strong and invincible.
Difficulty: *Easy*   **Objective:** *Interpretation*

Essay

11. Students should explain why they chose the poem about which they are writing. Their essays should include quotations from the chosen poem. Evaluate students' essays for clarity and coherence.
Difficulty: *Easy*   **Objective:** *Essay*

12. For "Dream Deferred," students should identify the similes and make connections between the vivid images of decay and neglect and the speaker's implied warning in the final line. Students' analysis of "Dreams" should identify the two metaphors for life and explore the emotional weight of those images. Discussion of "I Wandered Lonely as a Cloud" should note the ways in which Wordsworth personifies the daffodils and uses metaphors in the final stanza. Students should focus on personification in an analysis of "Rocking." Discussion of "Sonnet on Love XIII" should note the poet's use of paradox, especially in lines 1–2 and 10–12.
Difficulty: *Average*   **Objective:** *Essay*

13. Students should understand that part of the poem deals with the speaker's experience in the field with the daffodils and part of it deals with the speaker's memory of the daffodils and the effect they have on him. In line 21, "they" refers to the daffodils. The speaker's "inward eye" is his visual memory. In the final stanza, the speaker remembers the daffodils and realizes that he can always summon the beauty of the daffodils and feel the joy of his experience again. To the speaker, the daffodils represent the joy and beauty that can be found in nature.
Difficulty: *Challenging*   **Objective:** *Essay*

14. Students may say that both "Dreams Deferred" and "Dreams" are advising readers to pursue their dreams rather than let them wither; that "I Wandered Lonely as a Cloud" is advising readers to notice and treasure nature's gifts of beauty; that "Rocking" is advising readers to treat loved ones gently; and that "Sonnets on Love XIII" advises readers to appreciate and strengthen the bonds of love they feel.
Difficulty: *Average*   **Objective:** *Essay*

Oral Response

15. Oral responses should be clear, well organized, and well supported by appropriate examples from the selections.
   Difficulty: *Average*   **Objective:** *Oral Interpretation*

Selection Test A, p. 35

Critical Reading

1. **ANS:** A	**DIF:** Easy	**OBJ:** Literary Analysis
2. **ANS:** C	**DIF:** Easy	**OBJ:** Comprehension
3. **ANS:** B	**DIF:** Easy	**OBJ:** Comprehension
4. **ANS:** B	**DIF:** Easy	**OBJ:** Interpretation
5. **ANS:** C	**DIF:** Easy	**OBJ:** Literary Analysis
6. **ANS:** B	**DIF:** Easy	**OBJ:** Interpretation
7. **ANS:** D	**DIF:** Easy	**OBJ:** Interpretation
8. **ANS:** B	**DIF:** Easy	**OBJ:** Comprehension
9. **ANS:** A	**DIF:** Easy	**OBJ:** Interpretation
10. **ANS:** D	**DIF:** Easy	**OBJ:** Reading
11. **ANS:** C	**DIF:** Easy	**OBJ:** Comprehension
12. **ANS:** D	**DIF:** Easy	**OBJ:** Literary Analysis

Vocabulary and Grammar

13. **ANS:** D	**DIF:** Easy	**OBJ:** Vocabulary
14. **ANS:** C	**DIF:** Easy	**OBJ:** Grammar

Essay

15. Students should explain why they chose the poem they are writing about. Their essays should also include a discussion of the poem's figures of speech. Evaluate students' essays for clarity and coherence.
   Difficulty: *Easy*
   Objective: *Essay*

16. In their essays, students should explain why they chose the poem and discuss all or most of the following elements: sound effects, imagery, figurative language, tone, and pauses. Evaluate students' essays for clarity and coherence and for specific references to the text. You may choose to have your students answer this question as an open-book essay.
   Difficulty: *Easy*
   Objective: *Essay*

17. Students may say that "Dreams Deferred" and "Dreams" advise readers to pursue their dreams rather than let them wither; "I Wandered . . ." advises readers to notice and treasure nature's gifts of beauty; "Rocking" advises readers to treat loved ones gently; and "Sonnets on Love XIII" advises readers to appreciate and strengthen the bonds of love they feel.
   Difficulty: *Average*
   Objective: *Essay*

Selection Test B, p. 38

Critical Reading

1. **ANS:** D	**DIF:** Average	**OBJ:** Interpretation
2. **ANS:** C	**DIF:** Average	**OBJ:** Literary Analysis
3. **ANS:** D	**DIF:** Average	**OBJ:** Literary Analysis
4. **ANS:** D	**DIF:** Average	**OBJ:** Interpretation
5. **ANS:** C	**DIF:** Average	**OBJ:** Comprehension
6. **ANS:** D	**DIF:** Average	**OBJ:** Interpretation
7. **ANS:** C	**DIF:** Average	**OBJ:** Interpretation
8. **ANS:** B	**DIF:** Average	**OBJ:** Reading
9. **ANS:** C	**DIF:** Average	**OBJ:** Literary Analysis
10. **ANS:** C	**DIF:** Average	**OBJ:** Interpretation
11. **ANS:** C	**DIF:** Average	**OBJ:** Literary Analysis
12. **ANS:** D	**DIF:** Challenging	**OBJ:** Literary Analysis
13. **ANS:** D	**DIF:** Average	**OBJ:** Interpretation

Vocabulary and Grammar

14. **ANS:** B	**DIF:** Average	**OBJ:** Vocabulary
15. **ANS:** C	**DIF:** Average	**OBJ:** Vocabulary
16. **ANS:** C	**DIF:** Average	**OBJ:** Grammar

Essay

17. Students should point out that "Dream Deferred" focuses on the frustration and potential violence caused by postponed or unfulfilled dreams, while "Dreams" focuses on the empowering aspects of hope-giving dreams. Evaluate students' essays for conciseness, clarity, coherence, and specific reference to the elements listed.
   Difficulty: *Average*
   Objective: *Essay*

18. For "Dream Deferred," students should identify the similes and make connections between the vivid images of decay and neglect and the speaker's implied warning in the final line. Students' analysis of "Dreams" should identify the two metaphors for life and explore the emotional weight of these images. Discussion of "I Wandered Lonely as a Cloud" should note the ways in which Wordsworth personifies the daffodils and the poet's use of metaphors in the final stanza. Students should focus on personification in an analysis of "Meciendo." Finally, discussion of "Sonnet on Love XIII" should note the poet's use of paradox, especially in lines 1–2 and 10–12.
   Difficulty: *Average*
   Objective: *Essay*

19. Students should understand that part of the poem deals with the speaker's experience in the field with the daffodils, and part of it deals with the speaker's memory of the daffodils and the effect they have on him. The speaker's "inward eye" is his visual memory. In the quoted lines, the speaker is remembering the daffodils

Unit 4 Resources: Poetry
© Pearson Education, Inc. All rights reserved.
245

and realizing that he can always summon the beauty of the daffodils and feel the joy of his experience again. To the speaker, the daffodils represent the joy and beauty that can be found in nature.

Difficulty: *Challenging*

Objective: *Essay*

20. Students may say that both "Dreams Deferred" and "Dreams" are advising readers to pursue their dreams rather than let them wither; that "I Wandered . . ." is advising readers to notice and treasure nature's gifts of beauty; that "Rocking" is advising readers to treat loved ones gently; and that "Sonnets on Love XIII" advises readers to appreciate and strengthen the bonds of love they feel.

Difficulty: *Average*

Objective: *Essay*

Poetry Collection: Richard Brautigan, Emily Dickinson, Stanley Kunitz

Vocabulary Warm-up Exercises, p. 42

A. 1. virtue
2. hireling
3. ecology
4. assent
5. demur
6. grace

B. Sample Answers

1. F; The *extremity* is the outer edge, and the planets that are closest to the sun are not on the edge of our solar system.
2. F; People can be *mutually* happy with each other, but you cannot be *mutually* happy with yourself.
3. T; Being *maimed* may cause a permanent injury and probably would require medical attention for life.
4. F; A *discerning* person shows good judgment, so it might be a good idea to believe what a *discerning* person had to say.
5. F; *Prevail* means to "achieve success after a struggle," so if you give up, you cannot *prevail*.
6. T; A *grievous* concern is very serious and would cause someone to be very worried or upset.

Reading Warm-up A, p. 43

Sample Answers

1. (agree); *Disagree* means the opposite of *assent*.
2. (the interaction of creatures and their environment); During breaks from farm work, Muir explored the countryside.
3. (object); *Protest* is a synonym for *demur*.
4. moral goodness; (nature)
5. To earn money; A *hireling* worker would care most about how much a job paid because *hireling* means "doing something for the money."
6. (decency); "climb the mountains and get their good tidings"

Reading Warm-up B, p. 44

Sample Answers

1. Most members of the Second Continental Congress *mutually* agreed to make the bald eagle the national symbol. *Mutually* means that more than one person agreed.
2. (understanding); Franklin believed the bald eagle was "too lazy to fish for himself," but that is not the case.
3. (permanent injuries); A bald eagle has sharp claws and dives at high speeds, so its attack might seriously injure a cow and leave it *maimed*.
4. (seriously harmed); It would do *grievous* damage because if the eggs cannot hatch, no new bald eagles will be born and the species could become extinct.
5. (farthest edge); the eagle's loss had an impact on the other plants and animals in the chain.
6. After its long struggle; recovered; *Triumph* is a synonym for *prevail*.

Writing About the Big Question, p. 45

A. 1. comprehension, understanding
2. exchange, discuss
3. relationship, communication
4. informed
5. interpretation, understanding

B. Sample Answers

1. My ties to my older brother became deeper when I realized how much stress his sports injury was causing him; my best friend's advice about after-school activities helped me avoid getting into trouble.
2. Yesterday after school, I started to **discuss** my older brother's feelings about his ankle injury with him. I was able to feel **empathy** with his stress about not being able to play football for the rest of this season.

C. Sample Answer

As a result of advances in computer technology, communication between people has become much faster and cheaper. Electronic mail, for example, allows people all over the world to communicate 24/7, provided they have access to a computer and a telephone line. There are some drawbacks to e-mail, though, because it is not nearly as personal as a letter or a phone call.

Literary Analysis: Figurative Language, p. 46

Sample Answers

1. metaphor—"Mutually programming harmony" directly compares the coexistence of mammals and computers to computer programs.

   simile—In "like pure water," the poet compares the coexistence of mammals and computers to pure water touching a clear sky. The comparison uses the word *like*.
2. metaphor—Without using a comparative word, such as *like* or *as*, the poet compares "Hope" to a little bird that sings without stopping even in a storm.
3. personification—"Bulldozers, drunk with gasoline" gives the machines a human quality. Also, "the virtue of the

soil" gives the soil human characteristics, such as the ability to be virtuous.

4. paradox—The lines express two apparent contradictions.

Reading: Read Fluently, p. 47

1. Major pause at the end of line 9; minor pauses at the end of lines 1, 2, 5, and 7; no pause at all at the end of lines 3, 4, 6, and 8

2. Minor pauses after *trees, grub-dominions, halls,* and *crowns;* no pause at all after *underground, mole,* and *shook*

Vocabulary Builder, p. 48

A. 1. B; 2. A 3. D; 4. A

B. Sample Answers

1. Yes, because an airplane pilot should be insightful and observant.
2. Preliminaries take place before the main event.
3. No, because *abash* means "to frighten or make uncomfortable."
4. It suggests a violent action or event.

C. Sample Answers

1. They undermine it, because *subvert* literally means "turn under."
2. You dislike them, because *aversion* literally means "turning away from."
3. No, because no opposing argument can prevail against an *incontrovertible* statement.

Enrichment: Computers in the Workplace, p. 49

A. Sample Answers

1. Students should understand that basic computer and word-processing skills are probably expected in most office jobs. Administrative jobs probably require a knowledge of accounting skills, and designers need to know computer graphics programs.
2. People can now work more quickly and efficiently, and people have access to more information. Some tasks can be performed with more precision.
3. Students might feel that computers should not replace the human mind in certain situations. They might believe that computers will further isolate people from one another and from the tasks they are performing.
4. Students might say that computers have in many ways saved people from mundane tasks, although machines do not control people.

B. Students should research their career choices thoroughly and then present their findings to the rest of the class.

Poetry Collections: Langston Hughes, William Wordsworth, Gabriela Mistral, Jean de Sponde; Richard Brautigan, Emily Dickinson, Stanley Kunitz

Integrated Language Skills: Grammar, p. 50

A. 1. with feathers (object is "feathers"); in the soul (object is "soul")
2. of our labors (object is "labors"); to nature (object is "nature")
3. in the love (object is "love"); for you (object is "you")

B. Examine students' paragraphs for correct usage and identification of prepositional phrases.

Open-Book Test, p. 53

Short Answer

1. This simile compares computers to flowers.
   Difficulty: *Average*   **Objective:** *Literary Analysis*
2. Students may say that he does like to think of these things because he uses words like "harmony" and "peacefully" to describe the scenarios or that he does not like to think of these things because he uses a sarcastic tone of parenthetical expressions.
   Difficulty: *Challenging*   **Objective:** *Interpretation*
3. feathers, perches, sings the tune without the words, asked a crumb
   Difficulty: *Easy*   **Objective:** *Literary Analysis*
4. Dickinson means that hope comforts people during difficult times.
   Difficulty: *Average*   **Objective:** *Interpretation*
5. One sentence, because a reader should use the punctuation and not the ends of lines to determine where to stop reading.
   Difficulty: *Average*   **Objective:** *Reading*
6. The "majority" decide what is madness and what is sense. This is paradoxical because it is contradictory. The designation of something as "madness" is not decided in a logical way.
   Difficulty: *Challenging*   **Objective:** *Literary Analysis*
7. The speaker believes a person with good judgment can see that what is called madness is sometimes sense, and vice versa.
   Difficulty: *Average*   **Objective:** *Vocabulary*
8. Sample answers: The bulldozers are "drunk with gasoline" and are forcing the trees, the "great-grandfathers of the town," "to their knees."
   Difficulty: *Average*   **Objective:** *Literary Analysis*
9. The poet sees the ghosts of children race in the shade and then disappear.
   Difficulty: *Easy*   **Objective:** *Interpretation*

© Pearson Education, Inc. All rights reserved.

10. Sample answer: Preliminaries—overthrowing the privet row, uprooting the forsythia and hydrangea; War Events—hacking at the roots, attacking the trees' crowns.

   Difficulty: *Average* **Objective:** *Vocabulary*

Essay

11. In their essays, students should identify and define one example of each of the four figures of speech, using examples from one or all of the poems in the collection. For example, in "The War Against the Trees," the speaker refers to "the bulldozers, drunk with gasoline" which is a personification, because it gives the nonhuman object of bulldozers the human characteristic of being drunk or intoxicated.

   Difficulty: *Easy* **Objective:** *Essay*

12. Students who choose "All Watched Over by Machines of Loving Grace" should point out that Brautigan offers a chillingly utopian vision of harmony and coordination between technology and nature. Those who choose "The War Against the Trees" should note that Kunitz pessimistically laments the disappearance of the natural world under the pitiless ax of technology and progress. Students should include specific references to figures of speech in the poem.

   Difficulty: *Average* **Objective:** *Essay*

13. In discussing "All Watched Over by Machines of Loving Grace," students should note the similes in lines 7–8 and 14–15 and the use of personification in lines 22–23. Students who choose "'Hope' is a thing with feathers—" should note Dickinson's use of metaphor and personification. Students who choose "Much Madness is divinest Sense—" should discuss paradox as the dominant figure of speech, but should also note the metaphorical image of the Chain in the last line. Finally, students who choose "The War Against the Trees" should single out Kunitz's use of personification and metaphor in some or all of the following lines: 3, 9, 13, 16, 18, 21, and 26.

   Difficulty: *Challenging* **Objective:** *Essay*

14. Some students may say that in Brautigan's vision, computer technology seems to have strengthened humans' ability to communicate and coexist with our "mammal brothers and sisters"; others may say that in the poet's vision, humans seem to have devolved into a state of mute, but content, uselessness.

   Difficulty: *Average* **Objective:** *Essay*

Oral Response

15. Oral responses should be clear, well organized, and well supported by appropriate examples from the selections.

   Difficulty: *Average* **Objective:** *Oral Interpretation*

Poetry Collection: Richard Brautigan, Emily Dickinson, Stanley Kunitz

Selection Test A, p. 56

Critical Reading

1. ANS: C	DIF: Easy	OBJ: Comprehension
2. ANS: C	DIF: Easy	OBJ: Literary Analysis
3. ANS: B	DIF: Easy	OBJ: Comprehension
4. ANS: A	DIF: Easy	OBJ: Comprehension
5. ANS: C	DIF: Easy	OBJ: Reading
6. ANS: D	DIF: Easy	OBJ: Interpretation
7. ANS: C	DIF: Easy	OBJ: Interpretation
8. ANS: C	DIF: Easy	OBJ: Literary Analysis
9. ANS: B	DIF: Easy	OBJ: Reading
10. ANS: C	DIF: Easy	OBJ: Literary Analysis
11. ANS: A	DIF: Easy	OBJ: Interpretation
12. ANS: B	DIF: Easy	OBJ: Interpretation

Vocabulary and Grammar

13. ANS: D	DIF: Easy	OBJ: Vocabulary
14. ANS: C	DIF: Easy	OBJ: Vocabulary

Essay

15. In their essays, students should include an accurate definition of the figure of speech they have chosen. The essays should have at least one main idea supported by specific examples drawn from the selections.

   Difficulty: *Easy*

   Objective: *Essay*

16. In their essays, students should identify a single work, state its theme, and support the theme statement with relevant details. Students should also evaluate the theme and give reasons and examples to support their evaluation.

   Difficulty: *Easy*

   Objective: *Essay*

17. Some students may say that in Brautigan's vision, computer technology seems to strengthen humans' ability to communicate, because mammal brothers and sisters seem to be in harmony and co-exist with technology. Other students may say that in the poet's vision, communications is weakened because people seem to be watched over by technology, in a passive and mute relationship.

   Difficulty: *Average*

   Objective: *Essay*

© Pearson Education, Inc. All rights reserved.

Selection Test B, p. 59

Critical Reading

1. ANS: A	DIF: Average	OBJ: Literary Analysis
2. ANS: A	DIF: Average	OBJ: Interpretation
3. ANS: A	DIF: Average	OBJ: Comprehension
4. ANS: B	DIF: Challenging	OBJ: Comprehension
5. ANS: A	DIF: Average	OBJ: Interpretation
6. ANS: D	DIF: Average	OBJ: Literary Analysis
7. ANS: A	DIF: Average	OBJ: Reading
8. ANS: C	DIF: Challenging	OBJ: Literary Analysis
9. ANS: C	DIF: Average	OBJ: Interpretation
10. ANS: B	DIF: Average	OBJ: Literary Analysis
11. ANS: C	DIF: Average	OBJ: Interpretation
12. ANS: C	DIF: Average	OBJ: Literary Analysis

Vocabulary and Grammar

13. ANS: C	DIF: Average	OBJ: Vocabulary
14. ANS: C	DIF: Average	OBJ: Vocabulary
15. ANS: B	DIF: Average	OBJ: Grammar
16. ANS: A	DIF: Challenging	OBJ: Grammar

Essay

17. Students should point out that Brautigan offers a utopian vision of harmony and coordination between technology and nature in his poem, while Kunitz pessimistically laments the disappearance of the natural world under the pitiless axe of technology and "progress." Evaluate essays for clarity, coherence, and students' specific references to images and figures of speech in each poem.

Difficulty: *Average*

Objective: *Essay*

18. In discussing "All Watched Over by Machines of Loving Grace," students should note the similes in lines 7–8 and 14–15 and the use of personification in lines 22–23. Students who choose "'Hope is the thing with feathers—'" should note Dickinson's use of metaphor and personification. Analysis of "The War Against the Trees" should single out Kunitz's use of personification and metaphor in some or all of the following lines: 3, 9, 13, 16, 18, 21, and 26. Finally, students who choose "Much Madness is divinest Sense" should discuss paradox as the dominant figure of speech in the poem.

Difficulty: *Challenging*

Objective: *Essay*

19. Some students may say that in Brautigan's vision, computer technology seems to have strengthened humans' ability to communicate and co-exist with our "mammal sisters and brothers;" others may say that in the poet's vision, humans seem to have devolved into a state of mute, but content, uselessness.

Difficulty: *Average*

Objective: *Essay*

Poetry Collection: Walter Dean Myers; Alfred, Lord Tennyson; May Swenson

Vocabulary Warm-up Exercises, p. 63

A. 1. crawls
2. bait
3. dripping
4. peeping
5. beaming
6. disgrace

B. Sample Answers

1. T; An audience that *exploded* with, or burst into, laughter means the comedian is successful.
2. T; Someone who *flirts* with danger shows a playful interest in it but does not take the risks seriously and could end up hurt or in serious trouble.
3. F; If the bases were *loaded*, there would be a player on each of the three bases.
4. T; If you are *ripping* through a field, you are moving very quickly. A player is more likely to move quickly than a referee.
5. F; Since trees tend to attract lightning, you should not stand under one if there is a *thunderbolt*, which is thunder accompanied by lightning.
6. T; A confused person often frowns, causing the forehead to be *wrinkled*.

Reading Warm-up A, p. 64

Sample Answers

1. to feel a little unsettled when you are in a brand new place; It would be a *disgrace* to cheat on a test.
2. (water); The icicles hanging from our roof were *dripping* as the sun melted them.
3. (worm); A brand new shiny guitar would be *bait* for me.
4. (hears birds); Birds that are *peeping* make high sounds.
5. (delight); My face might be *beaming* if I were chosen as class president.
6. time; The traffic near the mall *crawls* on weekends.

Reading Warm-up B, p. 65

Sample Answers

1. good ideas; Someone whose mind is *loaded* with good ideas might write stories.
2. (nonstop); Where were all those ideas that usually were *rushing* nonstop through her head?
3. (forehead); Clothes and paper can be *wrinkled*.
4. (idea); A *thunderbolt* that is striking hits suddenly and powerfully.
5. playfully teasing; *Flirts* means "shows an attraction for or interest in, in a playful way."
6. the audience at the poetry festival; I *exploded* with anger last week when my puppy tore my new sweater.

Writing About the Big Question, p. 66

A. 1. illuminate
2. understanding, comprehension
3. resolution
4. react, respond
5. respond, react

B. Sample Answers

1. I woke up Saturday morning to smell the wonderful aroma of fresh pancakes; when I stroked the kittens, I couldn't believe how fluffy their fur was.
2. When I woke up, I was keenly **aware** of the smell of the pancakes Dad was making in the kitchen. Saturdays have a basic **meaning** that makes everyone happy at our house: NO SCHOOL!

C. Sample Answer

By reading someone else's interpretation of a common experience, a reader can learn to question his or her assumptions. Everyone reacts to the same experience a little differently. We are all individuals with a unique personality. I like to share viewpoints with my parents, friends, and classmates. When I share and keep an open mind, I never stop learning.

Poetry Collection: Walter Dean Myers; Alfred, Lord Tennyson; May Swenson

Literary Analysis: Sound Devices, p. 67

Sample Answers

Students may give one or more of the following examples.
"Summer": Alliteration: Bugs buzzin; cousin to cousin; Running and ripping; Lazy days, daisies lay **Assonance:** Bugs buzzin; Lazy days, daisies lay **Consonance:** Sweat is what you got days **Onomatopoeia:** buzzin; peeping
"The Eagle": Alliteration: clasps the crag with crooked hands; lonely lands **Assonance:** sea beneath him **Consonance:** None **Onomatopoeia:** None
"Analysis of Baseball": Alliteration: Ball hits bat; bad doesn't hit ball; Ball bounces off bat; done on a diamond, for fun; Ball hates to take bat's bait **Assonance:** it hits mitt, Ball hates to take bat's bait, Ball fits mitt **Consonance:** the bat and the mitt **Onomatopoeia:** thuds, dud, thwack, pow

Reading: Read Fluently, p. 68

Sample Answers

Students may give one or more of the following examples.
"Summer"
Sight: Juices dripping; Running and ripping; Old men sleeping; daisies lay beaming
Hearing: Bugs buzzin; Birds peeping
Smell: None
Taste: Juices dripping
Touch: Sweat is what you got days; running and ripping
"The Eagle"
Sight: He clasps the crag with crooked hands; Close to the sun; Ring'd with the azure world; wrinkled sea beneath him

crawls; watches from his mountain walls; like a thunderbolt he falls
Hearing: like a thunderbolt he falls
Smell: None
Taste: None
Touch: He clasps the crag with crooked hands
"Analysis of Baseball"
Sight: Ball bounces off bat, flies air; Bat waits for ball to mate; Ball flirts, bat's late; Ball fits mitt; sails to a place; bases loaded, about 40,000 fans exploded; done on a diamond
Hearing: thuds ground (dud); Ball goes in (thwack) to mitt, and goes out (thwack) to mitt; ball gets hit (pow); about 40,000 fans exploded
Smell: None
Taste: None
Touch: Ball hits bat; ball fits mitt

Vocabulary Builder, p. 69

A. 1. B; 2. C 3. A
B. Sample Answers

1. Blue-green is the color closest to azure.
2. Clasping hands—gripping or holding someone's hand—in greeting or farewell is a friendly gesture.
3. Yes, it would help, because an analysis involves a close scrutiny of each part of a whole.

C. Sample Answers

1. Because she felt the two theories were *analogous*, and she couldn't wait to point out the similarities between them.
2. The *anachronisms* in that novel showed that the author had an inaccurate grasp of the historical setting.
3. The *Analects* are a collection of teachings by the ancient Chinese philosopher Confucius.

Enrichment: Seasons in Literature, p. 70

Sample Answers

Spring: E. E. Cummings, "in Just—"; Richard Wilbur, "A Storm in April"; Edna St. Vincent Millay, "Spring"
Summer: Robert Lowell, "This Golden Summer"; William Shakespeare, "Sonnet 18" ("Shall I compare thee to a summer's day?") and *A Midsummer Night's Dream;* Ray Bradbury, "All Summer in a Day"
Autumn: Jean Toomer, "Harvest Song"; Ted Hughes, "November"; William Shakespeare, "Sonnet 73" ("That time of year thou mayest in me behold"); Percy Bysshe Shelley, "Ode to the West Wind"; John Keats, "To Autumn"
Winter: E. E. Cummings, "what if a much of a which of a wind"; Robert Frost, "Stopping by Woods on a Snowy Evening"; William Carlos Williams, "These"; William Shakespeare, *The Winter's Tale*

Open-Book Test, p. 71

Short Answer

1. Sample answers: *buzzin, dripping, ripping,* and *peeping* are examples of onomatopoeia because their sounds imitate their meanings.
   Difficulty: *Average* **Objective:** *Literary Analysis*

2. Sample answer: The first stanza describes the active "buzzin," "Running and ripping" side of summer; the second stanza describes the slow-moving, "Old men sleeping / Lazy days" side of the season.
   Difficulty: *Average* **Objective:** *Interpretation*

3. Sample answers: "Bugs buzzin," "cousin to cousin," "Lazy days, daisies lay"
   Difficulty: *Easy* **Objective:** *Literary Analysis*

4. Sample answers: The phrases "He clasps the crag" and "like a thunderbolt he falls" describe the eagle as fierce and powerful.
   Difficulty: *Easy* **Objective:** *Interpretation*

5. The "azure world" is the blue sky.
   Difficulty: *Average* **Objective:** *Vocabulary*

6. The sense of sight most helps the reader understand the poem because most of the images in the poem are visual; for example, "wrinkled sea."
   Difficulty: *Challenging* **Objective:** *Reading*

7. The second line, "Close to the sun in lonely lands," contains consonance because the /n/ sound is repeated in stressed syllables in the words *sun, lonely,* and *lands.* Also, the third line contains consonance with /d/ in *Ring'd, world, stands.*
   Difficulty: *Challenging* **Objective:** *Literary Analysis*

8. Some students may say that the poem's sound effects seem to suggest that she enjoys the sounds and rhythms of baseball. Others may say that the poem's focus on a ball, a bat, and a mitt make the game sound juvenile.
   Difficulty: *Challenging* **Objective:** *Interpretation*

9. Two sentences
   Difficulty: *Average* **Objective:** *Reading*

10. Sample answer: Alliteration— "It's about / the ball, / the bat"; Consonance— "the bat, / and the mitt"; Assonance— "it / hits / mitt"; Onomatopoeia— "(thwack)"

    Students should note that the sound devices imitate the sounds of the game of baseball.
    Difficulty: *Average* **Objective:** *Literary Analysis*

Essay

11. Students may respond that Myers seems to feel affectionate and reminiscent about summer; Lord Tennyson seems to regard the eagle with awe; and Swenson seems to enjoy the sights, sounds, and atmosphere of baseball. Students should support what they say with references to the text and should explain whether and why they share the poets' sentiments.
    Difficulty: *Easy* **Objective:** *Essay*

12. Students should correctly identify the sound devices and provide appropriate examples from one of the poems. Students should make connections between a poet's use of sounds and the mood the poem creates. For example, they might point out that the use of onomatopoetic words in "Summer" and in "Analysis of Baseball" results in a playful tone.
    Difficulty: *Average* **Objective:** *Essay*

13. Students should either identify specific musical selections that could accompany and enhance each poem or indicate the features that an ideal soundtrack would possess. For example, the selection for "Summer" might be a slow-paced, moody piece of jazz, and the selection for "The Eagle" might be a stirring selection by Beethoven.
    Difficulty: *Challenging* **Objective:** *Essay*

14. Students may respond that "Summer" caused them to appreciate more deeply the fun and relaxation of summer; that "The Eagle" caused them to appreciate the majestic beauty of the bird; or that "Analysis of Baseball" changed the way they watch or listen to the game. Students' responses should be supported with appropriate evidence from the text.
    Difficulty: *Average* **Objective:** *Essay*

Oral Response

15. Oral responses should be clear, well organized, and well supported by appropriate examples from the selections.
    Difficulty: *Average* **Objective:** *Oral Interpretation*

Selection Test A, p. 74

Critical Reading

1. ANS: B	DIF: Easy	OBJ: Interpretation
2. ANS: C	DIF: Easy	OBJ: Literary Analysis
3. ANS: B	DIF: Easy	OBJ: Reading
4. ANS: D	DIF: Easy	OBJ: Interpretation
5. ANS: A	DIF: Easy	OBJ: Comprehension
6. ANS: C	DIF: Easy	OBJ: Comprehension
7. ANS: A	DIF: Easy	OBJ: Literary Analysis
8. ANS: C	DIF: Easy	OBJ: Comprehension
9. ANS: B	DIF: Easy	OBJ: Literary Analysis
10. ANS: B	DIF: Easy	OBJ: Interpretation
11. ANS: D	DIF: Easy	OBJ: Reading

Vocabulary and Grammar

12. ANS: A	DIF: Easy	OBJ: Vocabulary
13. ANS: C	DIF: Easy	OBJ: Grammar
14. ANS: C	DIF: Easy	OBJ: Grammar

Essay

15. In their essays, students should identify specific examples of onomatopoeia in the poem chosen. Students should also comment on how the use of onomatopoetic

© Pearson Education, Inc. All rights reserved.

words contributes to the selection's overall mood: for example, laziness in "Summer" or playfulness in "Analysis of Baseball." You may choose to have your students answer this question as an open-book essay.

Difficulty: *Easy*

Objective: *Essay*

16. In their essays, students should identify a favorite poem and give two reasons to support their choice. Evaluate students' essays for clarity, coherence, specific mention of sound devices, and effective support for their choice.

Difficulty: *Easy*

Objective: *Essay*

17. Students may respond that "The Eagle" caused them to appreciate the majestic beauty of the bird; or that "Analysis of Baseball" changed the way they watch or listen to the game. Students' responses should be supported with appropriate evidence from the text.

Difficulty: *Average*

Objective: *Essay*

Selection Test B, p. 77

Critical Reading

1. ANS: B	DIF: Average	OBJ: Comprehension
2. ANS: D	DIF: Challenging	OBJ: Literary Analysis
3. ANS: D	DIF: Average	OBJ: Literary Analysis
4. ANS: C	DIF: Average	OBJ: Comprehension
5. ANS: D	DIF: Average	OBJ: Interpretation
6. ANS: C	DIF: Average	OBJ: Interpretation
7. ANS: C	DIF: Average	OBJ: Comprehension
8. ANS: C	DIF: Average	OBJ: Reading
9. ANS: C	DIF: Average	OBJ: Interpretation
10. ANS: B	DIF: Average	OBJ: Literary Analysis
11. ANS: B	DIF: Average	OBJ: Interpretation
12. ANS: C	DIF: Average	OBJ: Comprehension
13. ANS: D	DIF: Average	OBJ: Literary Analysis
14. ANS: C	DIF: Average	OBJ: Reading
15. ANS: B	DIF: Average	OBJ: Literary Analysis
16. ANS: C	DIF: Average	OBJ: Interpretation

Vocabulary and Grammar

17. ANS: A	DIF: Average	OBJ: Vocabulary
18. ANS: C	DIF: Average	OBJ: Vocabulary
19. ANS: B	DIF: Challenging	OBJ: Grammar

Essay

20. Students should correctly identify the sound devices and provide appropriate examples from one of the poems. Students should make connections between a poet's use of sounds and the mood the poem creates. For example, they might point out that the use of onomatopoetic words in "Summer" and in "Analysis of Baseball" results in a playful tone.

Difficulty: *Average*

Objective: *Essay*

21. In their essays, students should offer a detailed account of a soundtrack for each poem. If students do not identify a specific piece of music, they should indicate the features that an ideal soundtrack would possess. For example, the soundtrack for "Summer" might be a slow-paced, moody piece of jazz, and the soundtrack for "The Eagle" might be a stirring selection by Beethoven. You might have small groups discuss their choices and actually create soundtracks for their oral readings of the poems in this collection.

Difficulty: *Challenging*

Objective: *Essay*

22. Students may respond that "Summer" caused them to appreciate more deeply the fun and relaxation of summer; that "The Eagle" caused them to appreciate the majestic beauty of the bird; or that "Analysis of Baseball" changed the way they watch or listen to the game. Students' responses should be supported with appropriate evidence from the text.

Difficulty: *Average*

Objective: *Essay*

Poetry Collection: Yusef Komunyakaa, Lewis Carroll, Edgar Allan Poe

Vocabulary Warm-up Exercises, p. 81

A.
1. balmy
2. Glistening
3. lanky
4. dunk
5. slam
6. hook

B. Sample Answers

1. I might feel a little embarrassed if I were *outmaneuvered* in a checkers game.
2. I think that global terrorism is the greatest *menace* to world peace.
3. My *intention* is to become a pediatrician.
4. Employees might make a *clamor* if the employer announced cuts in pay.
5. I might join a protest group if I heard that people were being *slain*.
6. I was very proud of my *endeavor* to help clean up the litter on Route 347.

Reading Warm-up A, p. 82

Sample Answers

1. (tall); A *lanky* player can reach farther and jump higher because he or she is tall and lean.
2. a player shoots over the shoulder; When the player shoots, his or her arm makes the shape of a *hook*.

3. Very tall players; Players have to leap high to *dunk* the ball because they have to be above the basket to push the ball through it.
4. (the ball); When players *slam* a ball, they throw it through the basket with a lot of force.
5. (the stadium lights); My mom's freshly waxed car was *glistening* as it sat in the driveway.
6. (cold and wet); I like going to the park on a *balmy* day.

Reading Warm-up B, p. 83

Sample Answers
1. This huge, snakelike monster; A *menace* is something dangerous.
2. (the outraged citizenry); When the citizenry raise a *clamor*, they make a lot of noise and let their opinions be known.
3. giving up without a fight; It is my *intention* to go to college.
4. to vanquish his opponent; If the knight failed in his *endeavor*, the dragon might eat the maiden.
5. (the wicked dragon); the clever and fearless knight; When the knight *outmaneuvered* the dragon, he gained an advantage by using skillful movements.
6. (killer); I saw a movie in which the monster was *slain* by an arrow shot right through its heart.

Writing About the Big Question, p. 84

A. 1. react, respond
2. communication, comprehension
3. discuss
4. meaning
5. interpretation

B. Sample Answers
1. I argued with my best friend over which project we should choose for the science fair; I disagreed with Toby when he said that our baseball team needed better coaching.
2. Tony wanted to **discuss** the baseball team and the coach the other day. I listened to his **interpretation** of the strategy Coach Billings used in the game last Friday, but I didn't think Toby was well **informed.**

C. Sample Answer
By reading about the meaning that someone finds in certain sounds, a reader can learn to appreciate a poem better. For example, I never realized how carefully Edgar Allan Poe chose his words to create a certain mood in each section of his poem "The Bells." After I listened to Robin's report on sound effects, I reread "The Bells" aloud. The different word choices and the sound of the words increased my understanding.

Poetry Collection: Yusef Komunyakaa, Lewis Carroll, Edgar Allan Poe

Literary Analysis: Sound Devices, p. 85

Sample Answers
Students may give one or more of the following examples.

"Slam, Dunk, & Hook": Alliteration: Like storybook sea monsters; A high note hung there; Muscles were a bright motor; Dribble, drive to the inside; our bodies spun on swivels of bone & faith **Assonance:** Swish of strings like silk; slapping a blackjack **Consonance:** the skullcap of hope **Onomatopoeia:** Swish; dunk; slapping

"Jabberwocky": Alliteration: gyre and gimble; Tumtum tree; beamish boy **Assonance:** vorpal sword **Consonance:** None **Onomatopoeia:** Bandersnatch; whiffling; burbled; snicker-snack; galumphing; chortled

"The Bells": Alliteration: a world of merriment their melody foretells; tintinnabulation; a world of happiness their harmony foretells; Brazen bells; a tale of terror now their turbulency tells; desperate desire; How the danger sinks and swells; the clamor and the clangor of the bells; the melancholy menace of their tone; muffled monotone; Runic rhyme **Assonance:** a world of merriment their melody foretells; crystalline delight; mellow wedding bells; the molten golden-notes; liquid ditty; euphony voluminously; resolute endeavor; the clamor and the clangor; the silence of the night; brute nor human; the moaning and the groaning **Consonance:** None **Onomatopoeia:** tinkle; tintinnabulation; jingling; tinkling; gush; shriek; twanging; jangling; wrangling; clangor; tolling; knells

Reading: Read Fluently, p. 86

Sample Answers
Students may give one or more of the following examples.

"Slam, Dunk, & Hook"

Sight: Mercury's Insignia on our sneakers; roundhouse Labyrinth; poised in midair; storybook sea monsters; corkscrew Up & dunk balls; Bug-eyed, lanky, All hands & feet; Tangled up in a falling; Muscles were a bright motor; Double-flashing to the metal hoop; Our backboard splintered; Glistening with sweat; drive to the inside, feint, and glide like a sparrow hawk

Hearing: Swish of strings; A high note hung there; dunk balls; girls cheered on the sidelines; Our backboard splintered; slapping a blackjack

Smell: None

Taste: None

Touch: Swish of strings like silk; dunk balls that exploded the skullcap of hope; Glistening with sweat; rolled the ball off our fingertips; slapping a blackjack against an open palm; Dribble; Our bodies spun on swivels

© Pearson Education, Inc. All rights reserved.

"Jabberwocky"

Sight: the slithy toves did gyre and gimble in the wabe; the mome raths; He took his vorpal sword in hand; So rested he by the Tumtum tree, and stood awhile in thought; The Jabberwock with eyes of flame; The vorpal blade went snicker-snack; and with its head he went galumphing back

Hearing: came whiffling through the tulgey wood, and burbled as it came; O frabjous day! Callooh! Callay!; He chortled in his joy

Smell: None

Taste: None

Touch: The jaws that bite, the claws that catch; He took his vorpal sword in hand; And through and through, the vorpal blade went snicker-snack; Come to my arms

"The Bells"

Sight: the stars that oversprinkle all the heavens, seem to twinkle; the turtle-dove that listens, while she gloats on the moon; the deaf and frantic fire; the side of the pale-faced moon; they that dwell up in the steeple

Hearing: practically the entire poem

Smell: None

Taste: None

Touch: icy air of night; balmy air of night; the bosom of the palpitating air; we shiver with affright; the rust within their throats

Vocabulary Builder, p. 87

A. 1. B; 2. D; 3. A; 4. C

B. Sample Answers

1. He spoke in a *monotone*, with no variation in tone and mood.
2. Making a *feint* to her right, the soccer player plunged to her left instead.
3. He was determined to make an *endeavor* at finishing the assignment that evening, and so he stayed up until midnight.

C. Sample Answers

1. They have one mate, since the prefix *mono-* means "one" or "single."
2. The person is interested in just one subject, since *monomania* is a disorder marked by excessive interest in a single subject.
3. A *monologue* is spoken by just one character.

Enrichment: Physical Education, p. 88

Students should identify the game or sport and limit their instructions to a *portion* of that game. The terms and expressions they list and define should be those needed to understand the portion of the game and its context. In their instructions, students should give clear and logical directions. Remind them to define or explain any game-related terms or jargon that a newcomer will not understand.

Poetry Collections: Walter Dean Myers; Alfred, Lord Tennyson; May Swenson; Yusef Komunyakaa, Lewis Carroll, Edgar Allan Poe

Integrated Language Skills: Grammar, p. 89

A. 1. with many sports fans; adverb phrase; modifies *popular*
2. in the late nineteenth century; adverb phrase; modifies *was invented*
3. of basketball; adjective phrase; modifies *inventor*
4. of nine players; adjective phrase; modifies *teams*

B. Examine students' paragraphs for correct usage and identification of adjective phrases and adverb phrases.

Open-Book Test, p. 92

Short Answer

1. Alliteration. The initial consonant /t/ sound is repeated four times.
   Difficulty: *Average*   **Objective:** *Literary Analysis*
2. Sample answer: golden wedding bells predict happiness; brass alarum bells tell of terror; iron bells reveal mourning and fear of death.
   Difficulty: *Average*   **Objective:** *Interpretation*
3. Sample answer: The stanzas are alike in their similar use of repetition, alliteration, and onomatopoeia.
   Difficulty: *Challenging*   **Objective:** *Literary Analysis*
4. Sample answer: The tolling of the iron funeral bells would most likely cause my heart to beat rapidly in fear.
   Difficulty: *Average*   **Objective:** *Vocabulary*
5. It suggests that they have fast, light feet and godlike powers on the basketball court.
   Difficulty: *Easy*   **Objective:** *Interpretation*
6. The short-*a* vowel sound is repeated in the first stressed syllables of *slapping* and *blackjack*. These sounds imitate the sound of a hand slapping a basketball.
   Difficulty: *Easy*   **Objective:** *Literary Interpretation*
7. *Bone* is paired with *faith*, *slipknot* with *joy*, *we* (the players) with *beautiful* and *dangerous*.
   These pairings suggest that basketball is both a physical and a spiritual/emotional experience.
   Difficulty: *Average*   **Objective:** *Interpretation*
8. The warning could be summarized *Beware of vicious beasts*. The boy does not heed it, but rather engages the Jabberwock in battle.
   Difficulty: *Average*   **Objective:** *Interpretation*
9. The boy slays the Jabberwock and lugs away its head. The senses of hearing ("snicker-snack") and sight ("galumphing") help the reader picture these events.
   Difficulty: *Average*   **Objective:** *Reading*

© Pearson Education, Inc. All rights reserved.

10. Students may respond that the sounds of the nonsense words suggest certain meanings; that the context gives clues to the words' meanings; or that a word's position within a sentence gives a clue about its part of speech.

Difficulty: *Challenging*   **Objective:** *Interpretation*

Essay

11. Students should compare and contrast two poems and articulate the criteria they use to evaluate each poem's entertainment value. In general, students may say that "Slam, Dunk, & Hook" entertains readers with vivid descriptions of playing the fast-paced game of basketball; "Jabberwocky" entertains with clever sound effects and descriptions of fantastical creatures; and "The Bells" entertains by using sound devices that effectively imitate the sounds of various bells.

Difficulty: *Easy*   **Objective:** *Essay*

12. Students may note that in the poem, basketball brings the players together in a network of friendship and support. It allows them to feel powerful and beautiful; to work out their grief; and to imagine becoming more than they presently are. Students may also respond that in this poem, basketball is used to symbolize an active, positive response to life's challenges.

Difficulty: *Average*   **Objective:** *Essay*

13. Students should mention that the serious tale of a young boy slaying a terrible monster is made humorous by playful coined words such as "frumious" and "Bandersnatch," and by the description of ridiculous, imaginary creatures such as "toves" and "raths." Students should discuss Carroll's use of alliteration ("gyre and gimble"), onomatopoeia ("snicker-snack," "galumphing"), and assonance (as in "vorpal sword"), and observe that these words and others like them conjure comical moods (i.e., "Tumtum tree") or darker, more serious moods (i.e., "the tulgey wood").

Difficulty: *Challenging*   **Objective:** *Essay*

14. Students may respond that the father's initial advice to "Beware the Jabberwock" had absolutely no impact on the boy; or that the advice itself spurred him to do the opposite, i.e., engage the Jabberwock in battle. Students may also say the poem suggests that in order to grow up and become independent from one's parents, a young person must learn to rely not on the parent's warnings and advice, but rather on his or her own instincts and abilities.

Difficulty: *Average*   **Objective:** *Essay*

Oral Response

15. Oral responses should be clear, well organized, and well supported by appropriate examples from the selections.

Difficulty: *Average*   **Objective:** *Oral Interpretation*

Poetry Collection: Yusef Komunyakaa, Lewis Carroll, Edgar Allan Poe

Selection Test A, p. 95

Critical Reading

1. ANS: D	DIF: Easy	OBJ: Comprehension
2. ANS: A	DIF: Easy	OBJ: Interpretation
3. ANS: A	DIF: Easy	OBJ: Literary Analysis
4. ANS: D	DIF: Easy	OBJ: Reading
5. ANS: B	DIF: Easy	OBJ: Literary Analysis
6. ANS: B	DIF: Easy	OBJ: Comprehension
7. ANS: B	DIF: Easy	OBJ: Interpretation
8. ANS: B	DIF: Easy	OBJ: Literary Analysis
9. ANS: B	DIF: Easy	OBJ: Reading
10. ANS: A	DIF: Easy	OBJ: Literary Analysis
11. ANS: C	DIF: Easy	OBJ: Interpretation

Vocabulary and Grammar

12. ANS: D	DIF: Easy	OBJ: Vocabulary
13. ANS: C	DIF: Easy	OBJ: Vocabulary
14. ANS: A	DIF: Easy	OBJ: Grammar

Essay

15. Evaluate students' writing for clarity, coherence, thorough treatment of sound devices, and specific references to the text. You may choose to have your students answer this question as an open-book essay.

Difficulty: *Easy*
Objective: *Essay*

16. In their essays, students' poems should compare and contrast two of the poems and should include specific references to the sound effects in each one. In general, students may point out that "Slam, Dunk, & Hook" entertains readers with its vivid descriptions of playing the fast-paced sport of basketball even as it includes some serious themes. "Jabberwocky" is probably the clearest example of a poem written to entertain, with its clever sound effects and its descriptions of fantastic creatures. "The Bells" entertains readers by using a host of devices that effectively imitate the sounds of various types of bells.

Difficulty: *Easy*
Objective: *Essay*

17. Students may respond that the father's advice to "beware the Jabberwock" had no impact or change on the boy's behavior. He did not beware, but engaged the Jabberwock in battle. Others may say that the advice itself spurred the boy to do battle carefully, which led to his success.

Difficulty: *Average*
Objective: *Essay*

© Pearson Education, Inc. All rights reserved.

Selection Test B, p. 98

Critical Reading

1. ANS: B   DIF: Average   OBJ: Literary Analysis
2. ANS: A   DIF: Average   OBJ: Literary Analysis
3. ANS: A   DIF: Average   OBJ: Interpretation
4. ANS: C   DIF: Challenging   OBJ: Interpretation
5. ANS: C   DIF: Average   OBJ: Reading
6. ANS: C   DIF: Average   OBJ: Interpretation
7. ANS: D   DIF: Average   OBJ: Comprehension
8. ANS: D   DIF: Average   OBJ: Literary Analysis
9. ANS: A   DIF: Average   OBJ: Literary Analysis
10. ANS: A   DIF: Average   OBJ: Comprehension
11. ANS: B   DIF: Challenging   OBJ: Comprehension
12. ANS: C   DIF: Average   OBJ: Literary Analysis
13. ANS: C   DIF: Average   OBJ: Reading
14. ANS: D   DIF: Challenging   OBJ: Interpretation
15. ANS: B   DIF: Average   OBJ: Comprehension

Vocabulary and Grammar

16. ANS: B   DIF: Average   OBJ: Vocabulary
17. ANS: C   DIF: Average   OBJ: Vocabulary
18. ANS: B   DIF: Average   OBJ: Grammar
19. ANS: A   DIF: Average   OBJ: Grammar

Essay

20. Students may select a wide range of activities for their comparisons. These activities could include jobs, hobbies, other sports, arts and music, or similar activities. In their essays, students should indicate the way these activities are similar to the qualities of play in "Slam, Dunk, & Hook." Comparisons may include distraction from difficulties, sheer pleasure of participation, identity and status with peers, release of pent-up energy, positive rather than negative activity, pursuit of excellence, and competition. Students should identify the quality in the poem as well as make the point about the chosen activity.

   Difficulty: *Average*
   Objective: *Essay*

21. In their essays, students should mention that the serious tale of a young boy slaying a terrible monster is made humorous by playful coined words (such as "frumious" and "Bandersnatch") and by the description of ridiculous, imaginary creatures (such as "toves" and "raths"). Students should also discuss Carroll's use of alliteration (as in "gyre and gimble"), onomatopoeia (as in "snicker-snack" and "galumphing"), and assonance (as in "vorpal sword").

   Difficulty: *Challenging*
   Objective: *Essay*

22. Students may respond that the father's initial advice to "beware the Jabberwock" had absolutely no impact on the boy; or that the advice itself spurred him to do the opposite, i.e., engage the Jabberwock in battle. Students may also say the poem suggests that in order to grow up and become independent from one's parents, a young person must learn to rely not on the parent's warnings and advice, but rather his or her own instincts and abilities.

   Difficulty: *Average*
   Objective: *Essay*

Poetry by Mary Tall Mountain, Naomi Shihab Nye, Student Writers

Vocabulary Warm-up Exercises, p. 102

A.
1. icy
2. prickly
3. flash
4. splurge
5. overripe
6. rippled

B. Sample Answers

1. If you receive a <u>penalty</u> in a sports game, you have made a bad play because a *penalty* is a punishment.
2. If a friend was acting <u>peculiar</u>, it means that he or she is acting strangely. So, if the friend wants to talk to you, you should try to find out what is wrong.
3. If an idea comes <u>unbidden</u>, it means that it comes suddenly, so the person has not been thinking about it already.
4. A <u>startled</u> animal might react to a loud noise by running, jumping, or hiding because the fact that it is *startled* means that it is surprised or not expecting the noise.
5. Having a <u>shade</u> of luck means having only a little bit of luck, so that would not automatically mean that everything was going well.

Reading Warm-up A, p. 103

Sample Answers

1. <u>spread</u>; Pemmican got more and more popular as more people tried pemmican and experienced its value as a high-nutrition fast food.
2. (thorny); <u>bushes</u>
3. <u>lost their best flavor and vitamins</u>; One way to avoid letting fruit become *overripe* is to eat it right away.
4. <u>buy in great quantities</u>; I enjoy movies and would *splurge* on a DVD of every movie I love if I could.
5. (cold); *Freezing* is a synonym for *icy*, and *boiling* is an antonym for *icy*.
6. <u>catch people's eyes</u>; Advertisers like packages that *flash* because they think people are likelier to buy something that attracts their attention.

Reading Warm-up B, p. 104

Sample Answers

1. their differences are not small but great; A *shade* is "a little bit of something."
2. (to call so many different peoples and their languages Athabaskan); *Unusual* is a synonym for *peculiar.*
3. (punishment); A serious *penalty* for speeding might be having your driver's license taken away.
4. (pinch); If you ate a sour berry, your mouth might *squinch* up in response.
5. frighten off; *Alarmed* is a synonym for *startled.*
6. (uninvited); Every season arrives *unbidden* because we cannot control when a season comes and goes. The seasons change whether we want them to or not.

Writing About the Big Question, p. 105

A. 1. aware
2. react, respond
3. informed
4. empathy

B. Sample Answers

1. Last night after dinner, my parents and I talked about violence on TV; when I wrote my report on Hurricane Katrina, I understood the storm and its effects better.
2. When I wrote my report on Hurricane Katrina, I gained a better **understanding** of the storm and its effects. The suffering the storm created led to my feeling **empathy** with the victims.

C. Sample Answer

1. When a writer responds strongly to an experience, his or her word choices in a poem usually communicate deep emotion. You can tell from Mary Tall Mountain's poem, for example, how deeply the speaker loves and respects her aunt. In Naomi Shihab Nye's poem "Daily," the word choices and images make the reader aware of the speaker's emotional attachment to her daily activities, even though these chores may seem routine and ordinary.

Poetry: Mary Tall Mountain, Naomi Shihab Nye, Student Writers

Literary Analysis: Imagery, p. 106

Sample Answers

1. **Senses:** sight and touch. **Imagery:** I can see the tanned skin of old Sokoya, and as I watch, I can see the emotion that causes her skin to "ripple." I can feel the wind as it chafes the skin and turns it tan.
2. **Senses:** hearing and sight. **Imagery:** As Sokoya speaks the word "Nothing," I hear her voice. I can see her watching the river, and at that moment, the sun glints on the water, causing it to "flash."
3. **Senses:** taste, touch, sight, and hearing. **Imagery:** I can feel the motions of slicing the tortillas and scrambling the eggs. I can feel the "crisp" strips and the weight of the clay bowl. I can see the golden fried strips, the yellow scrambled eggs, and the gray bowl.
4. **Senses:** sight and touch. **Imagery:** I can see the speaker dusting and polishing the table. I can feel how worn and scarred it is. I can see the clean table shining.
5. **Senses:** hearing, touch. **Imagery:** I can hear the crash made by the tree and feel the violence with which the wind pulled the tree's roots out of the earth and slammed it into the ground.

Vocabulary Builder, p. 107

Sample Answers

A. 1. The performance was so dramatic and exciting that we were *awestruck.*
2. While the storm was passing over, we were standing *amid* howling winds.
3. Because of the hot weather and *lack of rainfall*, the flowers in our garden look shriveled.
4. The furniture is so *old* that it looks scarred and unstable.

B. 1. B; 2. C; 3. A; 4. C

Open-Book Test, p. 109

Short Answer

1. Sample answers: "We always think you're coming back" reflects the value of family and community. "We'll see you some place else" reflects the belief in a hereafter.
   Difficulty: *Easy* **Objective:** *Interpretation*
2. Yes, Sokoya's old face is described in the poem as a "net of wrinkle," and *shriveled* means "shrunken and wrinkled."
   Difficulty: *Average* **Objective:** *Vocabulary*
3. The poet considers the activities sacred. The speaker says the hands that perform these tasks "are churches that worship the world."
   Difficulty: *Challenging* **Objective:** *Interpretation*
4. Sample answer: "Daily": loosened soil; T-shirts we fold; covers I straighten / smoothing edges; page I type." "There Is No Word for Goodbye": wind-tanned skin; touched me light as a bluebell. Most of the touch images in "Daily" are associated with daily, household tasks. In "There Is No Word for Goodbye," touch images are associated with nature.
   Difficulty: *Average* **Objective:** *Literary Analysis*
5. "There Is No Word for Goodbye" uses the sparest imagery. This reflects the simple wisdom of Sokoya and also the sparseness of language itself and language's inability to express ideas such as *goodbye.*
   Difficulty: *Challenging* **Objective:** *Literary Analysis*
6. Sample answer: "There Is No Word for Goodbye": "She touched me light as a bluebell"; "Daily": ". . . seeds we plant . . . with measured fingertips".
   Difficulty: *Average* **Objective:** *Literary Analysis*
7. The author means that surviving the storm has made him appreciate all the ordinary aspects of everyday life,

such as pretty scenery, a safe home, and family members.

Difficulty: *Average*   **Objective:** *Interpretation*

8. He means that for a moment, Adam thought he was going to die.

Difficulty: *Average*   **Objective:** *Interpretation*

9. Sample response: "There Is No Word for Goodbye": wise black pools of her eyes; "The Day of the Storm": old oak trees thrown around as if they were small branches; "Hope": the remains of an airliner strewn all over the football field; "Daily": T-shirts we fold into/perfect white squares.

Difficulty: *Easy*   **Objective:** *Literary Analysis*

10. Students may say that "Daily" appeals most strongly to the sense of touch in its descriptions of the various tactile domestic chores the speaker performs. Accept all reasonable, well-supported responses.

Difficulty: *Average*   **Objective:** *Literary Analysis*

Essay

11. Students may note that Nye's imagery in "Daily" is abundant and draws from the recognizable world of everyday chores, while TallMountain's imagery in "There Is No Word for Goodbye" is the sparest, comparing Sokoya's face and touch to natural objects. Students should also identify one or more emotions that seem connected to each image.

Difficulty: *Easy*   **Objective:** *Essay*

12. Students who found "The Day of the Storm" more vivid and moving may cite its rich imagery and suspenseful narrative, while those who connected more strongly with "Hope" may cite that essay's brevity, power, and understated affirmation of the father-son bond. Evaluate students' essays for clarity and adequate support.

Difficulty: *Average*   **Objective:** *Essay*

13. Students should clearly distinguish the ways in which the speaker or main character of each work affirms a certain type of faith or confidence and should give examples of imagery that support this faith and whether it is shaken or strengthened. For example: faith in our connection to our ancestors, in the continuity of everyday life and work, or in a sense of safety, security, and home. Evaluate students' essays for clarity, coherence, and support for main ideas.

Difficulty: *Challenging*   **Objective:** *Essay*

14. Students may respond that the older woman's words in "There Is No Word for Goodbye" caused the speaker to appreciate familial bonds more deeply and to see that people who love each other remain connected even when far apart. Or students may say that images of ordinary things in "Daily" change the way we look and appreciate the everyday things in our lives that we might otherwise overlook or take for granted.

Difficulty: *Average*   **Objective:** *Essay*

Oral Response

15. Oral responses should be clear, well organized, and well supported by appropriate examples from the selections.

Difficulty: *Average*   **Objective:** *Oral Interpretation*

Selection Test A, p. 112

Critical Reading

1. ANS: C	DIF: Easy	OBJ: Comprehension
2. ANS: B	DIF: Easy	OBJ: Literary Analysis
3. ANS: B	DIF: Easy	OBJ: Comprehension
4. ANS: D	DIF: Easy	OBJ: Interpretation
5. ANS: C	DIF: Easy	OBJ: Literary Analysis
6. ANS: B	DIF: Easy	OBJ: Interpretation
7. ANS: C	DIF: Easy	OBJ: Literary Analysis
8. ANS: C	DIF: Easy	OBJ: Literary Analysis
9. ANS: C	DIF: Easy	OBJ: Comprehension
10. ANS: C	DIF: Easy	OBJ: Interpretation
11. ANS: D	DIF: Easy	OBJ: Interpretation

Vocabulary

12. ANS: C	DIF: Easy	OBJ: Vocabulary
13. ANS: A	DIF: Easy	OBJ: Vocabulary

Essay

14. In their essays, students should identify the lasting power of community and family as the main idea in "There Is No Word for Goodbye." The vivid descriptions of the aunt show the speaker's love and respect for her aunt. In "Daily," the speaker celebrates the beauty, joy, and dignity of doing each day's work. The careful descriptions of ordinary routine show the speaker's respect or reverence for the rituals of daily life. Evaluate students' essays for clarity, coherence, and specific reference to the selections.

Difficulty: *Easy*

Objective: *Essay*

15. Naomi Shihab Nye's imagery includes a number of concrete sensory details involved in her daily chores. Mary Tall Mountain's imagery includes a few vivid concrete details about the aunt's appearance. Much of her poem, though, reports the conversation between aunt and speaker. Evaluate students' essays for clarity, coherence, and specific references to the texts.

Difficulty: *Easy*

Objective: *Essay*

16. Students may respond that the older woman's words in "There Is No Word for Goodbye" causes the speaker to appreciate family bonds more deeply and to see that people who love one another remain connected even when far apart.

Difficulty: *Average*

Objective: *Essay*

Selection Test B, p. 115

Critical Reading

1. ANS: C	DIF: Average	OBJ: Comprehension
2. ANS: A	DIF: Average	OBJ: Literary Analysis
3. ANS: B	DIF: Average	OBJ: Interpretation
4. ANS: C	DIF: Challenging	OBJ: Interpretation
5. ANS: B	DIF: Average	OBJ: Literary Analysis
6. ANS: B	DIF: Average	OBJ: Comprehension
7. ANS: C	DIF: Average	OBJ: Literary Analysis
8. ANS: B	DIF: Average	OBJ: Literary Analysis
9. ANS: D	DIF: Challenging	OBJ: Literary Analysis
10. ANS: A	DIF: Average	OBJ: Interpretation
11. ANS: C	DIF: Challenging	OBJ: Literary Analysis
12. ANS: A	DIF: Challenging	OBJ: Interpretation
13. ANS: B	DIF: Average	OBJ: Interpretation

Vocabulary

14. ANS: B	DIF: Average	OBJ: Vocabulary
15. ANS: D	DIF: Average	OBJ: Vocabulary
16. ANS: C	DIF: Average	OBJ: Vocabulary

Essay

17. In their essays, students should identify and discuss the major images of the poem selected and also comment on how the poet's use of imagery relates to the main idea in the selection. Evaluate students' essays for clarity, coherence, and support for main ideas.

    Difficulty: *Average*

    Objective: *Essay*

18. Students should clearly distinguish the ways in which the speaker in each of the three poems affirms a certain type of faith or confidence. Evaluate students' essays for clarity, coherence, and support for main ideas.

    Difficulty: *Challenging*

    Objective: *Essay*

19. Students may respond that the older woman's words in "There Is No Word for Goodbye" caused the speaker to appreciate familial bonds more deeply, and to see that people who love one another remain connected even when far apart. Or students may say that images of ordinary things in "Daily" change the way we look and appreciate the everyday things in our lives that we might otherwise overlook or take for granted.

    Difficulty: *Average*

    Objective: *Essay*

Writing Workshop

Descriptive Essay: Integrating Grammar Skills, p. 119

A. Students should put a check before sentences 1, 2, and 4.

B. Sample Answers

1. In New England, many towns have a town green.
2. A large square in the town center, the green is a centuries-old tradition.
3. Long and attractive, our town green is lined with trees.
4. Facing the green, fine shops sell a variety of goods.

Benchmark Test 7, p. 120

MULTIPLE CHOICE

1. ANS: D
2. ANS: B
3. ANS: A
4. ANS: C
5. ANS: D
6. ANS: A
7. ANS: C
8. ANS: B
9. ANS: D
10. ANS: A
11. ANS: A
12. ANS: C
13. ANS: D
14. ANS: A
15. ANS: D
16. ANS: C
17. ANS: D
18. ANS: A
19. ANS: B
20. ANS: D
21. ANS: B
22. ANS: A
23. ANS: C
24. ANS: B
25. ANS: D
26. ANS: C
27. ANS: D

28. ANS: C

29. ANS: D

30. ANS: A

31. ANS: D

32. ANS: A

33. ANS: D

34. ANS: B

ESSAY

35. Paragraphs or poems should describe a scene in nature and use sensory images.

36. Editorials should clearly state an opinion and provide data to support it.

37. Essays should have a logical organization and include figurative language and details that appeal to the senses.

Poetry Collection: Ernest Lawrence Thayer, William Stafford, Sandra Cisneros

Vocabulary Warm-up Exercises, p. 128

A. 1. shattered
2. kindling
3. defiance
4. occurred
5. cyclone
6. pulsing

B. Sample Answers

1. No. A *confident* person would be relaxed and in control.

2. No. A person who sees *grandeur* would be pleased and amazed.

3. A *haughty* response shows a great dislike for my question, and the person probably feels that he or she is better than I am.

4. I might be happy at first to have all my wishes *indulged,* but I might discover that getting everything I wish for is not really good for me.

5. Musical instruments would create sounds that *rebounded,* or bounced back, especially in a room that had nothing to absorb the sound.

6. The class would be more comfortable in a bus because students would be very crowded if they all tried to squeeze into a car the size of a *sedan.*

Reading Warm-up A, p. 129

Sample Answers

1. The word *cyclone* usually refers to a powerful windstorm that starts over the ocean somewhere in the tropics; The *cyclone* is 50 miles off shore and approaching quickly, so get to a safe place as quickly as possible.

2. tree or wooden house; *Kindling* is material, such as small pieces of wood or sticks, used to start a fire.

3. The largest known tornado outbreak; A synonym for *occurred* is *happened.*

4. (flashed); The *pulsing* satellite caught our attention as we gazed at the stars.

5. (glass); The car's windshield was *shattered* when a rock hit it while we were driving on the freeway.

6. get to a safe place immediately; lie flat in the nearest ditch and cover your head; *Defiance* of a tornado's power could result in serious injuries; a tornado is far more powerful than any human.

Reading Warm-up B, p. 130

Sample Answers

1. (car); My aunt's *sedan* is dark red with black cloth seats and a sunroof.

2. that we could win; They might feel *confident* because they have won many games.

3. The Eagles were an excellent team; A team wins by playing well and not by taking a *haughty* or superior attitude toward the other team.

4. my desire to close my eyes for a few seconds; It would have been more sensible for him to have *indulged* his desire for rest after the game was over.

5. how wonderful it would be to win the championship; The huge rooms with their beautiful ceilings help create the *grandeur* of the fine arts museum.

6. (the ball); *Rebounded* means "bounced back."

Writing About the Big Question, p. 131

A. 1. resolution
2. relationship
3. understanding
4. exchange
5. illuminate

B. Sample Answers

1. When Raúl and I talked about hip-hop music the other day, I changed my mind about the style; Dad sold me on the idea of using our summer vacation to visit some of the national parks in our region.

2. Dad and I started to **discuss** summer vacation the other day. He persuaded me that I could become a lot better **informed** about geography and the environment if we visited some of the national parks in our region.

C. Sample Answer

When a crowd communicates its support or disapproval, a person might react by joining in or by standing aside. Cheering a great play at a soccer game, for example, gives me a good feeling. However, booing players for a mistake is not very sportsmanlike, in my opinion. Also, I don't feel that booing an opposing team is fair at any time.

Literary Analysis: Narrative Poetry, p. 132

Sample Answers

1. The poem tells the story of the tense final moments of a baseball game.
2. The most important characters are Casey and the umpire (or the pitcher on the opposing team).
3. Casey strikes out, and the Mudville team loses.
4. He mentions the deathlike silence, the joyous yell, 5,000 applauding tongues, the muffled roar, and the fans' shouts of "Kill the umpire!" and "Fraud!"
5. The speaker, a man, remembers when he was fifteen and found a wrecked motorcycle.
6. The speaker has an inner conflict: He wants to ride the motorcycle, yet he feels obliged to return it to its owner.
7. Details creating suspense include the damage caused by the tornado and the repetition of Mama and Papa's version of events.
8. The atmosphere is a little sad and ironic.

Reading: Paraphrasing, p. 133

Sample Answers

1. As the pitch flew toward the plate, Casey eyed the ball scornfully. He did not swing at the pitch, saying that he did not like it, but the umpire called it a strike.
2. When I was fifteen, I admired the shiny sides and the headlights of the motorcycle, and then I walked it to the road and stood beside it, thinking about it as if it were a friend.
3. When the storm hit, Papa was on the front porch. The tornado was so powerful that it split the large black oak tree.

Vocabulary Builder, p. 134

A. 1. C; 2. A; 3. B

B. Sample Answers
  1. The large crowd might have blocked an onlooker's view of the marchers.
  2. We might have felt angry and hurt because of Jean's hostility.
  3. Nathaniel's comments came before, or *preceded*, his performance.

C. Sample Answers
  1. Lucy was greatly interested in the comments by the authors in the *preface* at the beginning of the report.
  2. At the parade, Mayor Vargas was clearly visible because she *preceded* all the other marchers.
  3. Thinking about tomorrow's history test, Mark had a *premonition* that several questions would relate to the chapter review.

Enrichment: Mathematics, p. 135

1. A. 54; B. 128; C. 141
2. A. 41; B. 95; C. 169
3. 714 home runs
4. 18 years

5. Have students compare their research results to see if they agree on current totals for Bonds and Sosa.

Open-Book Test, p. 136

Short Answer

1. Sample answer: Flynn and Blakey get on base; Casey comes to bat; Casey gets a strike; the fans yell at the umpire; Casey gets a second strike; the crowd screams "Fraud!"; Casey strikes out.
   Students may say the event that creates the most suspense is Casey's second strike.
   Difficulty: *Average* **Objective:** *Literary Analysis*
2. Sample answer: Flynn gets on first base and Blakey hits the ball hard enough to reach second and advance Flynn to third.
   Difficulty: *Easy* **Objective:** *Reading*
3. Students may say Casey does not like the ball the pitcher throws. His comment may show that he is confident or overconfident in his ability to hit the ball.
   Difficulty: *Average* **Objective:** *Interpretation*
4. Sample answer: Yes, the fans are most likely twisting and turning in anticipation and excitement as they wait for the next pitch.
   Difficulty: *Average* **Objective:** *Vocabulary*
5. The reader assumes the speaker will ride the motorcycle, but instead the speaker finds the injured motorcyclist and helps him to the motorcycle.
   Difficulty: *Average* **Objective:** *Reading*
6. Sample answer: Childhood dream: "I thought about / hills, and patting the handle got back a / confident opinion"; Adult reality: I found / the owner, just coming to, where he had flipped solidus / over the rail.
   Difficulty: *Easy* **Objective:** *Interpretation*
7. The speaker has chosen to act responsibly instead of following his childish desires. He has, in this moment, become a man.
   Difficulty: *Challenging* **Objective:** *Interpretation*
8. Sample answer: Papa was on the porch and saw the twister splinter a tree, throw a car into the yard, and make the back door rattle. Mama was in the kitchen and missed it.
   Difficulty: *Easy* **Objective:** *Literary Analysis*
9. Papa seems proud that he saw the action. Mama seems jealous, or envious, that she "missed it."
   Difficulty: *Average* **Objective:** *Interpretation*
10. Sample answer: Mama reveals that the twister knocked out the electricity.
   Difficulty: *Challenging* **Objective:** *Literary Analysis*

Essay

11. Students' essays should identify elements of plot, setting, character, and mood in a single poem and should explain which of these elements is dominant in the poem. Evaluate essays for clarity, coherence, and appropriate textual support.
   Difficulty: *Easy* **Objective:** *Essay*

12. Students should compare and contrast the use of suspense in the two poems. Students may point out that the suspense in "Casey at the Bat" mounts as the fans grow more and more excited while Casey faces the next pitch. The suspense in "Fifteen" is psychological, revolving around what action the speaker will choose to take.
    Difficulty: *Average*   **Objective:** *Essay*

13. Students should point out that, like a story, "Casey at the Bat" includes elements such as plot, characters, setting, mood, dialogue, and suspense; but that, unlike a short story, the poem uses stanzas, meter, and rhyme. Students may conclude that the poetic elements help to carry the action forward and to build the story's suspense, giving readers, in effect, the same intense emotional experience as that experienced by the fans.
    Difficulty: *Challenging*   **Objective:** *Essay*

14. Students may respond that in situations such as this one, people tell and retell their story as a way of asserting control in a situation that has otherwise made them feel helpless. Accept all other reasonable responses.
    Difficulty: *Average*   **Objective:** *Essay*

Oral Response

15. Oral responses should be clear, well organized, and well supported by appropriate examples from the selections.
    Difficulty: *Average*   **Objective:** *Oral Interpretation*

Selection Test A, p. 139

Critical Reading

1. ANS: B	DIF: Easy	OBJ: Comprehension
2. ANS: A	DIF: Easy	OBJ: Reading
3. ANS: C	DIF: Easy	OBJ: Literary Analysis
4. ANS: A	DIF: Easy	OBJ: Reading
5. ANS: D	DIF: Easy	OBJ: Interpretation
6. ANS: B	DIF: Easy	OBJ: Reading
7. ANS: C	DIF: Easy	OBJ: Literary Analysis
8. ANS: C	DIF: Easy	OBJ: Interpretation
9. ANS: D	DIF: Easy	OBJ: Comprehension
10. ANS: A	DIF: Easy	OBJ: Reading
11. ANS: D	DIF: Easy	OBJ: Literary Analysis

Vocabulary and Grammar

12. ANS: B	DIF: Easy	OBJ: Vocabulary
13. ANS: D	DIF: Easy	OBJ: Vocabulary
14. ANS: A	DIF: Easy	OBJ: Grammar

Essay

15. Students' essays should include specific mention and discussion of the elements of plot, setting, character, and mood. Evaluate essays for clarity and coherence.

Difficulty: *Easy*
Objective: *Essay*

16. Students' essays should focus on two of the poems in the collection and should present a well-organized comparison-and-contrast discussion. Students may point out that the suspense in "Casey at the Bat" mounts as the fans grow more excited and Casey faces increasingly long odds. The suspense in "Fifteen" is psychological, revolving around what action the speaker will choose to take. Finally, the suspense in "Twister Hits Houston" involves the conflict of humans vs. nature.
    Difficulty: *Easy*
    Objective: *Essay*

17. Students may respond that the characters Mama and Papa in "Twister Hits Houston" give their eyewitness description of a natural disaster of a cyclone and its effect. They relate that the cyclone destroyed property and electric power, but did not harm them.
    Difficulty: *Average*
    Objective: *Essay*

Selection Test B, p. 142

Critical Reading

1. ANS: C	DIF: Average	OBJ: Interpretation
2. ANS: C	DIF: Average	OBJ: Literary Analysis
3. ANS: D	DIF: Average	OBJ: Interpretation
4. ANS: A	DIF: Average	OBJ: Comprehension
5. ANS: C	DIF: Challenging	OBJ: Interpretation
6. ANS: A	DIF: Average	OBJ: Reading
7. ANS: A	DIF: Average	OBJ: Comprehension
8. ANS: C	DIF: Average	OBJ: Comprehension
9. ANS: B	DIF: Challenging	OBJ: Interpretation
10. ANS: D	DIF: Average	OBJ: Reading
11. ANS: C	DIF: Challenging	OBJ: Interpretation
12. ANS: B	DIF: Average	OBJ: Comprehension
13. ANS: A	DIF: Average	OBJ: Reading
14. ANS: C	DIF: Average	OBJ: Interpretation
15. ANS: D	DIF: Challenging	OBJ: Interpretation

Vocabulary and Grammar

16. ANS: A	DIF: Average	OBJ: Vocabulary
17. ANS: C	DIF: Average	OBJ: Vocabulary
18. ANS: B	DIF: Average	OBJ: Grammar
19. ANS: B	DIF: Average	OBJ: Grammar

Essay

20. Students should produce a well-organized comparison-contrast essay focusing on two of the poems. Students should show that they have an accurate understanding of the plot in each narrative poem, and they should comment on the poem's theme or message. In general, the theme of

"Casey at the Bat" might be linked with the expectations people have of heroes, the theme of "Fifteen" might concern the tension between dreams and responsible choices, and the theme of "Twister Hits Houston" might touch on people's reactions to moments of extreme stress.

Difficulty: *Average*
Objective: *Essay*

21. Students should point out that a narrative poem and a short story both tell a story, include descriptions, and have characters. Narrative poetry, unlike a short story, consists of rhyming lines with a certain rhythm. Narrative poetry also makes use of inverted word order and more poetic language than does a short story.

Difficulty: *Average*
Objective: *Essay*

22. Students may respond that in situations such as this one, people tell and retell their story as a way of asserting control in a situation that has otherwise made them feel helpless. Accept all other reasonable responses.

Difficulty: *Average*
Objective: *Essay*

Poetry Collection: Edgar Allan Poe, Edwin Muir, Richard Wilbur

Vocabulary Warm-up Exercises, p. 146

A.
1. dank
2. impenetrable
3. dazed
4. pondered
5. iridescent
6. Undaunted

B. Sample Answers
1. T; A *commotion* is some kind of loud activity, and it would keep me awake.
2. T; If I *hauled*, or pulled, something heavy like an air conditioner up the stairs, my arms might be sore.
3. F; An *ominous* piece of news would be frightening and unpleasant.
4. F; A silly limerick would probably not be deeply moving and would not *pierce* my heart.
5. F; Most prisoners would not want to serve more time in prison but would want to be released from *servitude* as quickly as possible.
6. F; Swans are very graceful when they are in the water, so they are not *ungainly*.

Reading Warm-up A, p. 147

Sample Answers
1. (I [the narrator]); The narrator might be *undaunted* because he or she wants very much to have a pet and would not give up hope.
2. (feathers); A diamond might be *iridescent*.
3. (confused); The narrator thinks the bird may be ill because if he is *dazed*, he is not acting as he usually does.

4. expression on his face; *Impenetrable* means "not able to be understood."
5. my next move; If the narrator *pondered*, he or she thought seriously for a while, so there must not have been an easy solution to the problem.
6. (miserable); On a *dank* day, I would wear warm clothes and I might wear a raincoat or carry an umbrella.

Reading Warm-up B, p. 148

Sample Answers
1. were expected to work hard; Before the Civil War, many African Americans were held in *servitude*.
2. (Newborn foals); A synonym for *ungainly* is *clumsy*.
3. startle; try to flee; A group of people celebrating and making lots of noise or two people arguing loudly could make a *commotion* that would startle a horse.
4. pulled; I have *hauled* huge boxes of books out of our basement.
5. (threatened); Trains and cars were *ominous* developments because they meant that people no longer needed horses for transportation as much as before.
6. Stories about horses; These stories might *pierce* the heart because the horses in them face a tragedy.

Writing About the Big Question, p. 149

A.
1. comprehension, understanding
2. respond
3. aware
4. interpretation
5. discuss, exchange, resolution

B. Sample Answers
1. When I told Mom my grade on the math test, her face glowed; Ruth didn't say anything, but you could tell she was disappointed that we couldn't get tickets to the concert.
2. When I told Mom my grade on the math test, I wondered how she would **respond**. Although she didn't say anything, the proud glow on her face communicated her **meaning** clearly.

C. Sample Answer

Having empathy for someone who is in a difficult situation might make a person realize that life is a series of ups and downs, at least for most of us. I realized this truth when my friend Jessica lost her pet cat the other day. I never knew how hard the loss of a pet could be on its owner.

Literary Analysis: Narrative Poetry, p. 150

Sample Answers
1. The speaker in "The Raven" is a gloomy, depressed young man.
2. The poem takes place late at night during a bleak, dreary December.
3. The poem tells the story of a depressed man who, in despair over the loss of his beloved Lenore, is haunted by thoughts of death.

© Pearson Education, Inc. All rights reserved.

4. In "The Horses," the speaker recalls a seven-day war that destroyed much of human civilization. He also recalls the mysterious arrival a year later of herds of wild horses.

5. The poem is set on a drastically destroyed planet Earth, where people live in a relatively primitive state.

6. The poem ends on an optimistic, hopeful note.

7. In "The Writer," the speaker tells about his daughter trying to write a story. He also recalls the time two years earlier when a starling succeeded in escaping from his daughter's room.

8. The overall mood is reflective and affectionate.

Reading: Paraphrasing, p. 151

Sample Answers

1. I was impatient for the morning because I was thinking of my lost love, Lenore, and reading had not stopped my sadness.

2. However, the horses refused to leave. They acted as if they had been told to locate us and to renew the old bond between human beings and horses.

3. I remember the starling trapped in my daughter's room two years ago, and how we tiptoed in and raised a window.

Vocabulary Builder, p. 152

A. 1. B; 2. A; 3. C

B. Sample Answers

1. The professor's lecture was so *impenetrable* that we all failed completely to grasp his main ideas.

2. The *iridescent* fabric of the tablecloth caught our eye immediately because the colors were so appealing.

3. He *pondered* his dilemma, avoiding any contact at the party so he could be by himself.

C. Sample Answers

1. No, it cannot be changed, because *immutable* means "unable to be changed."

2. No, because *impersonal* means "not personal" or "indifferent."

3. No, because he or she is behaving in an inappropriate or improper fashion.

Enrichment: Animals in Mythology and Folklore, p. 153

Students' reports should contain specific information on some or all of the elements listed. Evaluate students' reports for accuracy, thorough coverage, and overall interest.

Poetry Collections: Ernest Lawrence Thayer, William Stafford, Sandra Cisneros, Edgar Allan Poe, Edwin Muir, Richard Wilbur

Integrated Language Skills: Grammar, p. 154

A. 1. a figure of speech involving deliberate exaggeration; hyperbole

2. the oral poet credited with composing the *Iliad* and *Odyssey*; Homer

3. his pointed satire on human life and behavior; *Gulliver's Travels*

B. Examine students' paragraphs for correct usage and identification of appositive phrases.

Open-Book Test, p. 157

Short Answer

1. Sample answer: The embers faded and died upon the floor.
   Difficulty: *Average*   **Objective:** *Reading*

2. Sample answer: The speaker is very sad because his love, Lenore, has died. He is trying to overcome his sorrow by reading books of ancient learning.
   Difficulty: *Average*   **Objective:** *Interpretation*

3. Students may say the darkness represents death, fear, or loneliness.
   Difficulty: *Easy*   **Objective:** *Interpretation*

4. Sample answer: Stanza 10—friendly, but afraid the raven might leave him; Stanza 14—desperate to hear whatever message the bird may be bringing; Stanza 18—hatred for the raven and its single repeated word.
   At the end of the poem, the speaker seems to have gone mad.
   Difficulty: *Average*   **Objective:** *Literary Analysis*

5. The survivors of the war no longer want to listen to people who represent the old, violent, now-destroyed world.
   Difficulty: *Average*   **Objective:** *Interpretation*

6. Sample answer: The tractors are "like dank sea-monsters couched and waiting." They lay still and damp, waiting to be used again.
   Difficulty: *Easy*   **Objective:** *Reading*

7. Sample answer: The tractors seem more archaic because they are rusty, old, and useless, while the horses seem fresh and new.
   Difficulty: *Average*   **Objective:** *Vocabulary*

8. Sample answer: They are alike because they are both trying to achieve a kind of freedom: the bird from the room in which he is trapped and the daughter from the burden of the story she wants to tell.
   Difficulty: *Challenging*   **Objective:** *Literary Analysis*

9. A bird gets trapped in a room in the speaker's house. The bird hurts itself by flying into a closed window. Finally, it flies through an open window and is free.
   Difficulty: *Easy*   **Objective:** *Literary Analysis*

10. Sample answer: The "It" may refer to writing or to finding your way in life. The speaker probably wishes his daughter both creative success and a larger joy in life.
    Difficulty: *Challenging*   **Objective:** *Interpretation*

© Pearson Education, Inc. All rights reserved.

Essay

11. Students should identify the setting of one of the poems and discuss the connection between it and the story's plot, mood, or theme. For example, the speaker's chamber in "The Raven" contributes to the mystery and intensity of the mood. The stark descriptions of the setting in "The Horses" are linked to the desolate mood that dominates the first half of the poem. The daughter's room in "The Writer"—also the room in which the starling was trapped—is connected to the poem's themes of effort and liberation.

    Difficulty: *Easy*   **Objective:** *Essay*

12. Students should compare and contrast the raven and the starling, the raven and the horses, or the horses and the starling. Students may observe that the raven provides the speaker of that poem with an opportunity (or excuse) to descend further into his melancholy; the horses bring hope and companionship to desolate, shell-shocked humans; and the starling reminds the speaker of the urgency a young writer—or any young person—might feel at the beginning of his or her life's journey.

    Difficulty: *Average*   **Objective:** *Essay*

13. Students should note that in the first story, an entire civilization ends and the survivors reject all it stood for—including its technology—and turn toward a new, quieter kind of life; and that in the second story, the coming of the horses puts an end to the humans' despair and ushers in a new, more natural and communal era. Both stories work together to warn humans against self-destruction and to urge a greater respect for the natural, nontechnological world.

    Difficulty: *Challenging*   **Objective:** *Essay*

14. Students should point out that the speaker in "The Raven" expects the bird to say something that will relieve his grief and misery over the lost Lenore; instead, the bird simply repeats the word "nevermore," which sends the speaker into a state of madness. Students should also note that in "The Horses," the speaker and other survivors expect the radio to provide information about the war and the state of the world, but instead, the radios remain silent, and the survivors must learn to depend on themselves and their immediate world for consolation.

    Difficulty: *Average*   **Objective:** *Essay*

Oral Response

15. Oral responses should be clear, well organized, and well supported by appropriate examples from the selections.

    Difficulty: *Average*   **Objective:** *Oral Interpretation*

Poetry Collection: Edgar Allan Poe, Edwin Muir, Richard Wilbur

Selection Test A, p. 160

Critical Reading

1. ANS: C   DIF: Easy   OBJ: Interpretation
2. ANS: A   DIF: Easy   OBJ: Literary Analysis

3. ANS: C   DIF: Easy   OBJ: Reading
4. ANS: B   DIF: Easy   OBJ: Interpretation
5. ANS: A   DIF: Easy   OBJ: Comprehension
6. ANS: C   DIF: Easy   OBJ: Interpretation
7. ANS: B   DIF: Easy   OBJ: Comprehension
8. ANS: C   DIF: Easy   OBJ: Reading
9. ANS: C   DIF: Easy   OBJ: Literary Analysis
10. ANS: D   DIF: Easy   OBJ: Comprehension
11. ANS: B   DIF: Easy   OBJ: Interpretation
12. ANS: C   DIF: Easy   OBJ: Interpretation

Vocabulary and Grammar

13. ANS: C   DIF: Easy   OBJ: Vocabulary
14. ANS: D   DIF: Easy   OBJ: Vocabulary
15. ANS: A   DIF: Easy   OBJ: Grammar

Essay

16. In their essays, students should include specific details of setting from one of the poems. Students should discuss the connection between the poem's setting and two of the following: plot, mood, theme, or the poem's total effect. For example, the elaborately decorated chamber of the speaker in "The Raven" contributes to the mystery and intensity of the mood. The stark descriptions in "The Horses" are linked to the desolate mood that dominates the first half of the poem. The descriptions of the daughter's room and the starling in "The Writer" are connected to the poem's themes of effort and liberation.

    Difficulty: *Easy*

    Objective: *Essay*

17. Students should point out that the speaker in "The Raven" expects the bird to say something that will relieve his grief and misery over the lost Lenore; instead, the bird only repeats the word "nevermore." This sends the speaker into madness. In "The Horses," the speaker and other survivors expect the radio to give information about the war and the state of the world. Instead the radios remain silent, and the survivors must learn to depend on themselves and their immediate world for consolation.

    Difficulty: *Average*

    Objective: *Essay*

Selection Test B, p. 163

Critical Reading

1. ANS: B   DIF: Average   OBJ: Literary Analysis
2. ANS: A   DIF: Challenging   OBJ: Interpretation
3. ANS: C   DIF: Average   OBJ: Comprehension
4. ANS: B   DIF: Challenging   OBJ: Interpretation
5. ANS: D   DIF: Challenging   OBJ: Interpretation
6. ANS: A   DIF: Average   OBJ: Reading
7. ANS: C   DIF: Average   OBJ: Comprehension
8. ANS: B   DIF: Challenging   OBJ: Literary Analysis

© Pearson Education, Inc. All rights reserved.

9. ANS: B	DIF: Challenging	OBJ: Interpretation
10. ANS: C	DIF: Average	OBJ: Reading
11. ANS: C	DIF: Average	OBJ: Interpretation
12. ANS: C	DIF: Average	OBJ: Comprehension
13. ANS: B	DIF: Average	OBJ: Comprehension
14. ANS: C	DIF: Challenging	OBJ: Interpretation
15. ANS: B	DIF: Average	OBJ: Interpretation

Vocabulary and Grammar

16. ANS: C	DIF: Average	OBJ: Vocabulary
17. ANS: B	DIF: Average	OBJ: Vocabulary
18. ANS: C	DIF: Average	OBJ: Grammar
19. ANS: C	DIF: Average	OBJ: Grammar

Essay

20. Students may suggest that the narrative poem is more effective or more dramatic in capturing and conveying the speaker's desolate state of mind, which is essential to the story's plot. Students should point out Poe's haunting use of repetition to heighten the effect of the speaker's distraught mood. If written in the form of a story, the speaker's train of thought would most likely be interrupted, and thus the impact of his state of mind would be diminished. Finally, in the narrative poem, the speaker's use of first-person point of view, rhyme, and other sound effects enhances and makes more direct his growing distress.
Difficulty: *Average*
Objective: *Essay*

21. In their essays, students should note that the first story concerning the war is an account of how the world, almost totally destroyed by an apocalyptic conflict, has declined into a demoralizing state of sleep and silence. Students should contrast this narrative with the consoling appearance of the horses, who seem to offer companionship and hope. The poem's theme may concern the capacity of human beings for causing destruction and also their capacity for resilience and hope.
Difficulty: *Average*
Objective: *Essay*

22. Students should point out that the speaker in "The Raven" expects the bird to say something that will relieve his grief and misery over the lost Lenore; instead, the bird simply repeats the word "nevermore," which sends the speaker into a state of madness. Students should also note that in "The Horses," the speaker and other survivors expect the radio to provide information about the war and the state of the world, but instead, the radios remain silent, and the survivors must learn to depend on themselves and their immediate world for consolation.
Difficulty: *Average*
Objective: *Essay*

Poetry Collection: Emily Dickinson, Robert Frost, T. S. Eliot

Vocabulary Warm-up Exercises, p. 167

A. 1. stifled
2. defy
3. despair
4. equally
5. outwardly
6. hence

B. Sample Answers
1. No. A <u>fiend</u> is an evil person, and most people would not want to be friendly with someone who is that bad.
2. No. When the police have legally searched a house, they have not *rifled* through it because they are not trying to steal something.
3. People would admire the achievement of a weak team that beat a strong team, so its *stature* would become greater. The reputation or *stature* of the strong team would become lower.
4. No, most people probably would not be eager to perform an act of <u>heroism</u> because the great courage that is needed means there is great danger.
5. At a wedding, a *respectable* outfit would be formal, like a suit for a man or a nice dress for a woman.

Reading Warm-up A, p. 168

Sample Answers
1. (tough characters); (Battlefield toughs); <u>cause as much unhappiness and irritation to others</u>
2. (break the rules); If everyone decided to *defy* the rules, there would be chaos.
3. <u>However, that outside appearance was hiding an amazing ability inside.</u> *Externally* is a word and *on the surface* is a phrase that are synonyms for *outwardly*.
4. (same degree); I enjoy reading and walking *equally* because one exercises my mind and the other my body.
5. <u>love of music and the skill to produce it</u>; (set free); *Stifled* means "stopped from being expressed."
6. (From this time); *Hence* refers to the part of Armstrong's life after he learned music.

Reading Warm-up B, p. 169

Sample Answers
1. <u>followed the rules and contributed to society</u>; Someone who is *respectable* behaves in a way that earns the *respect* of others.
2. (courage); Most people admire someone who shows *heroism* because it often involves risking one's life for others.
3. (admire them and hold them in high regard); <u>Individual officers strived to be polite and helpful to law-abiding citizens.</u>

4. (bushes); In a city, you might find *undergrowth* in a park because that is where you will find the most trees.

5. (who committed a cold-blooded murder); The qualities that make a person a *fiend* include evil and lack of pity.

6. searched through tourists' pockets and purses and stolen their vacation money; A desk that had been *rifled* might have all the drawers pulled out, and the things that were inside might be scattered all over.

Writing About the Big Question, p. 170

A. 1. communication
2. exchange, discuss
3. illuminate, meaning
4. relationship

B. Sample Answers

1. When I talked to my best friend Aleesha, she showed me how to develop better search terms to use on the Internet; Paula showed me how to improve my serve in tennis by tossing the ball higher.

2. Aleesha showed me the other day that my **understanding** of Internet search terms was incomplete. Good **communication** with her made me aware that search terms have to be as specific as possible.

C. Sample Answer

Other people can make someone aware of his or her potential by giving valuable tips and encouragement. For example, Mr. Gonzalez, our band teacher, sees hidden talent in every player. When I thought I couldn't possibly learn to play the trumpet, he worked with me for over two months. He patiently reassured me that I could master the instrument. His encouragement helped me tremendously. Eventually, I realized that I had the talent to become a good trumpet player.

Poetry Collection: Emily Dickinson, Robert Frost, T. S. Eliot

Literary Analysis: Rhyme and Meter, p. 171

Sample Answers

1. The rhyme scheme is *abcbdeeef*.
2. The last line comes after three successive lines ending with the same sound.
3. The meter is somewhat irregular with two or three stresses in each line.

Reading: Paraphrasing, p. 172

Sample Answers

1. Then I took the other road, which looked just as attractive. Maybe it was better, because it seemed grassy and fresh. But actually both roads appeared about the same.

2. We could often be heroic if we did not let our fears damage our confidence in achieving our goals.

3. When the Foreign Office or the Admiralty discover that documents are missing, it is useless to trace them. Macavity's committed another crime.

Vocabulary Builder, p. 173

A. 1. C; 2. A; 3. D; 4. B

B. Sample Answers

1. You would be likely be surprised, or even stunned, since *levitation* refers to the ability to raise one's body into the air without any visible means of support.

2. The burglars would have searched rapidly.

3. The person disclosing a secret would not keep it, but rather reveal it.

C. Sample Answers

1. Yes, because you are in a state or condition of complete surprise or shock.

2. It is an addition.

3. It is in a state or condition of being done later.

Enrichment: Workplace Skills, p. 174

Sample Answers

A. 1. My long-term goal is to study abroad somewhere in South America for my junior year of high school.

2. My goal is a year and a half away.

3. I will need to continue learning Spanish and to maintain a good grade point average.

4. I should enroll for second-year Spanish, get information from the academic counseling office about programs for study abroad, and maybe take a conversational Spanish course over the summer.

5. My short-term goals will take place over months and years.

B. My long-term goal is to study abroad somewhere in South America for my junior year of high school. The short-term goals I have set are completing first-year Spanish with at least a B. I plan to take second-year Spanish my sophomore year. This summer and next summer, I will practice my speaking skills by joining a conversational Spanish club sponsored by the recreational department in my town.

Open-Book Test, p. 175

Short Answer

1. Sample paraphrase: We never know how great we are until we are challenged. Then, if we try, we will achieve great things.
   Difficulty: *Average*   **Objective:** *Reading*

2. No, greatness is our natural state; we distort ourselves to remain small and insignificant.
   Difficulty: *Challenging*   **Objective:** *Vocabulary*

3. The diverging roads are important choices in life.
   Difficulty: *Challenging*   **Objective:** *Interpretation*

4. The rhyme Scheme is *ababb*. No, there is only one rhyme scheme.
   Difficulty: *Challenging*   **Objective:** *Literary Analysis*

5. Yes, the speaker has a difficult time choosing because the roads are equally attractive, or "fair." Although the

speaker says his choice "has made all the difference," he does not say whether it was for the better or the worse.

Difficulty: *Average* **Objective:** *Interpretation*

6. Sample answer: The speaker may remember his choice fondly or regret it.

Difficulty: *Easy* **Objective:** *Interpretation*

7. The steady rhythm echoes the rhythm of a person's steps on a walk through the woods.

Difficulty: *Easy* **Objective:** *Literary Analysis*

8. The type of rhyme is exact rhyme. The words "thumbs" and "sums" end with the same vowel and consonant sounds.

Difficulty: *Average* **Objective:** *Literary Analysis*

9. Macavity puzzles the police because he can never be found at the scene of a crime he commits.

Difficulty: *Average* **Objective:** *Vocabulary*

10. Sample answer: Eliot may be suggesting that criminals are the rotten teeth of society.

Difficulty: *Challenging* **Objective:** *Interpretation*

Essay

11. In general, students should note that the speaker in "The Road Not Taken" wonders about life decisions that he did *not* take. The message of the poem may be that choices are necessary but also irreversible. In "We never know how high we are," the chief conflict lies between self-confidence and fear. The speaker asserts that people are capable of reaching their goals if they will only focus on confidence rather than yielding to fears or misgivings.

Difficulty: *Easy* **Objective:** *Essay*

12. Some students may say that the speaker's ambivalence and lingering sense of regret may make him a weak mentor, while others may say that his awareness of the importance of life's choices would make him a wise life guide. Evaluate students' responses for clarity, logic, and ample textual support.

Difficulty: *Average* **Objective:** *Essay*

13. Students may point out that Dickinson and Frost use relatively simple meters and rhyme schemes in their poems. Eliot, by contrast, uses a rollicking meter and humorous rhymes to develop a comic poem. Evaluate students' essays for clarity, coherence, and sufficient textual support.

Difficulty: *Challenging* **Objective:** *Essay*

14. Students who choose "We never know how high we are" may say that they hope to communicate to their younger self the idea that they can achieve anything they hope to achieve and that only their own fear and self-doubt can limit them. Students who choose "The Road Not Taken" may wish to warn their younger self that even minor choices in life can have significant effects and that no choice should be made carelessly.

Difficulty: *Average* **Objective:** *Essay*

Oral Response

15. Oral responses should be clear, well organized, and well supported by appropriate examples from the selections.

Difficulty: *Average* **Objective:** *Oral Interpretation*

Selection Test A, p. 178

Critical Reading

1. ANS: B	DIF: Easy	OBJ: Comprehension
2. ANS: A	DIF: Easy	OBJ: Interpretation
3. ANS: C	DIF: Easy	OBJ: Interpretation
4. ANS: B	DIF: Easy	OBJ: Reading
5. ANS: C	DIF: Easy	OBJ: Literary Analysis
6. ANS: C	DIF: Easy	OBJ: Comprehension
7. ANS: D	DIF: Easy	OBJ: Literary Analysis
8. ANS: D	DIF: Easy	OBJ: Literary Analysis
9. ANS: D	DIF: Easy	OBJ: Interpretation
10. ANS: D	DIF: Easy	OBJ: Comprehension
11. ANS: C	DIF: Easy	OBJ: Interpretation
12. ANS: C	DIF: Easy	OBJ: Interpretation

Vocabulary and Grammar

13. ANS: B	DIF: Easy	OBJ: Vocabulary
14. ANS: C	DIF: Easy	OBJ: Vocabulary
15. ANS: B	DIF: Easy	OBJ: Grammar

Essay

16. In Eliot's poem, the story of an unstoppable criminal is made humorous by the fact that the criminal is a cat. Eliot creates humor with his descriptions of the cat's unusual behavior and the unsuccessful attempts by people to stop him. References to well-known organizations and people, such as Scotland Yard and Napoleon, serve to enhance the humor.

Difficulty: *Easy*

Objective: *Essay*

17. In general, students should point out that the speaker in "The Road Not Taken" wonders meditatively about life decisions that he did *not* take. The message of the poem may be that choices are necessary but also irreversible. In "We never know how high we are," the chief conflict lies between self-confidence and fear. The speaker optimistically asserts that people are capable of reaching their goals if they will only focus on confidence rather than yield to fears or misgivings. Evalute students' essays for clarity, coherence, and specific reference to the texts.

Difficulty: *Easy*

Objective: *Essay*

© Pearson Education, Inc. All rights reserved.

18. Students who choose "We never know how high we are" may say that choices made in fear and self-doubt can limit their opportunities. Students who choose "The Road Not Taken" may say that even minor choices in life can have significant effects, and that no choice should be made carelessly.

Difficulty: *Average*
Objective: *Essay*

Selection Test B, p. 181

Critical Reading

1. ANS: D	DIF: Average	OBJ: Literary Analysis
2. ANS: B	DIF: Average	OBJ: Reading
3. ANS: D	DIF: Average	OBJ: Interpretation
4. ANS: C	DIF: Challenging	OBJ: Interpretation
5. ANS: B	DIF: Average	OBJ: Literary Analysis
6. ANS: A	DIF: Average	OBJ: Interpretation
7. ANS: C	DIF: Average	OBJ: Reading
8. ANS: C	DIF: Average	OBJ: Comprehension
9. ANS: C	DIF: Average	OBJ: Literary Analysis
10. ANS: C	DIF: Average	OBJ: Interpretation
11. ANS: D	DIF: Average	OBJ: Interpretation
12. ANS: C	DIF: Average	OBJ: Literary Analysis
13. ANS: D	DIF: Challenging	OBJ: Interpretation
14. ANS: B	DIF: Challenging	OBJ: Interpretation

Vocabulary and Grammar

15. ANS: B	DIF: Average	OBJ: Vocabulary
16. ANS: C	DIF: Average	OBJ: Vocabulary
17. ANS: D	DIF: Average	OBJ: Grammar
18. ANS: D	DIF: Average	OBJ: Grammar

Essay

19. Students should point out that Macavity is a mastermind of crime. He is dusty and unkempt, but he manages to appear respectable so that his victims do not suspect his true nature. He is also clever enough to commit his crimes quietly, without leaving a trace of evidence. People, especially the police, are continually frustrated by Macavity. Eliot provides humorous details about Macavity's crimes, which range from stealing jewels and milk to destroying property and attacking small dogs.

Difficulty: *Average*
Objective: *Essay*

20. Students may point out that Frost and Dickinson use relatively simple meters and rhyme schemes in their poems about serious themes. Eliot, by contrast, uses a rollicking meter and humorous rhymes to develop a poem on a comic subject: Macavity the Mystery Cat. Evaluate students' essays for clarity, coherence, and specific reference to the texts of the selections.

Difficulty: *Average*
Objective: *Essay*

21. Students should understand that the roads in Frost's poem are figurative roads in life. The speaker might anticipate sighing when he looks back and feels some regret about his decision. No matter how wonderful his life has been, he will probably always wonder how his life might have turned out had he taken the other road. When a person makes an important life decision, he or she does not often get the chance to revise or reverse it.

Difficulty: *Challenging*
Objective: *Essay*

22. Students who choose "We never know how high we are" may say that they hope to communicate to their younger self the idea that they can achieve anything they hope to achieve, and that only their own fear and self-doubt can limit them. Students who choose "The Road Not Taken" may wish to warn their younger self that even minor choices in life can have significant effects, and that no choice should be made carelessly.

Difficulty: *Average*
Objective: *Essay*

Poetry Collection: Robert Frost, E. E. Cummings, William Shakespeare

Vocabulary Warm-up Exercises, p. 185

A. 1. ballad
2. eventful
3. desire
4. favor
5. whatever
6. stranded

B. Sample Answers
1. T; *Mewling* means "crying weakly," and someone who is very sick might do that.
2. F; *Childishness* is behavior that is immature and inappropriate and not something people would aim to do to stay young.
3. T; If a friend says hello *unwillingly,* he or she does not want to say hi to you and that signals a problem.
4. F; *Saws* are sayings or proverbs that people often use, so many people have already heard them.
5. T; *Befriended* means "made friends with," so two enemies united in friendship against another person would be double trouble.
6. T; *Oblivion* is a state of unconsciousness, and someone driving should always be aware and alert.

Reading Warm-up A, p. 186

Sample Answers
1. (gas, oil, wood, paper); *Whatever* means "anything that."
2. (strong hope); I have the *desire* to travel the world and see all kinds of exotic places.
3. filled with dramatic moments and nonstop activity; *Dull* is an antonym for *eventful.*

© Pearson Education, Inc. All rights reserved.

4. <u>trapping</u>; <u>unable to get away</u>; A *stranded* car might have run out of gas or have some mechanical problem that keeps it from running. A safe way to respond would be to use a cell phone to call for help and then keep the doors locked and wait for assistance.

5. (musical story); Yes, I like a *ballad* because it is a song that tells a story.

6. (over wood); Romans would *favor* marble and stone because wood burns easily and marble and stone do not.

Reading Warm-up B, p. 187

Sample Answers

1. (unaware); *Unconsciousness* means the same as *oblivion*.

2. <u>accepted adult responsibilities</u>; Fish can only behave the way nature tells them to, so they cannot behave inappropriately or with *childishness*.

3. <u>they swim with great strength</u>; A person who went on a trip *unwillingly* might sulk, complain, and keep asking "Are we there yet?"

4. (quietly); *Crying* means the same as *mewling*.

5. <u>pilot fish</u>; The word *friend* is part of *befriended*, and that helps you know that *befriended* means "made friends with."

6. "<u>Live and let live</u>"; The expression "A stitch in time saves nine" is one of the *saws* I know. Like other *saws*, it is short and expresses a piece of advice.

Writing About the Big Question, p. 188

A. 1. communication
   2. resolution
   3. comprehension, understanding
   4. exchange, discuss
   5. empathy

B. Sample Answers

1. One topic for my documentary would be video games; another topic would be Internet search engines.

2. I would choose video games as the subject for a documentary because I believe that parents and children need to become better **informed** about the pros and cons of these popular games. In particular, I would like to explore how video games may affect a young person's **relationship** with his or her family and friends at school.

C. Sample Answer

Communication between two people can seem like action in a play when actors square off with each other in rapid dialogue. It's not just the words that are involved. Communication also takes place through non-verbal signals, such as facial expressions, gestures, posture, and movements.

Poetry Collection: Robert Frost, E. E. Cummings, William Shakespeare

Literary Analysis: Rhyme and Meter, p. 189

Sample Answers

1. The rhyme scheme is *ababcc*.

2. The last two lines introduce a new rhyme that is different from the alternating rhymes in the poem's first four lines.

3. The first five lines of the poem have a regular meter, but in the sixth line, the meter shifts. This change emphasizes the speaker's thought in the final line.

Reading: Paraphrasing, p. 190

Sample Answers

1. If the world had to end twice, the ice of hatred would be an effective agent of destruction.

2. Molly found a stranded, five-pointed starfish.

3. Life is like a play, with men and women taking the parts of actors. They are born and they die. During a lifetime, each human being plays many different parts. There are seven "acts," or phases, in a lifetime.

Vocabulary Builder, p. 191

A. 1. C; 2. B; 3. D; 4. A

B. Sample Answers

1. I think the amount of lemonade in that pitcher will *suffice* for lunch, so we will not need to make any more.

2. Their behavior was extremely *languid*, and we could not believe the lack of energy they displayed.

3. We were *stranded* in the middle of nowhere, so we felt dejected and desperate.

4. He dreamed of losing himself in *oblivion*, where he could escape reality by plunging into forgetfulness.

C. Sample Answers

1. Yes, because *fusion* means the act or condition of being blended or joined.

2. Yes, because an *admission* is the act of admitting something.

3. Yes, because a *delusion* is the state or condition of being deluded, or unstable.

Enrichment: Music, p. 192

A. Sample Answers

1. innocent, pure
2. playful, active
3. lovesick, obsessed
4. dutiful, courageous
5. respectable, self-satisfied

6. wise, reminiscent

7. regretful, lively interests

B. Students should select a variety of music. You might have students compare their suggestions for music and encourage them to play samples in class.

Poetry Collections: Robert Frost, Emily Dickinson, T. S. Eliot; Robert Frost, E. E. Cummings, William Shakespeare

Integrated Language Skills: Grammar, p. 193

A. 1. to collect; adjective

2. to keep the smooth round stone; noun

3. to find; adverb

4. to admit her fear of the little crab; adverb

5. to enjoy the warm, sunny afternoon; adjective

B. Examine students' paragraphs for correct usage and identification of infinitive phrases.

Open-Book Test, p. 196

Short Answer

1. Frost links fire to desire and ice to hate. Both emotions can cause destruction.
   Difficulty: *Challenging* **Objective:** *Interpretation*

2. In the first four lines, it is *-ire.* In the last five lines it is *-ice.*
   Difficulty: *Average* **Objective:** *Literary Analysis*

3. Line 2
   Difficulty: *Easy* **Objective:** *Literary Analysis*

4. The thing that chased Molly was probably a crab because it "raced sideways while blowing bubbles."
   Difficulty: *Easy* **Objective:** *Interpretation*

5. Sample answer: The words *star* and *were* are a slant rhyme at the ends of lines 5 and 6.
   Difficulty: *Average* **Objective:** *Literary Analysis*

6. Sample answer: Maggie found a shell that made a pretty sound. The sound of the shell made Maggie forget her worries.
   Difficulty: *Average* **Objective:** *Reading*

7. Entrances may refer to being born and exits to dying.
   Difficulty: *Average* **Objective:** *Interpretation*

8. The seven ages in order on the timeline are: baby, child in school, young person in love, soldier, judge, old man, elderly person near death.
   Students might add stages such as toddler, teenager, parent, active older person.
   Difficulty: *Easy* **Objective:** *Reading*

9. The meter is regular, with each line having five stressed and five unstressed syllables.
   Difficulty: *Challenging* **Objective:** *Literary Analysis*

10. Sample answer: He does see the human condition as *woeful,* because in his view people are "merely players" and their predictable lives end in sorrow and loneliness.
    Difficulty: *Average* **Objective:** *Vocabulary*

Essay

11. Students should note that Frost links fire and ice to the human emotions of desire and hatred, while Cummings links various ocean objects to human experiences—i.e., shells to daydreaming, starfish to friendship, crabs to fear, and sea stones to imagination. Students may say that Frost's overall theme is that extreme human emotions can destroy people, just as fire and ice can; and Cummings's theme is that people see themselves in nature. Accept all logical, well-supported responses.
    Difficulty: *Easy* **Objective:** *Essay*

12. Stages and qualities include infancy/helplessness, student/rebelliousness, lover/infatuation, soldier/self-absorption, justice/wisdom, old person/uselessness, elderly dying person/obliviousness. Students may agree or disagree with this portrait of life but should provide ample support for their ideas from both the poems and their own knowledge and experience.
    Difficulty: *Average* **Objective:** *Essay*

13. In their essays, students should discuss rhyme and meter in all three poems. In "Fire and Ice," Frost condenses his ideas into a few brief lines of varying meter and exact rhyme. In "maggie and milly and molly and may," Cummings uses longer lines and various types of end rhyme. And in "The Seven Ages of Man," Shakespeare uses a form known as blank verse, which consists of unrhymed lines in a regular meter.
    Difficulty: *Challenging* **Objective:** *Essay*

14. Students should note that a shell sends Maggie a message about happy things, a starfish sends Milly a message about friendship, a crab sends Molly a message about fear, and a sea stone sends May a message about the entire world. Students may conclude that these messages change their recipients for the better or worse—making them happier or more afraid—or that the messages reflect each girl's personality.
    Difficulty: *Average* **Objective:** *Essay*

Oral Response

15. Oral responses should be clear, well organized, and well supported by appropriate examples from the selections.
    Difficulty: *Average* **Objective:** *Oral Interpretation*

Poetry Collection: Robert Frost, E. E. Cummings, William Shakespeare

Selection Test A, p. 199

Critical Reading

1. ANS: A   DIF: Easy   OBJ: Comprehension
2. ANS: B   DIF: Easy   OBJ: Reading
3. ANS: D   DIF: Easy   OBJ: Literary Analysis
4. ANS: C   DIF: Easy   OBJ: Interpretation
5. ANS: D   DIF: Easy   OBJ: Literary Analysis

6. ANS: A	DIF: Easy	OBJ: Comprehension
7. ANS: C	DIF: Easy	OBJ: Literary Analysis
8. ANS: A	DIF: Easy	OBJ: Interpretation
9. ANS: A	DIF: Easy	OBJ: Interpretation
10. ANS: D	DIF: Easy	OBJ: Comprehension
11. ANS: C	DIF: Easy	OBJ: Comprehension
12. ANS: B	DIF: Easy	OBJ: Interpretation

Vocabulary and Grammar

13. ANS: D	DIF: Easy	OBJ: Vocabulary
14. ANS: A	DIF: Easy	OBJ: Vocabulary
15. ANS: C	DIF: Easy	OBJ: Grammar

Essay

16. Students should point out that Frost dwells on human desire and hatred in "Fire and Ice" in order to present a pessimistic vision of human nature. Cummings, by contrast, dwells on pleasure, recreation, and discovery at the seashore. Frost's use of brief lines, irregular meter, and a relatively complex rhyme scheme contributes to an ominous mood in his poem. Cummings uses a rollicking meter in long lines together with slant rhyme and exact rhyme in order to create a playful, upbeat mood.

Difficulty: *Easy*

Objective: *Essay*

17. Evaluate students' essays for clarity, coherence, thorough coverage of some or all of the seven ages, and adequate support from the text.

Difficulty: *Easy*

Objective: *Essay*

18. Students should note that a shell sends Maggie a message about happy things, a starfish sends Milly a message about friendship, a crab sends Molly a message about fear, and a sea stone sends May a message about the entire world.

Difficulty: *Average*

Objective: *Essay*

Selection Test B, p. 202

Critical Reading

1. ANS: B	DIF: Average	OBJ: Comprehension
2. ANS: A	DIF: Challenging	OBJ: Interpretation
3. ANS: C	DIF: Average	OBJ: Literary Analysis
4. ANS: C	DIF: Average	OBJ: Literary Analysis
5. ANS: B	DIF: Average	OBJ: Reading
6. ANS: D	DIF: Challenging	OBJ: Interpretation
7. ANS: C	DIF: Average	OBJ: Interpretation
8. ANS: C	DIF: Average	OBJ: Interpretation
9. ANS: B	DIF: Average	OBJ: Interpretation
10. ANS: C	DIF: Average	OBJ: Interpretation
11. ANS: C	DIF: Average	OBJ: Interpretation

12. ANS: D	DIF: Average	OBJ: Interpretation
13. ANS: A	DIF: Average	OBJ: Interpretation
14. ANS: B	DIF: Average	OBJ: Reading

Vocabulary and Grammar

15. ANS: B	DIF: Average	OBJ: Vocabulary
16. ANS: D	DIF: Average	OBJ: Vocabulary
17. ANS: D	DIF: Average	OBJ: Grammar
18. ANS: D	DIF: Average	OBJ: Grammar

Essay

19. Students should note that Frost's description of the destruction of the world by fire and ice represents the destructive nature of human desire and hatred. Students may also note that while humans continually fear things outside themselves, human activities have proven to be as destructive and frightening as any natural disaster. Evaluate essays for clarity, coherence, and adequate support.

Difficulty: *Average*

Objective: *Essay*

20. In their summaries, students should recognize the essential features of each of the seven ages: disgusting, helpless infancy; lazy childhood; the obsessive, ridiculous lover; the impulsive soldier; the corrupt, mid-life judge; the foolish, frugal old man; and the dying man, who lacks teeth, eyes, taste, and—finally—life itself. Students should draw the conclusion that, in Shakespeare's depiction of man's seven ages, he conveys the message that life has little consequence and many unattractive features.

Difficulty: *Average*

Objective: *Essay*

21. In their essays, students should discuss rhyme, rhythm, and meter in all three poems, relating these features to the elements listed. In general, students should comment on the pessimistic irony of Frost in "Fire and Ice," on the affirmative enthusiasm of Cummings's poem, and on the detached, lightly ironic description of human life and behavior in Shakespeare's "The Seven Ages of Man."

Difficulty: *Challenging*

Objective: *Essay*

22. Students should note that a shell sends Maggie a message about happy things, a starfish sends Milly a message about friendship, a crab sends Molly a message about fear, and a sea stone sends May a message about the entire world. Students may conclude that these messages change their recipients for the better or worse—making them happier or more afraid—or that the messages reflect each girl's personality.

Difficulty: *Average*

Objective: *Essay*

© Pearson Education, Inc. All rights reserved.

Poetry by Alice Walker, Bashō, Chiyojo,
Walt Whitman, William Shakespeare

Vocabulary Warm-up Exercises, p. 206

A.
1. vanished
2. husky
3. robust
4. madly
5. heavily
6. grievances

B. Sample Answers
1. There is nothing I enjoy more than *smelling* a fragrant garden.
2. A precious memory is something to *remember as long as possible.*
3. He always looks so *neat* in his starched shirts.
4. Summon your friends when you want *company.*
5. During the intermission of the game, we watched *the half-time show.*
6. Her melodious voice was *soft and pleasant.*

Reading Warm-up A, p. 207

Sample Answers
1. (large amounts); understanding and acceptance
2. complaints of unfairness; People can work out *grievances* with friends by talking about what has made them upset.
3. (strong); Yes, most people would want their best friendships to be *robust*, or strong and healthy.
4. (wild and crazy); *Calmly* is the opposite of *madly.*
5. (tired); talked to people; *Croaky* could mean the same as *husky* in this passage.
6. disappear without a trace; A "*vanished* friendship" is a friendship that has disappeared. The friends have lost touch or had a fight and never made up.

Reading Warm-up B, p. 208

Sample Answers
1. break from effort; A vacation or a restful weekend is an *intermission* from work that people today enjoy.
2. strength, endurance, and determination; (Gathering)
3. (ironed); A *starched tablecloth* would look very neat and clean.
4. (smells); *Fragrant* is used to describe pleasant smells, so the word would not belong in the sentence if Washington's mother burned the food.
5. (valuable); *Worthless* is the opposite of *precious.*
6. pleasant tune; I think the sound of wind chimes in a light breeze is *melodious.*

Writing About the Big Question, p. 209

A.
1. communication, relationship
2. aware, comprehension
3. discuss, react/respond

4. interpretation, illuminate, meaning

B. Sample Answers
1. Choices will vary.
2. Answers will vary but should focus on a change of perception and on a description of the feelings that resulted.

C. Sample Answer
A powerful poem makes us aware of a new angle of vision on a person, a place, or an event. Because a poem is so compressed, the emotion it conveys can make a deep impression on the reader. If you read a poem aloud, it is almost as if the speaker is in the same room with you. A good poem makes you take part in a dialogue with the speaker.

Poetry by Alice Walker, Bashō, Chiyojo,
Walt Whitman, William Shakespeare

Literary Analysis: Lyric Poetry, p. 210

Sample Answers
Walker: free verse; daughter remembering older generation; admiration; "Headragged Generals / Across mined / Fields / Booby-trapped / Ditches"
Bashō: haiku; observer of nature; serenity; "fragrant blossoms"
Chiyojo (1): haiku; person addressing dragonfly catcher; envy; "how far have you gone today"
Chiyojo (2): haiku; person exclaiming with enthusiasm; liberation; "like the willow tree"
Whitman: free verse; observer of society; enthusiasm; "the carpenter singing his as he measures his plank or beam"
Shakespeare: sonnet; person recalling sorrowful memories; sadness but then consolation; "then can I drown an eye"

Vocabulary Builder, p. 211

Sample Answers
A.
1. Because she is stout of heart, she faces her future with great *courage.*
2. The film was 3 hours long with *an* intermission; we were grateful for the break.
3. His face was *sad* as he recounted to us his many woes of the past year.
4. So many misfortunes in a single day caused her to wail with *grief.*

B. 1. C; 2. D; 3. B; 4. B

Open-Book Test, p. 213

Short Answer
1. The poet finds the women's efforts remarkable because they themselves had no education: "How they knew what we / *Must* know / Without knowing a page / Of it / Themselves."

Difficulty: *Average* **Objective:** *Interpretation*

© Pearson Education, Inc. All rights reserved.

2. Sample answer: Discrimination, unjust laws, racial hatred, hard physical labor, and a lack of education caused the women sorrow and suffering.
   Difficulty: *Average*　**Objective:** *Vocabulary*

3. Each haiku contains a single striking image from nature.
   Difficulty: *Easy*　**Objective:** *Literary Analysis*

4. Sample answer: "I hear America singing, the varied carols I hear."
   Difficulty: *Easy*　**Objective:** *Interpretation*

5. Whitman uses free verse, which does not follow a set rhythm or rhyme scheme. Just as each line of the poem is different, so is the song of each American.
   Difficulty: *Challenging*　**Objective:** *Literary Analysis*

6. Sample answer: The speaker changes from feeling sad about the past to feeling optimistic. This change happens when he thinks about his friend.
   Difficulty: *Challenging*　**Objective:** *Interpretation*

7. Both poems are written in free verse. Both express a feeling of admiration.
   Difficulty: *Average*　**Objective:** *Literary Analysis*

8. Sample answer: Both the women and the speaker are powerful and in motion. However, unlike a blossomless willow tree, the women are bearing the "flowers" of educated children, and their motions are not "mad" but intentional.
   Difficulty: *Challenging*　**Objective:** *Literary Analysis*

9. Sonnet 30 uses a regular rhyme scheme. Its rhyming sounds—for example, *flow/woe, night/sight,* and *foregone/moan*—mimic the sound of moaning and wailing.
   Difficulty: *Average*　**Objective:** *Literary Analysis*

10. Students' choice of images will vary. Students should select one as the most powerful and identify the feeling it conveys.
    Difficulty: *Average*　**Objective:** *Literary Analysis*

Essay

11. Students should identify two poems and describe their moods and speakers. Students should also express a preference for one or the other poem and an opinion regarding the relative power of the poems. Evaluate essays for logic, clarity, and appropriate support.
    Difficulty: *Easy*　**Objective:** *Essay*

12. In their essays, students should briefly identify a theme of each lyric poem and then explain how the various elements of the poem work to convey that theme. Students may choose to focus on Whitman's appreciation of diversity, Shakespeare's celebration of friendship, the haiku's respect for the environment, or Walker's celebration of courage and determination. Students should conclude by identifying and explaining the message they consider most crucial for future generations.
    Difficulty: *Average*　**Objective:** *Essay*

13. Students should cite specific details that illustrate the lyric forms they choose. For example, haiku and sonnets require concise expression and rigorous control of elements such as imagery, rhyme, and syllable count. Free verse often uses lists to pile up images and details. Evaluate students' essays for unity, coherence, and specific references to the selection.
    Difficulty: *Challenging*　**Objective:** *Essay*

14. Students may respond that "Women" caused them to think differently about the civil rights movement; that one of the haiku caused them to think differently about simple natural sights, sounds, or smells; that "I Hear America Singing" caused them to think differently about the diversity of people in our country; or that Sonnet 30 caused them to think differently about memories or friendship.
    Difficulty: *Average*　**Objective:** *Essay*

Oral Response

15. Oral responses should be clear, well organized, and well supported by appropriate examples from the selections.
    Difficulty: *Average*　**Objective:** *Oral Interpretation*

Selection Test A, p. 216
Critical Reading

1. ANS: C	DIF: Easy	OBJ: Interpretation
2. ANS: C	DIF: Easy	OBJ: Comprehension
3. ANS: D	DIF: Easy	OBJ: Literary Analysis
4. ANS: B	DIF: Easy	OBJ: Literary Analysis
5. ANS: A	DIF: Easy	OBJ: Interpretation
6. ANS: B	DIF: Easy	OBJ: Comprehension
7. ANS: C	DIF: Easy	OBJ: Literary Analysis
8. ANS: B	DIF: Easy	OBJ: Interpretation
9. ANS: D	DIF: Easy	OBJ: Comprehension
10. ANS: B	DIF: Easy	OBJ: Interpretation
11. ANS: B	DIF: Easy	OBJ: Interpretation
12. ANS: A	DIF: Easy	OBJ: Comprehension

Vocabulary

13. ANS: C	DIF: Easy	OBJ: Vocabulary
14. ANS: B	DIF: Easy	OBJ: Vocabulary

Essay

15. In their essays, students should explain why the poems chosen can be classified as lyric poetry. Students should support their statements with specific references to the poems, including references to speaker, imagery, and sound devices. Evaluate students' writing for clarity, coherence, and unity.
    Difficulty: *Easy*
    Objective: *Essay*

16. In their essays, students should identify and discuss specific images from the two poems selected and clearly relate these images to the speaker's emotion or the poem's overall mood. For example, students who choose "Women" might single out images of war including booby-traps, mines, and generals. Students should note the speaker's admiration for the determination and toughness of the women. In the haiku, images such as the temple bells, the dragonfly catcher, and the madly tossing willow tree highlight the speakers' emotions of serenity, adventuresome wandering, and exuberance. In "I Hear America Singing," the earthy, concrete imagery relating to different occupations reflects the speaker's zestful appreciation of America's diversity. In Sonnet 30, images such as moans, sighs, and drowned eyes highlight the speaker's deep melancholy before he is cheered by the thoughts of his friend.

Difficulty: *Easy*

Objective: *Essay*

17. Students may respond that "Women" caused them to think differently about the civil rights movement; that one of the haiku caused them to think differently about simple natural sights, sounds, or smells; that "I Hear America Singing" caused them to think differently about the diversity of people in our country; or that Sonnet 30 caused them to think differently about memories or friendship.

Difficulty: *Average*

Objective: *Essay*

Selection Test B, p. 219

Critical Reading

1. ANS: B	DIF: Average	OBJ: Literary Analysis
2. ANS: C	DIF: Challenging	OBJ: Interpretation
3. ANS: A	DIF: Average	OBJ: Interpretation
4. ANS: A	DIF: Average	OBJ: Interpretation
5. ANS: C	DIF: Average	OBJ: Interpretation
6. ANS: C	DIF: Average	OBJ: Literary Analysis
7. ANS: B	DIF: Average	OBJ: Comprehension
8. ANS: A	DIF: Challenging	OBJ: Interpretation
9. ANS: B	DIF: Challenging	OBJ: Interpretation
10. ANS: C	DIF: Average	OBJ: Comprehension
11. ANS: B	DIF: Average	OBJ: Literary Analysis
12. ANS: C	DIF: Challenging	OBJ: Interpretation
13. ANS: A	DIF: Average	OBJ: Interpretation
14. ANS: D	DIF: Average	OBJ: Literary Analysis
15. ANS: B	DIF: Challenging	OBJ: Interpretation

Vocabulary

16. ANS: B	DIF: Average	OBJ: Vocabulary
17. ANS: C	DIF: Average	OBJ: Vocabulary
18. ANS: C	DIF: Average	OBJ: Vocabulary

Essay

19. In their essays, students should briefly identify the theme of each lyric and then focus on why students think a particular life lesson from one of the poems is most important for the next generation. For example, they might choose Whitman's appreciation of diversity as a requirement for social harmony, or they might choose Shakespeare's celebration of friendship. Students concerned with the environment might select Bashō's haiku. Finally, students might choose Walker's celebration of courage and determination as an inspiring model for the next generation. Students should support their choice of life lesson with reasons why they think it is most important.

Difficulty: *Average*

Objective: *Essay*

20. In their essays, students should include specific discussion of details relevant to the lyric forms they choose. For example, haiku and sonnets require concise expression and rigorous control of elements such as imagery, rhyme, and syllable count. Free verse often uses lists to pile up images and details. Evaluate students' essays for unity, coherence, and specific reference to the selections.

Difficulty: *Average*

Objective: *Essay*

21. Students may respond that "Women" caused them to think differently about the civil rights movement; that one of the haiku caused them to think differently about simple natural sights, sounds, or smells; that "I Hear America Singing" caused them to think differently about the diversity of people in our country; or that Sonnet 30 caused them to think differently about memories or friendship.

Difficulty: *Average*

Objective: *Essay*

Writing Workshop

Response to Literature: Integrating Grammar Skills, p. 223

A. 1. among; 2. as; 3. between; 4. among; 5. as if

B. 1. We watched a tennis match between Sol and Roberto.

2. Sol played as if (*or* as though) he needed a good nap.

3. correct

4. He moved up to the net, just as he practiced.

5. Among the three of them, who do you think will take home the trophy?

Vocabulary Workshop—1, p. 224

Sample Answers

notorious → famous

tumultuous → passionate

amusing → enjoyable

irritable → angry

Vocabulary Workshop—2, p. 225

Sample Answers

1. Boy, that could be good or bad. . . .
2. Bizarre, now I am sure that is an insult!
3. Unique sounds a little better, like I have my own wonderful style. . .
4. No one has ever dressed this way before, Wow, I like that. Or do I?

Benchmark Test 8, p. 227

MULTIPLE CHOICE

1. ANS: A
2. ANS: D
3. ANS: D
4. ANS: B
5. ANS: D
6. ANS: C
7. ANS: C
8. ANS: B
9. ANS: A
10. ANS: D
11. ANS: A
12. ANS: D
13. ANS: A
14. ANS: C
15. ANS: D
16. ANS: B
17. ANS: D
18. ANS: B
19. ANS: B
20. ANS: A
21. ANS: C
22. ANS: B
23. ANS: D
24. ANS: A
25. ANS: B
26. ANS: B
27. ANS: B
28. ANS: C
29. ANS: A
30. ANS: C
31. ANS: B
32. ANS: A
33. ANS: B

ESSAY

34. Students' descriptions of their bedrooms should be detailed and display an organizing principle.
35. Students may choose to provide words that describe any of the poetic techniques. For example, they may focus on sound devices, imagery, or figurative language.
36. Students' descriptive poems should employ exact end rhyme.

Vocabulary in Context 4, p. 233

MULTIPLE CHOICE

1. ANS: B
2. ANS: A
3. ANS: D
4. ANS: A
5. ANS: C
6. ANS: A
7. ANS: A
8. ANS: D
9. ANS: B
10. ANS: B
11. ANS: A
12. ANS: D
13. ANS: C
14. ANS: B
15. ANS: A
16. ANS: C
17. ANS: B
18. ANS: C
19. ANS: B
20. ANS: D

© Pearson Education, Inc. All rights reserved.